PATHWAYS TO DIVINE AWARENESS

The Art of Conscious Creation

VINOD KUMAR

BookLeaf Publishing
India | USA | UK

Pathways to Divine Awareness:
The Art of Conscious Creation © 2026
Vinod Kumar

Presentation by *BookLeaf Publishing*

Web: www.bookleafpub.com
E-mail: info@bookleafpub.com

ISBN: 9789367392331

First edition 2026

DEDICATION

To my beloved father, who left us on 24th February 2025 but remains a guiding light in wisdom and love. His strength, kindness, and values continue to inspire my path of conscious creation.

CONTENTS

PREFACE

"**Pathways to Divine Awareness: The Art of Conscious Creation** " is a soulful guide through the profound themes that define our human experience. This collection of 108 poems, each consisting of 7 verses, is not merely a literary endeavour but an exploration of the timeless truths that connect us to ourselves, each other, and the world around us. With its rich blend of poetic artistry, philosophy, and wisdom, the book seeks to inspire readers to embrace life's challenges and opportunities with renewed purpose and clarity.

The world we live in is ever-changing, demanding adaptability, introspection, and resilience. In the face of uncertainty and complexity, we often seek anchors—principles and insights that ground us, heal us, and guide us toward growth. This book is one such anchor. It illuminates universal concepts such as gratitude, forgiveness, purpose, self-discovery, and the art of embracing change. These themes are not isolated but interconnected, offering a holistic approach to understanding life's dynamic nature and our place within it.

The poetry in this book draws inspiration from the profound wisdom of nature, the transformative power of science, and the enduring philosophies of great thinkers.

It speaks to the silent strength of resilience, the quiet grace of acceptance, and the boundless potential of human creativity. The book gently guides you through the foundations of conscious creation, where you'll learn the importance of intention, self-belief, and the power of attention. These fundamental principles lay the groundwork for living with greater awareness and control over your thoughts, emotions, and actions. By embracing these teachings, you'll understand how your mind and spirit shape the reality around you.

This is a book for those who seek more than inspiration; it is for those who long to evolve. The accompanying interpretations for each poem deepen understanding, connecting the beauty of the verses to practical insights for daily living. The Practical Guidance sections encourage active reflection, urging readers to take steps toward meaningful self-improvement.

To fully immerse yourself in this journey, approach the book as a companion for self-discovery. Begin with a curious and open heart, ready to explore the themes that resonate most with your current experiences. Each poem is a lens through which you can view life's challenges and joys with greater depth. Read slowly, allowing the words to settle in your mind and stir your emotions.

After reading each poem, take time to reflect on its explanation and guidance. These sections are designed to bridge the abstract beauty of poetry with Practical Guidance. Journal your thoughts, noting any personal insights or areas where the poem's message feels particularly relevant. Let the reflective questions guide you toward deeper self-awareness and intentional change.

The poems are not meant to be rushed through but savoured like a conversation with your inner self. Revisit them as life unfolds—what resonates today may take on new meaning tomorrow. As you engage with the themes, challenge yourself to integrate their lessons into your life, whether through daily habits, mindful reflection, or purposeful action.

This book is more than a collection of words; it is an invitation to transform your perspective, embrace your strengths, and confront your fears. It is a reminder that life's greatest gifts often lie hidden in its challenges and that within each of us exists the power to shape our reality.

As you read, let these poems awaken the dormant parts of your soul. Allow them to inspire courage where there is fear, resilience where there is doubt, and gratitude where there is longing. Let this be a journey of self-discovery, growth, and the conscious evolution of the life you are meant to live.

Welcome to this shared exploration of life's truths. May this book serve as a guiding light, leading you toward wholeness, purpose, and the infinite possibilities of being.

ACKNOWLEDGEMENT

I extend my heartfelt gratitude to Late Dr. Sunny Satin, whose teachings in hypnotherapy and profound guidance inspired me to embark on this transformative path. Your wisdom continues to echo in every step of my journey.

My deep appreciation goes to Dr. Dalbir Singh, whose encouragement to embrace and uphold human values has profoundly shaped my perspective and this work.

To my wife, Anshu, a constant source of inspiration and strength, whose dedication to practicing the principles contained in this book exemplifies its essence. Your unwavering support has been instrumental in bringing this work to life.

I also express my gratitude to my father-in-law, Professor Onkar Mal, whose words and encouragement inspired me to write and pursue my creative aspirations.

To my beloved daughters, Avi and Vaani, your unconditional love and inspiration have been the driving forces behind this endeavour. You remind me daily of the beauty of purpose and perseverance.

I am equally thankful to my brother, Sanjay Kumar, for his invaluable inspiration, and to my friends and colleagues, who have enriched my journey with their camaraderie and support.

This book is a reflection of all the guidance, love, and encouragement I have received, and I am profoundly grateful to each one of you for being a part of this journey.

CHAPTER 1

Foundation of Conscious Creation

1

Awakening to Conscious Creation

Within us all, a spark does lie,
A force of change that can't deny.
A flicker, a flame, ready to soar,
Awakening the soul to so much more.

From the depths of silence, a voice will rise,
Guiding us toward truth, no disguise.
Conscious creation, a gift so pure,
Shaping our lives, it will endure.

The mind, a canvas, blank and wide,
Where our thoughts and dreams collide.
With every thought, with every breath,
We create the life we seek beneath.

In the stillness, we begin to see,
The power we hold to set us free.
The choices we make, both small and grand,
Are the brushstrokes of life's command.

The seed is planted with focused thought,
Through intention, the world is sought.
Awake, arise, let your vision take flight,
Consciously shaping your day and night.

The path is clear, once you align,
With the soul's calling, so divine.
Awakened hearts, awakened minds,
In the dance of creation, one finds.

To create with purpose, to live with grace,
Is the art of life we must embrace.
Awake, and know the power you hold,
To create a world that's brave and bold.

INTERPRETATION

Consciousness is the foundation of all creation

In the vast expanse of our existence, there is a latent power within every human being that, when awakened, has the capacity to shape the very fabric of reality. This power is not external or distant; it lies deep within, waiting for recognition and activation. Our thoughts, intentions, and actions are the mediums through which we engage in conscious creation. This is a process of realisation — that we are not mere passengers in life, but active participants and creators of our journey.

When we awaken to this truth, we come into alignment with the natural flow of the universe. In the Vedas, it is said that *"Tat Tvam Asi"* (Thou art that), which signifies the inherent divinity within every being. The realisation of this connection, the recognition of the inherent oneness of existence, triggers the awakening of conscious creation. Our thoughts are powerful tools; they are the seeds from which our reality grows. This knowledge, when deeply understood, elevates our capacity to manifest a life of meaning, joy, and purpose.

As we awaken, we align with the divine will, not in a passive sense, but as active creators. This is not a distant ideal, but a practical truth embedded in our daily choices, thoughts, and actions. To live consciously is to engage with the world with full awareness, to choose our responses with intention, and to take responsibility for the realities we bring into existence.

STANZA-WISE INTERPRETATION

- **Stanza 1:** The poem begins by stating that within every person, there lies a spark of potential for change, a force that cannot be denied. This spark represents the divine essence, the latent consciousness that can be awakened through focused awareness. It is the beginning of a journey of self-realisation.
- **Stanza 2:** This stanza focuses on the pivotal moment when awareness is triggered, and we begin to recognise our ability to influence our reality through conscious thought and action.
- **Stanza 3:** Here, the mind is compared to a blank canvas, emphasising how our thoughts are the brushstrokes that shape our reality. This stanza suggests that through conscious creation, we take responsibility for the life we manifest.
- **Stanza 4:** The poem emphasises that the choices we make are significant. Whether small or large, they play a role in crafting our lives. Just as an artist creates their masterpiece with deliberate strokes, we too create our lives with intentional thoughts and actions.
- **Stanza 5:** The act of conscious creation begins with a single thought or intention. Just like a seed planted in the soil, a focused thought grows and begins to shape our reality, manifesting the world we desire.
- **Stanza 6:** This stanza highlights the clarity that comes when we align our actions with our true purpose. Awakening to our higher self allows us to move in the direction of our true desires, with full awareness and alignment.

- **Stanza 7:** The final stanza encourages us to recognise the immense power within. By living with purpose, grace, and intention, we create the life we desire. The poem calls the reader to embrace the role of creator in their own life and in the world around them.

PHILOSOPHICAL INSIGHTS

This topic speaks to the transformative power of conscious creation. It emphasises that each individual holds the inherent ability to shape their reality through the awakening of their inner consciousness. As described in the Upanishads, the idea of *Brahman* (the ultimate reality) residing within every being points to the divine potential we all possess. Conscious creation is not a mere philosophical concept but a lived experience — a practical realisation of the divine will manifesting through human thought and intention.

In Indian philosophy, the idea of *Karma* also aligns with conscious creation — our actions and intentions shape our future. This topic invites the reader to awaken to their creative power, take responsibility for their reality, and live in alignment with their true self and purpose. The realisation that we are co-creators of our own destiny empowers us to live with intentionality, purpose, and fulfilment.

PRACTICAL GUIDANCE

Where is your focus? Are you consciously creating the life you desire, or are you merely drifting through life, letting circumstances dictate your path?

Begin by grounding yourself in the present moment. Take time each day to reflect on your thoughts and actions. Observe where your attention is going — is it aligned with your goals and values? Practice mindfulness and meditation to deepen your awareness and clarity. Set daily intentions that are aligned with your higher purpose, and watch how your world begins to shift in alignment with your conscious creations. As you awaken to this power, trust that you are the creator of your reality. Let your thoughts and actions become the building blocks of a life you love.

2

The Sacred Power of Attention

Where attention flows, energy goes,
Like a river that endlessly grows.
The mind, a vessel, holds the key,
To shape the world, to set it free.

In silence, we learn to direct,
The focus of thought, a force to select.
Through intention, our path is made clear,
With attention, we draw what we hold dear.

Each thought, a seed we plant in the mind,
Attention nurtures what we choose to find.
The more we focus, the more we grow,
A garden of thoughts we tend and sow.

What we attend to, we invite in,
It shapes our reality, where we begin.
Our focus is the light that guides the way,
Illuminating the night, brightening the day.

In stillness, we hold the power to see,
The world we create through what we decree.
With attention, we bring our dreams alive,
In the heart of creation, we thrive.

The power of attention, pure and true,
Guides our thoughts and actions through.
Where we place our gaze, we open the door,
To possibilities, forevermore.

Attention is sacred, a gift divine,
It shapes our world, it shapes our mind.
Place it wisely, with love and grace,
For it is the force that creates your space.

INTERPRETATION

Attention is the guiding force of creation

Our attention is one of the most powerful tools we possess. It is through attention that we direct our energy, influence our thoughts, and ultimately create the reality we experience. In Indian philosophy, the concept of *dhyana* (meditation) points to the practice of focusing the mind to achieve clarity and spiritual insight. Just as a garden is shaped by the care it receives, our lives are shaped by where we place our focus and attention.

Attention is not a passive act but an active one. When we focus on something, we give it life, allowing it to grow and manifest in our world. This is the fundamental truth of creation: *what we focus on, we bring into existence.* The Vedic scriptures often speak of the power of the mind in shaping reality, and attention is the key to unlocking this potential. It is said in the Upanishads, *"Yad Bhavam Tad Bhavati"* (As is the feeling, so is the experience), highlighting the profound impact our focus and attention have on our inner and outer worlds.

When we consciously direct our attention, we align ourselves with the flow of the universe, shaping our lives with purpose and clarity. The practice of mindfulness, which comes from the ancient wisdom of India, is a powerful way to refine our attention and harness its full potential.

STANZA-WISE INTERPRETATION

- **Stanza 1:** This stanza emphasises that attention is the force that guides our energy. Where we focus, our energy follows, influencing the reality we experience. Just like a river's flow, attention directs the course of our lives.
- **Stanza 2:** Attention is the tool we use to direct our thoughts and actions. By intentionally focusing, we clear the path for our desired outcomes. In this sense, attention is not passive but active — it shapes and influences our journey.
- **Stanza 3:** The more we focus our attention, the more it grows, much like nurturing a seed into a plant. Our thoughts are seeds, and attention is the nurturing force that helps them grow into tangible outcomes.
- **Stanza 4:** This stanza highlights that what we give our attention to is what we attract into our lives. Attention is the light that illuminates our path, guiding us toward what we seek and transforming our world with focused energy.
- **Stanza 5:** Attention allows us to create the world we envision. In stillness, when we direct our attention inward, we can shape our inner and outer realities. Our dreams take form as we focus our energy on them.
- **Stanza 6:** Attention, when used with wisdom and intention, leads to the manifestation of our desires. The more we focus on our goals and align our attention with our values, the more we draw those desires into our lives.

- **Stanza 7:** The poem concludes by reinforcing the sacredness of attention. It is through this sacred act of focus that we shape our environment and our experiences. The poem encourages the reader to use attention wisely, for it is the force that creates their world.

PHILOSOPHICAL INSIGHTS

This topic delves into the sacred power of attention and its transformative impact on our lives. Attention is not merely the act of noticing something but is a powerful force that shapes our thoughts, actions, and the reality we experience. As taught in *Indian spiritual practices*, particularly *dhyana* (meditation), the mind is a tool that can be trained to focus and create. When we consciously direct our attention, we begin the process of conscious creation. What we focus on expands, and our lives are shaped by this simple but profound truth.

The poem highlights that our attention is sacred and divine, capable of guiding us toward our higher purpose. By being mindful of where we place our focus, we can align ourselves with the flow of the universe, creating a life of intention and fulfilment.

PRACTICAL GUIDANCE

Where does your attention go each day? Are you aware of the power it holds in shaping your reality?

Start by practising mindfulness daily. Take a few moments each day to center yourself, focusing your attention on your breath. Observe where your attention naturally flows and consciously redirect it toward your intentions and goals. You can also use affirmations to reinforce the power of your attention, reminding yourself that what you focus on becomes your reality. With every task you undertake, try to remain present and fully engaged. By mastering your attention, you become the creator of your life's unfolding.

3

The Science of Thought

Each thought we think, a seed we sow,
A spark of creation, where dreams will grow.
Through the mind's eye, the world takes shape,
Manifesting in life, no thought escapes.

The whispers within, whether joy or fear,
Shape the life that we hold dear.
What we harbor, the body reflects,
The mind and soul, it deeply affects.

From ancient wisdom, the Vedas say,
"Yad Bhavam Tad Bhavati," each day.
As is the thought, so becomes the deed,
A truth profound, a timeless creed.

Negative thoughts, like shadows, impair,
Their weight too heavy for the soul to bear.
The mind, when tainted, the body will ache,
A cycle of suffering, we must not partake.

But in the light of positivity lies,
The power to rise, to touch the skies.
Through mindful practice, our thoughts refine,
The path to joy becomes divine.

Meditate deeply, let clarity reign,
In the stillness, release the pain.
A single thought, like a guiding star,
Can take you closer to who you are.

The science of thought, a gift supreme,
To create, to heal, to live the dream.
Choose with care, for what you seek,
Will shape your world, complete and unique.

INTERPRETATION

Thoughts hold the power to shape our lives

Thoughts are the seeds of our reality, influencing not only our actions but also our mental and physical well-being. As ancient Indian teachings affirm, "*Yad Bhavam Tad Bhavati*" (as is the thought, so is the experience), thoughts are the foundation of creation. Positive or negative, each thought sets into motion a ripple of effects, manifesting in tangible ways in our lives. The poem emphasizes the responsibility we hold to cultivate positive, empowering thoughts and the caution required to avoid harbouring negativity, as it can harm both body and mind.

This principle finds echoes in modern psychology, particularly in the understanding of neuroplasticity, which highlights that repeated thoughts rewire the brain. Just as the mind can be shaped by fear or negativity, it can also be trained to foster optimism and growth. Indian philosophies, such as Sankhya and Raja Yoga, teach that the mind is both a creator and a reflector, shaping the inner and outer worlds based on the vibrations of thought it emits. Therefore, the realization of the power of thought is not just enlightening but also transformative, urging us to take conscious control of our mental energy.

Negative thoughts are like toxins, not just for the soul but for the physical body. Chronic stress, anxiety, and a pessimistic mindset can lead to ailments and a diminished quality of life. Conversely, cultivating positivity through deliberate practice—meditation, mindfulness, and affirmations—becomes a source of healing and alignment with higher energies. The poem serves as a guide to understanding this profound truth and offers a roadmap to align thoughts with intentions, leading to the manifestation of desired outcomes.

STANZA-WISE INTERPRETATION

- **Stanza 1:** This stanza establishes the foundational idea that thoughts are seeds, and every thought manifests in some form in our reality. Our inner world shapes our outer world.
- **Stanza 2:** The connection between the mind, body, and emotions is explored. Thoughts have a direct impact on our physical and mental well-being, making their nature crucial.
- **Stanza 3:** Ancient wisdom is brought into focus, emphasizing the timeless truth that thoughts determine actions and outcomes, as taught in Indian scriptures like the Vedas and Upanishads.
- **Stanza 4:** Negative thoughts are shown as harmful, creating cycles of pain and suffering. The stanza warns against harboring negativity, as it adversely affects the mind and body.
- **Stanza 5:** This stanza highlights the transformative power of positive thoughts. They uplift the soul and enable individuals to align with their higher purpose and potential.
- **Stanza 6:** Meditation is introduced as a means to clear the mind and redirect thoughts. In stillness, clarity emerges, allowing us to cultivate positivity and release negativity.

- **Stanza 7:** The poem concludes by affirming the sacred science of thought. Thoughts are a divine gift that must be used with wisdom and intention to create a life of fulfillment and purpose.

PHILOSOPHICAL INSIGHTS

The essence of this poem lies in the timeless wisdom that "thoughts become things." Each thought, no matter how fleeting, carries energy that can shape our reality. This idea aligns beautifully with the ancient Indian understanding of the mind as a powerful tool for creation. The Upanishads and the Bhagavad Gita emphasize that mastery over one's thoughts is key to mastering life itself. The Sankhya philosophy further elaborates on the dual nature of the mind, capable of creating harmony or chaos depending on how it is directed.

Negative thoughts are like weeds in the garden of the mind; if left unchecked, they grow, choking out the positive seeds. These thoughts not only manifest in external experiences but also affect our internal state, leading to emotional and physical ailments. On the other hand, positive thinking acts as a divine catalyst, creating joy, success, and alignment with universal energies.

The poem also reflects the Vedic idea of *sankalpa*, or focused intention. It is through *sankalpa* that individuals manifest their higher purpose. By consciously choosing our thoughts, we align with the rhythms of the cosmos, allowing life to unfold with grace. This understanding offers a path to both inner peace and external success, making the practice of cultivating positive thoughts a sacred responsibility.

PRACTICAL GUIDANCE

What thoughts are shaping your world today? Are they nurturing growth, joy, and alignment, or sowing seeds of limitation and despair?

Begin each day by observing your thoughts with awareness and curiosity. If you notice negativity, acknowledge it but don't dwell on it. Instead, consciously replace it with a positive affirmation such as, "I am aligned with my purpose and capable of achieving my goals." Cultivate a habit of mindfulness through daily meditation. Sit in silence for 10 minutes, focusing on your breath, and allow clarity to emerge. Visualization can further enhance this practice—imagine your goals and aspirations vividly as if they have already been achieved, embracing the emotions of fulfilment and gratitude.

Incorporate gratitude into your daily routine. Each evening, reflect on three positive events or moments that occurred during the day. This simple practice rewires your mind to focus on positivity and abundance. Strengthen your commitment to positive thinking by surrounding yourself with uplifting influences—books, music, and people who inspire and motivate. Remember, the energy of your environment amplifies the vibrations of your thoughts. Finally, take guidance from the ancient wisdom of *sankalpa*, setting a daily intention aligned with your highest values and goals. Repeat it often to keep your thoughts focused on what truly matters. In moments of doubt or negativity, remind yourself that each thought is a step toward creating the reality you desire. Choose wisely, with love and grace, and allow the power of thought to transform your life.

4

Harnessing the Power of Intention

With every thought, a seed is sown,
A desire born, yet to be known.
Through intention, we begin the quest,
To manifest the dreams we hold in our chest.

The mind, a tool that shapes the way,
Guides the heart, lights the day.
Through focus and will, we carve the path,
Intention's force, the power that lasts.

What we desire, we set the stage,
Our will the fire, our thoughts the gauge.
Through intention, we become the dream,
The force of creation, flowing like a stream.

In clarity, the vision is born,
Through intention, the future is drawn.
It is not a wish, nor a fleeting hope,
But a steadfast will, helping us cope.

The universe responds, to the energy we send,
Our intentions strong, our hearts we lend.
With unwavering faith, the dreams we cast,
Unfold in the now, at last.

When intention is clear and true,
It transforms the world, it sees us through.
A tool of power, of strength and grace,
It creates the life we long to embrace.

Harness your power, set your sights,
For intention's force ignites the lights.
What you desire, with purpose and might,
Shines through the darkness, guiding the flight.

INTERPRETATION

Intention is the driving force behind manifestation

Our thoughts are powerful, and when aligned with our intentions, they create the world we experience. In Indian philosophy, intention is seen as the first step in the process of creation. The concept of *sankalpa* (resolution or intention) is key in this practice. It is not merely wishing for something, but a focused desire that directs energy towards a specific goal. This is like the concept of *karma*, where every intention, thought, or action creates an effect in the world.

In the Upanishads, the idea that our desires shape our reality is evident. *"As you think, so you become"* is a central teaching. When we set a clear intention, the universe begins to respond by providing the opportunities, the tools, and the circumstances we need to bring that intention into reality. The process of manifestation is not about chance but about aligning our inner state with the outer world, where the power of intention transforms into action.

The practice of *dhyana* (*meditation*) and mindfulness allows us to refine and direct our intentions more consciously. When we focus our energy on a desired outcome with a clear mind, we engage the laws of the universe to support our path.

STANZA-WISE INTERPRETATION

- **Stanza 1:** This stanza introduces the idea that every thought is a seed, and intention gives it life. It is through our focused desires that we begin the process of manifestation, planting the seeds of our dreams.

- **Stanza 2:** The mind plays a central role in shaping our reality. Through intention, we direct our thoughts and energies to create a path that aligns with our purpose, illuminating the way forward.
- **Stanza 3:** This stanza emphasises the power of intention to manifest our desires. Our thoughts, when directed by intention, shape the life we are creating, acting as a river that carries our dreams forward.
- **Stanza 4:** Here, the poem reveals that intention is not just a passing wish, but a steadfast will that shapes our future. It highlights the importance of clarity and purpose in setting our intentions.
- **Stanza 5:** This stanza speaks about the universe's response to our intentions. With faith and determination, the world begins to align with our desires, and the manifestation process begins.
- **Stanza 6:** The power of intention, when true and clear, transforms our lives. It is a force of strength and grace that enables us to overcome obstacles and move towards the life we want to create.
- **Stanza 7:** The poem concludes by encouraging the reader to harness their power of intention. When focused and purposeful, intention guides us through the darkness, helping us realize our dreams.

PHILOSOPHICAL INSIGHTS

This topic explores the power of intention as the catalyst for creation. In Indian spiritual traditions, intention is regarded as a powerful force that shapes our reality. The concept of *sankalpa* represents a conscious decision to direct our energy towards a specific goal. It is not simply a wish or desire, but a force that, when focused and aligned with the laws of the universe, can bring about manifestation. The teachings from the Vedic scriptures and the Upanishads emphasise that what we focus on and give our energy to becomes our reality. By harnessing the power of intention, we begin the process of consciously creating the life we desire.

PRACTICAL GUIDANCE

What is your intention today? Are your thoughts and actions aligned with your deepest desires?

To harness the power of intention, start by clearly identifying your goals. Set specific intentions each day, focusing your energy and thoughts on them. Practice mindfulness and meditation to refine your intentions, ensuring they are pure and aligned with your true purpose. Write down your intentions and visualize them as already achieved. Use affirmations to reinforce your belief in your ability to manifest them. Through consistent focus and a strong, clear intention, you can begin to see your dreams take shape in the world around you.

5

The Power of Self-Belief

The strength to rise, to stand, to fight,
Comes from within, a burning light.
A belief in self, unshaken, pure,
A force that makes the soul endure.

In moments of doubt, when hope seems lost,
Self-belief remains, no matter the cost.
It carries us through the darkest days,
Guiding us along, through endless maze.

The power of belief is not in the mind,
But in the heart, where strength we find.
It is the light that pushes us to grow,
The inner flame that we let flow.

Through trials and storms, belief is the key,
Unlocking the door to what we can be.
When we trust in ourselves, we walk the path,
With courage and love, the world's aftermath.

Self-belief is a force so strong,
It fuels the dreams, where we belong.
It turns the impossible into the real,
And makes our hearts forever heal.

The universe responds to our trust,
In ourselves, it's clear, it's a must.
Through self-belief, we create our space,
Living with joy, love, and grace.

Believe in yourself, trust in your soul,
For through belief, we make ourselves whole.
The power within will light the way,
Guiding you through every single day.

INTERPRETATION

Self-belief is the foundation of all success

At the core of all achievement lies a deep, unwavering belief in oneself. In Indian spiritual practices, self-belief aligns closely with the concept of *atman* (the true self). When we believe in our inner strength, we tap into the vast potential of the universe, unlocking the power to overcome any obstacle. The mind is often clouded by doubt and fear, but the *atman* remains pure, strong, and unshaken, holding the truth of who we truly are.

The Bhagavad Gita teaches that *Krishna* advises *Arjuna* to trust in himself, for self-belief is what enables the warrior to face his greatest challenges. Through belief, we align ourselves with the divine will, and the world responds by guiding us toward our destiny. Self-belief is not about arrogance or pride, but a grounded understanding of one's inherent worth and power to shape their reality.

STANZA-WISE INTERPRETATION

- **Stanza 1:** The poem begins by explaining that self-belief is an inner strength. It is the power within that allows us to rise above challenges and continue the journey with determination.
- **Stanza 2:** This stanza emphasises the resilience that self-belief provides. Even in the darkest times, our belief in ourselves gives us the strength to carry on, leading us through difficult situations.

- **Stanza 3:** The focus here is on the origin of self-belief — it comes not from the intellect but from the heart. It is an inner force that drives us forward, helping us grow and evolve.
- **Stanza 4:** Self-belief is portrayed as the key that opens doors to our highest potential. It is the courage to act that leads to our success, and trusting ourselves is the foundation of that courage.
- **Stanza 5:** This stanza highlights how self-belief transforms what seems impossible into achievable reality. It is the force that heals, enabling us to manifest our desires and move forward.
- **Stanza 6:** The poem points out that the universe supports those who trust in themselves. By holding onto self-belief, we create the space and opportunities for our growth.
- **Stanza 7:** The final stanza encourages the reader to cultivate self-belief, reminding them that through belief, we make ourselves whole, and it will guide us each day.

PHILOSOPHICAL INSIGHTS

The poem emphasises the immense power of self-belief, which is the bedrock of all personal growth and success. In Indian spirituality, belief in one's inner strength — the *atman* — is central to realizing one's true potential. The Bhagavad Gita stresses that when we trust ourselves and believe in our inherent divinity, we align with the universe's support, unlocking the ability to manifest our highest desires. This belief in oneself, rooted in love, trust, and courage, is what empowers us to face life's challenges and transform them into opportunities for growth.

PRACTICAL GUIDANCE

> *Do you truly believe in your own strength? Are you willing to trust in yourself, even in times of doubt?*

Start by acknowledging the power that lies within you. Reflect on your past successes and remind yourself of your inherent worth. Practice affirmations daily, such as "I am strong," "I am capable," and "I believe in my abilities." Each day, take small steps that reflect your belief in yourself. Trust your decisions, follow through on your commitments, and know that through self-belief, you have the power to shape your reality.

6

The Role of Patience in Creation

In the stillness, time unfolds,
A journey of patience, silent, bold.
For all things, the seed must wait,
In patience, creation finds its fate.

The world is born in moments slow,
Like rivers that over time will grow.
In patience, we learn to trust the way,
Knowing the seed will sprout one day.

The impatient mind seeks instant gain,
But patience, in time, breaks every chain.
In stillness, creation comes to life,
Out of the quiet, ends all strife.

Patience is not passive or weak,
It is strength, steadfast and sleek.
It is the art of waiting with grace,
Knowing that the right time will embrace.

Through patience, we learn the rhythm of flow,
Letting the forces of nature grow.
In the fullness of time, we see,
The fruits of patience, the gift to be.

The creator's hand moves at its pace,
In patience, there's beauty, time, and space.
Trust in the waiting, the calm, the still,
For all things come when it's time to fulfil.

Patience is a virtue, so they say,
For in waiting, we find our way.
Trust the process, let go of the haste,
For time is the artist, a masterpiece to create.

INTERPRETATION

Patience is essential for creation

In the process of creation, be it personal growth or manifestation, patience plays a vital role. In Indian philosophy, *tapas* (the practice of steady, disciplined effort) teaches that growth is gradual and requires time. It is in the silence and stillness of patience that we allow our desires and intentions to take form. *Karma* teaches us that the actions we perform today will bear fruit, but it is the patience in waiting for those results that guides us on our journey. The universe unfolds in its own time, and patience is a way of aligning ourselves with its natural rhythm.

In the Bhagavad Gita, *Krishna* teaches that patience is necessary to achieve our goals, and life itself requires patience to unfold in the most harmonious way. The virtue of patience allows us to trust the process, enabling us to stay grounded even when the results are not immediate. It is through patience that we cultivate inner peace and realize that creation takes time.

STANZA-WISE INTERPRETATION

- **Stanza 1:** This stanza speaks about how patience is the foundation for creation. Just as seeds must wait for time to grow, so must our desires and intentions.
- **Stanza 2:** The poem emphasises that while the world evolves slowly, patience is essential in the process. It highlights the importance of trusting that things will unfold in their own time.

- **Stanza 3:** The impatient mind seeks quick results, but true creation takes time. Patience allows us to surrender to the process, resulting in a more meaningful outcome.
- **Stanza 4:** Patience is not weakness; it is strength. This stanza teaches that patience involves perseverance and trust, allowing us to wait for the right time to act.
- **Stanza 5:** Through patience, we learn to align ourselves with the rhythm of the universe. This stanza reminds us that patience allows things to naturally evolve and grow.
- **Stanza 6:** The creator works at its own pace, and patience brings clarity and fulfilment. In the stillness of waiting, the world is shaped with precision and grace.
- **Stanza 7:** The poem ends by reminding us that patience is a virtue. It teaches us to trust the process, knowing that everything will come to fruition at the right time.

PHILOSOPHICAL INSIGHTS

This topic explores the role of patience in the process of creation. In Indian philosophy, patience is seen as a tool for inner peace and alignment with the divine rhythm of the universe. *Karma* teaches us that everything unfolds according to divine timing, and patience allows us to trust this process. The poem emphasises that the act of waiting is not passive but an active cultivation of faith and strength. It encourages the reader to embrace patience, trust in the unfolding process of creation, and know that all things come in their rightful time.

PRACTICAL GUIDANCE

Do you practice patience in your life? Are you willing to trust the timing of the universe?

Start by embracing patience in small ways. When you face challenges or setbacks, remind yourself that everything takes time. Trust the process, and allow things to unfold naturally. Practice mindfulness and meditation to help cultivate a calm and patient mindset. Every moment of waiting is an opportunity to align yourself with the rhythm of life and to cultivate inner peace. Let go of impatience, and trust that everything will come to you in its perfect time.

7

The Energy of Hope

Hope is the light that guides the way,
A life shining through the gray.
It lifts the heart, it soothes the soul,
Hope makes us whole, it makes us whole.

In the darkest hours, hope still shines,
A promise that the sun will rise.
Hope is the force that lifts us high,
A vision of the stars in the sky.

It is the strength to carry on,
When all seems lost, dreams are withdrawn
Hope gives us wings, to soar and fly,
To touch the stars, to reach the sky.

Hope is a light that never fades,
A guiding star that never sways.
It holds us steady through the storm,
And keeps us safe, it keeps us warm.

Hope is the energy that fuels the fire,
The fuel for the heart's deepest desire.
Through hope, we move, we grow, we rise,
Hope is the force that touches the skies.

In every trial, hope's the key,
It opens doors for you and me.
Through every challenge, every test,
Hope leads us to our very best.

Hope is the essence of life's song,
A melody that plays all along.
With hope in our hearts, we find the way,
To build a brighter, better day.

INTERPRETATION

Hope is the energy that propels us forward

In times of difficulty and despair, hope acts as the light that guides us through. Hope is not just a fleeting feeling but a powerful force that sustains us. In Indian philosophy, hope aligns with the concept of *shraddha* (faith) and *bhakti* (devotion). Hope is rooted in belief — the belief that no matter how dark it gets, there is always light on the other side. The Bhagavad Gita speaks about facing life's challenges with an unwavering belief in the divine, which sustains our hope.

Hope is the energy that fuels us to continue moving forward, to rise after every fall. The Upanishads say that the divine presence is always with us, even in times of hardship. Hope reminds us that we are never truly alone, and it provides us with the strength to keep going.

STANZA-WISE INTERPRETATION

- **Stanza 1:** This stanza introduces hope as the guiding light in difficult times. Hope brings light to the soul and helps us stay strong through adversity.
- **Stanza 2:** Even when things seem bleak, hope remains constant. It assures us that brighter days are ahead, and it serves as the guiding light through the darkness.
- **Stanza 3:** The poem emphasises that hope provides the strength to carry on. It allows us to continue pursuing our dreams and rise above challenges.

- **Stanza 4:** Hope is steady and unwavering, providing comfort during the storm. It helps us stay grounded and safe through life's trials.
- **Stanza 5:** Hope fuels the desire to grow and achieve. It keeps the fire of determination burning, enabling us to move toward our goals.
- **Stanza 6:** Hope is the key that unlocks new possibilities. It empowers us to face challenges with courage and confidence, knowing that we can overcome them.
- **Stanza 7:** The poem concludes by showing that hope is the essence of life's journey. It helps us find the way forward, no matter the obstacles.

PHILOSOPHICAL INSIGHTS

This topic highlights the power of hope as the sustaining force in our lives. In Indian spiritual teachings, hope is closely connected with faith (*shraddha*) and devotion (*bhakti*). It is the belief that no matter how difficult life gets, there is always hope for a brighter future. Hope is not just a passive feeling but an active force that propels us forward and helps us overcome challenges. The poem reminds us that through hope, we can rise above adversity, trust the process of life, and continue our journey toward self-fulfilment.

PRACTICAL GUIDANCE

How does hope influence your life? Are you holding onto hope in challenging times?

Practice cultivating hope by focusing on the possibilities, not the limitations. In moments of doubt, remind yourself of your inner strength and resilience. Reflect on past challenges that you've overcome, and let that inspire hope for the future. Use affirmations to keep your spirit high: "I am hopeful," "I trust the process," and "I am open to possibilities." Through every trial, hold onto the energy of hope, knowing it will guide you toward the life you wish to create.

8

The Infinite Potential of Love

Love is the force that binds us all,
A gentle breeze, a soothing call.
It lifts us higher, makes us whole,
It is the language of the soul.

In love, there is no fear, no doubt,
It is the light that shines throughout.
A power that heals, a bond so deep,
In love, our hearts awake from sleep.

Love is the answer, love is the key,
It opens the doors to all that can be.
With love, we transcend all pain,
And through love, we break every chain.

In love, we see beyond the face,
A divine light, a sacred grace.
Love is the truth that guides our way,
It makes us one, every single day.

When love flows freely, hearts unite,
It brings peace and endless light.
With every act, with every touch,
We heal the world, we make it such.

Love is the energy that fuels the heart,
It is the force that plays its part.
In love, we rise, we soar, we fly,
We reach for the stars, we touch the sky.

To love is to live with boundless grace,
It is the essence of the human race.
With love, we create, we build, we thrive,
For love is the reason we're alive.

INTERPRETATION

Love is the supreme force of creation

In Indian philosophy, love is regarded as the highest power in the universe, transcending all boundaries and limitations. It is the force that binds everything in the cosmos together. The Bhagavad Gita speaks of the divine love between *Krishna* and his devotees, which is pure, unconditional, and transformative. Love is the energy that sustains creation and enables us to experience oneness with the universe.

In Vedic teachings, love is seen not only as an emotion but as an essential quality of the soul (*atman*). It is through love that we connect with the divine and with all beings. When love flows from the heart, it heals, nurtures, and unites us. True love, as described in Indian spirituality, is without attachment or expectation, and it transcends ego, allowing the spirit to experience divine unity.

STANZA-WISE INTERPRETATION

- **Stanza 1:** This stanza introduces love as a universal force that connects and heals. It shows love's ability to bring us closer to our true selves and to the people around us.
- **Stanza 2:** The poem continues by describing love's transformative power. Love removes fear and doubt, awakening us to a higher consciousness and revealing the beauty of the world.

- **Stanza 3:** Love is shown as a liberating force. It frees us from the constraints of fear and negativity, allowing us to live with courage and strength.
- **Stanza 4:** This stanza emphasises the spiritual dimension of love. Love transcends physical appearance and allows us to connect with the soul's essence, guiding us toward enlightenment.
- **Stanza 5:** The poem portrays love as the source of unity. It suggests that when we act from a place of love, we create harmony and peace in the world.
- **Stanza 6:** Love is the energy that empowers us to reach new heights. It propels us toward our highest potential, urging us to overcome obstacles and achieve greatness.
- **Stanza 7:** The final stanza speaks of the essence of life being love. Love is the driving force behind all creation, and it is through love that we find our true purpose.

PHILOSOPHICAL INSIGHTS

This topic emphasises love as the ultimate creative force. In Indian spiritual traditions, love is not merely an emotion but a divine power that connects us to the universe and to one another. The Bhagavad Gita teaches that when we act from love and devotion, we transcend the ego and experience the divine presence within and around us. Love is the force that unites all beings, heals the soul, and creates a harmonious world. By embodying love, we align ourselves with the divine flow of the universe, leading to peace, fulfilment, and spiritual growth.

PRACTICAL GUIDANCE

How often do you allow love to guide your actions and thoughts? Can you embody love in every situation you face?

Start by practising self-love. Spend time each day connecting with your inner self, nurturing your own spirit with compassion. Extend this love to others by performing acts of kindness and understanding. Let go of expectations and attachments, and allow love to flow freely from you. Through meditation and reflection, connect with the divine presence within and cultivate a love that transcends boundaries. Let love guide your decisions, and notice how it transforms your experiences and relationships.

9

The Language of Silence

In the quiet of the soul, words are few,
Yet the meaning is clear, the truth shines through.
Silence speaks louder than any sound,
It is where the deepest truths are found.

In silence, the mind finds peace,
A moment where worries cease.
It is the space where we connect,
With the self, with love, and intellect.

Through silence, the heart finds its way,
It brings clarity to each new day.
In the stillness, we hear the call,
Of the universe, guiding us all.

Silence is the voice of the divine,
A presence that is pure, sublime.
In silence, we listen, we understand,
The whispers of the universe, at hand.

The greatest wisdom is often silent,
It speaks in ways that are so vibrant.
In quietude, the soul becomes whole,
And silence brings us to the goal.

In a world of noise, silence is rare,
Yet it is the place where we truly care.
When we pause, when we breathe,
We find the wisdom we seek to believe.

Silence is the essence of peace,
A place where all conflicts cease.
It is the language of the soul,
The truth that makes us whole.

INTERPRETATION

Silence is the language of the divine

In Indian philosophy, silence holds great significance as a means of spiritual communication. In *dhyana* (meditation), silence is the gateway to deeper awareness and connection with the *Atman* (the true self). It is in silence that we connect with our inner truth and the divine presence. The Bhagavad Gita emphasises the power of stillness, where the mind is quiet, and the soul is in tune with the universal consciousness.

The importance of silence in spiritual practices like *yoga* and meditation cannot be overstated. In these practices, silence allows for self-reflection and inner growth, helping us transcend the noise of the world and find clarity. Silence is not an absence of sound but a presence of awareness — it is in this space that we experience the deepest understanding of who we truly are.

STANZA-WISE INTERPRETATION

- **Stanza 1:** This stanza introduces silence as the ultimate communicator, where the deepest truths emerge. Silence reveals the clarity that words cannot express.
- **Stanza 2:** Silence brings peace to the restless mind. By quieting the noise, we can find the space for clarity and insight.
- **Stanza 3:** The poem describes how silence connects us with our innermost self. It is through stillness that we hear the guidance of the universe.

- **Stanza 4:** Silence is portrayed as the divine voice. It allows us to listen to the subtle whispers of the universe and the deeper truths that words cannot convey.
- **Stanza 5:** This stanza highlights that wisdom often comes in moments of silence. It is in quiet reflection that we are able to understand profound truths.
- **Stanza 6:** Silence is a rare commodity in the noisy world, yet it is the key to deep self-awareness and understanding. This stanza encourages the reader to embrace silence to find their own truth.
- **Stanza 7:** The final stanza reinforces the idea that silence is peace. It is the language of the soul, allowing us to reconnect with the divine and experience wholeness.

PHILOSOPHICAL INSIGHTS

This topic emphasises silence as a spiritual practice that connects us with the divine and our inner self. In Indian spirituality, silence is seen as the most profound language, one that transcends words and allows for deeper understanding. Meditation and *yoga* use silence to quiet the mind, fostering spiritual insight. The poem reveals that in silence, we find clarity, wisdom, and peace. It is the language of the soul, guiding us toward self-realisation and connection with the universe.

PRACTICAL GUIDANCE

How often do you take time for silence in your life? Can you embrace silence to connect with your true self?

Begin by practising moments of stillness throughout your day. Spend a few minutes in silence, simply breathing and being present. Allow your mind to settle and your heart to open. Use meditation or mindful breathing to experience the peace that silence brings. Reflect on your thoughts and feelings in silence, and allow the wisdom of your soul to emerge. By making space for silence, you invite clarity, peace, and divine guidance into your life.

10

Cultivating Gratitude

Gratitude is the key that opens the door,
To abundance, love, and so much more.
It turns ordinary moments into gold,
And fills the heart with stories untold.

In gratitude, we see the beauty,
In the simple, in the duty.
It is the lens that brightens the day,
Turning darkness into light, all the way.

Gratitude is the seed of peace,
It helps the heart find its release.
Through thankfulness, we heal the soul,
And make our lives completely whole.

When we are grateful, we align,
With the divine, the sacred sign.
It opens our hearts, it clears the mind,
And leaves all fears and doubts behind.

Gratitude is the energy of grace,
It brings us back to our true place.
It allows us to see the light,
And find the beauty in every fight.

With every breath, gratitude flows,
In the small things, the love it shows.
When we cultivate gratitude, we see,
The gifts of life, so abundantly free.

Gratitude is a song of joy,
A melody that none can destroy.
In its music, we find our way,
And create a brighter, better day.

INTERPRETATION

Gratitude is the foundation of a fulfilled life

In Indian philosophy, gratitude is closely tied to the concept of *seva* (selfless service) and *bhakti* (devotion). It is through gratitude that we recognise the divine presence in all things. The practice of being grateful aligns us with the flow of abundance in the universe, as we acknowledge and appreciate the blessings we have received. Gratitude helps us see the beauty in everyday life, allowing us to remain grounded and connected to our higher purpose.

The Bhagavad Gita teaches that those who are grateful and content are in harmony with the divine, and their actions are aligned with the greater good. Gratitude also fosters humility and helps us stay present in the moment, appreciating the small things that make life extraordinary.

STANZA-WISE INTERPRETATION

- **Stanza 1:** This stanza introduces gratitude as the key that opens doors to abundance and love. It transforms ordinary experiences into something precious, making life richer and more meaningful.
- **Stanza 2:** Gratitude helps us see the beauty in every situation, even in the simple and mundane. It brightens our perspective, turning even the darkest moments into light.
- **Stanza 3:** The practice of gratitude brings peace to the heart and mind. It heals the soul by shifting our focus from what we lack to what we already have.

- **Stanza 4:** When we express gratitude, we align ourselves with the divine energy of the universe. It clears our doubts and fears, bringing us closer to our true nature.
- **Stanza 5:** This stanza highlights the transformative power of gratitude. It brings us back to our center, helping us find peace and clarity in every situation.
- **Stanza 6:** Gratitude is the force that opens us to the abundance of life. By practising gratitude, we begin to recognise the gifts of life, both big and small.
- **Stanza 7:** The final stanza portrays gratitude as a song of joy, one that fills our hearts and guides us toward creating a brighter and more fulfilling life.

PHILOSOPHICAL INSIGHTS

This topic explores the power of gratitude in shaping our lives. In Indian spiritual practices, gratitude is seen as a way to align ourselves with the divine and the flow of abundance. By practising gratitude, we acknowledge the blessings in our lives, which opens us up to receiving even more. The poem highlights that gratitude transforms our perspective, heals our hearts, and brings peace. It encourages the reader to cultivate gratitude daily, as it is the foundation for a joyful, fulfilling life.

PRACTICAL GUIDANCE

How often do you practice gratitude in your life? Can you see the beauty in even the smallest moments?

Start by keeping a gratitude journal. Every day, write down three things you are grateful for, no matter how small. Take time each day to express thanks, whether it's for the people in your life, the opportunities you have, or the simple joys of being alive. Use meditation to reflect on your blessings and open your heart to more abundance. Let gratitude guide your actions and transform the way you view the world around you.

11

The Art of Acceptance

Acceptance is the door that opens wide,
It allows us to flow with the tide.
It is not giving up or giving in,
But embracing life, with peace within.

To accept is to surrender control,
To release the burden, and heal the soul.
It is the key to freedom's gate,
A choice that makes us whole, not late.

Acceptance is the courage to see,
What is, and let it simply be.
In the flow of life, we find our grace,
And in acceptance, we find our place.

It is not a passive act, but bold,
A strength that allows us to unfold.
In acceptance, we find the key,
To living fully, to being free.

In every trial, acceptance shows,
The path to peace, where wisdom grows.
By accepting, we let go of strife,
And live in harmony with life.

Acceptance helps us find the way,
Through struggles and hardships of the day.
It opens the heart, it clears the mind,
And helps us leave the past behind.

Acceptance is the essence of peace,
It brings our fears to a sweet release.
In acceptance, we are free to be,
The fullest version of you and me.

INTERPRETATION

Acceptance is the key to inner peace

In Indian spiritual practices, acceptance is a fundamental concept tied closely to equanimity (*upeksa*), the ability to remain steady and balanced in all circumstances. Acceptance does not mean passive resignation, but the active embrace of reality as it is. *Krishna* in the Bhagavad Gita teaches *Arjuna* to accept the challenges of life, as it is through acceptance that one gains strength and clarity.

By accepting life as it comes, we release resistance and allow ourselves to flow with the natural rhythm of existence. The Upanishads often speak of accepting the impermanence of the world, for only through acceptance can we transcend attachment and find true freedom. Acceptance brings us peace, and it is in this peace that we connect with our highest self, the *Atman*.

STANZA-WISE INTERPRETATION

- **Stanza 1:** This stanza introduces acceptance as a vital aspect of peace and well-being. By accepting life's flow, we stop fighting against what is and start embracing it fully.
- **Stanza 2:** Acceptance is described as a release of control. When we let go of trying to control everything, we find freedom and healing.
- **Stanza 3:** Acceptance is shown as a form of courage. It takes strength to face reality as it is, without resistance, and to allow life to unfold naturally.

- **Stanza 4:** This stanza emphasises that acceptance is not weakness, but an act of strength. By accepting life as it is, we open ourselves up to growth and freedom.
- **Stanza 5:** Acceptance is portrayed as a way to overcome conflict. By accepting situations and people as they are, we remove strife from our lives and make space for wisdom and peace.
- **Stanza 6:** This stanza highlights the role of acceptance in helping us move forward. It releases the past and opens us to the future, creating harmony in our lives.
- **Stanza 7:** The poem concludes by showing that acceptance is the ultimate form of peace. Through acceptance, we embrace life fully, finding harmony and fulfilment.

PHILOSOPHICAL INSIGHTS

This topic focuses on the transformative power of acceptance in our lives. In Indian philosophy, acceptance is seen as an essential practice for spiritual growth. By accepting life as it comes, we align ourselves with the natural order of the universe, freeing ourselves from attachment and resistance. Acceptance is not about resignation, but about embracing reality with wisdom, allowing us to move forward in peace and harmony. Through acceptance, we learn to live fully in the present moment, connecting with our highest self.

PRACTICAL GUIDANCE

How often do you resist what is happening in your life? Are you ready to embrace acceptance and flow with the natural rhythm of life?

Practice accepting things as they are, starting with small moments of discomfort. When faced with challenges, take a moment to breathe and accept them as part of your journey. Use meditation to cultivate equanimity, focusing on letting go of judgment and resistance. Reflect on the impermanence of all things and remind yourself that acceptance is the path to peace. With practice, you will find that acceptance frees your heart and mind, bringing you closer to the true peace that lies within.

12

The Strength of Awareness

Awareness is the light that guides,
A self-shining from inside.
It wakes us up, it makes us see,
The world as it is, with clarity.

In awareness, we find the truth,
The wisdom hidden since our youth.
It opens the mind, it clears the haze,
And leads us down enlightened ways.

Awareness is not just thought,
It's the state where truth is sought.
It is the space where we can be,
Free from illusion, calm and free.

In the present moment, we are whole,
Awareness connects the body and soul.
It's the bridge between what's seen and unseen,
The lens through which we're truly keen.

Through awareness, we face our fears,
We see our doubts, we wipe our tears.
It's the power that helps us grow,
And find the strength to let go.

Awareness is the art of now,
Living fully, without a vow.
It is the breath we take with grace,
The present moment, our sacred space.

In awareness, there's peace and light,
It calms the soul, it makes us right.
With awareness, we find our way,
And live in truth every single day.

INTERPRETATION

Awareness is the foundation of true knowledge

In Indian spiritual traditions, awareness (*chit*) is the essence of consciousness. The Upanishads and Bhagavad Gita both emphasise the importance of becoming fully aware of the present moment as a way of transcending the mind and connecting with the higher self. *Chit* refers to the pure consciousness, which is the basis of all awareness. It is the lens through which we can perceive the truth, without the distortions of the ego, desire, or illusion.

Awareness is the ability to observe without attachment or judgment. It is through awareness that we see things as they truly are, and in doing so, we gain clarity and insight. When we live in awareness, we are not swept away by the fluctuations of the mind or the distractions of the external world. Instead, we become centered in the present moment, grounded in the knowledge of our true nature.

The practice of mindfulness, a key concept in Indian philosophy, teaches us to be fully present, to observe without judgment, and to embrace the reality of the moment. Through awareness, we are able to break free from the constraints of the ego and connect with the infinite wisdom that resides within us.

STANZA-WISE INTERPRETATION

- **Stanza 1:** This stanza introduces awareness as the guiding light in our lives. It allows us to see the world clearly, without the distortions of the mind or emotions.

- **Stanza 2:** The poem describes how awareness helps us access deeper truths. By becoming aware, we remove the fog of illusion and gain insight into life's true nature.
- **Stanza 3:** Here, awareness is seen as the ability to rise above thoughts. It's a state of being where we experience life as it is, without the interference of preconceived notions.
- **Stanza 4:** The stanza highlights that awareness connects the body, mind, and soul. It is the key to living fully in the present moment, grounded in the truth of who we are.
- **Stanza 5:** Awareness is shown as the power to face our fears and doubts. By being fully aware, we can confront the obstacles in our lives and find the strength to overcome them.
- **Stanza 6:** This stanza emphasises that awareness is an ongoing practice. It is the art of living fully in the present, without the need for external validation or promises of the future.
- **Stanza 7:** The final stanza affirms that awareness brings peace and clarity. When we are fully aware, we are aligned with our true nature and live with a sense of purpose and truth.

PHILOSOPHICAL INSIGHTS

This topic focuses on the strength of awareness, which is central to spiritual growth and self-realisation. In Indian philosophy, awareness is seen as the key to understanding the true nature of reality. Through awareness, we are able to transcend the distractions and limitations of the mind and ego, allowing us to connect with our higher self. The poem highlights that awareness is not a passive state but an active, ongoing practice that brings clarity, peace, and a deeper understanding of life. By cultivating awareness, we become aligned with the present moment and the infinite wisdom within.

PRACTICAL GUIDANCE

How often do you live fully in the present moment? Are you aware of the thoughts and emotions that arise within you?

Start by practising mindfulness each day. Take a few moments to center yourself, breathing deeply and focusing on the present moment. Observe your thoughts without judgment, letting them come and go. Engage fully in each task you do, bringing your attention to every detail. Reflect on how awareness changes your perception of the world and helps you find peace. Through regular practice, you will develop a deeper connection with the present moment, allowing awareness to guide you toward a life of clarity, peace, and purpose.

13

Aligning with Divine Will

When the heart surrenders to the flow,
A path of grace begins to glow.
The will of the divine, pure and true,
Guides us to what we're meant to do.

In every moment, we must align,
With the divine purpose, so divine.
Through surrender, we find our place,
In the embrace of love and grace.

When we listen to the inner voice,
We align with the divine choice.
It is in stillness we understand,
The divine will, held in our hand.

The will of the divine is ever near,
A force of love, without fear.
It guides our actions, shapes our way,
And in it, we find peace each day.

To align with the divine is to trust,
In the unfolding of life, just and just.
When we surrender, the path is clear,
With divine will, we have no fear.

In every step, the divine will show,
The way to go, the seeds to sow.
Through surrender, we become one,
With the divine, beneath the sun.

Align with the divine, feel its flow,
For in this grace, our souls will grow.
It is through divine will we find,
Our true self, our peace of mind.

INTERPRETATION

Aligning with the divine will is the key to spiritual fulfilment

In Indian philosophy, the idea of aligning with the divine will or *Ishvara's* will is central to the teachings of the Bhagavad Gita. *Krishna* instructs *Arjuna* to surrender his will to the divine and follow the path that has been laid out for him. By surrendering our personal desires and aligning with the greater cosmic plan, we find harmony, peace, and purpose. Surrender is not about giving up, but about trusting the divine process and allowing life to unfold with grace. In *yoga*, the concept of *prapatti* (surrender) teaches us to yield our individual will to the greater cosmic order.

By aligning with the divine will, we allow our actions to be guided by a higher power, ensuring that we walk the path of righteousness and spiritual growth. Through surrender, we learn to trust, let go of control, and accept whatever comes our way as part of the divine plan.

STANZA-WISE INTERPRETATION

- **Stanza 1:** This stanza introduces the concept of **alignment** with the divine will. By surrendering to the flow of the universe, we find guidance and clarity.
- **Stanza 2:** Aligning with divine will requires us to trust in the divine purpose. Surrendering to it brings peace and purpose, allowing us to navigate life effortlessly.

- **Stanza 3:** The poem emphasises that the inner voice, or **intuition**, is a reflection of the divine will. By listening to it, we align ourselves with our true purpose.
- **Stanza 4:** The stanza shows how divine will is always near, guiding our actions and decisions. When we align with it, our path becomes clearer.
- **Stanza 5:** Aligning with the divine will means trusting the unfolding of life. It helps us release fear and uncertainty, as we understand that everything happens for a reason.
- **Stanza 6:** By aligning with the divine, we find purpose and direction. The poem reinforces that this surrender brings fulfilment and peace.
- **Stanza 7:** The final stanza calls on the reader to align with the divine will, reminding them that by doing so, they will discover their true self and find lasting peace.

PHILOSOPHICAL INSIGHTS

This topic explores the importance of aligning with the divine will. Indian spirituality teaches that true peace and fulfilment come when we surrender our personal desires and align ourselves with a greater cosmic purpose. The Bhagavad Gita and other Vedic scriptures emphasise that the divine will is always present and guiding us, and by yielding to it, we unlock our highest potential. This poem illustrates that by aligning with divine will, we achieve peace, clarity, and spiritual growth.

PRACTICAL GUIDANCE

Are you ready to surrender your personal will and align with the divine plan? Can you trust the flow of life and accept it as it comes?

Start by practising mindfulness and meditation to connect with your inner self and the divine presence. Reflect on areas in your life where you are resisting or trying to control outcomes, and surrender these aspects to the divine. Cultivate trust in the process of life and know that every step you take is guided by a higher purpose. Use affirmations to reinforce your belief in divine guidance: "I trust the divine will," "I am aligned with the greater purpose," and "I surrender to the flow of life."

14

The Energy of Forgiveness

Forgiveness is the key that sets us free,
A healing force for you and me.
It lightens the heart, it clears the mind,
In forgiveness, peace we find.

To forgive is to release the pain,
The anger, the hurt, the endless strain.
In forgiveness, we find our grace,
And let go of the past's embrace.

Forgiveness is not about the other,
It's about freeing ourselves from the bother.
It's an act of love, an act of might,
A choice to bring our souls to light.

Forgiveness is the path to peace,
A way to make the suffering cease.
In forgiveness, we let go of blame,
And find healing, without shame.

When we forgive, we release the chain,
The past no longer holds the reign.
In forgiveness, we break the tie,
And soar like eagles, high and high.

Forgiveness is the energy of the heart,
A new beginning, a fresh start.
It allows us to live in love,
To rise above, like a dove.

In forgiveness, we find our strength,
We let go of the past's length.
With forgiveness, we heal the soul,
And make ourselves once again whole.

INTERPRETATION

Forgiveness is the powerful energy that heals and liberates

In Indian spirituality, forgiveness is not simply an emotional act but a profound spiritual practice. The teachings of the Bhagavad Gita emphasise that forgiveness is essential for spiritual growth. *Krishna* teaches *Arjuna* that one must rise above anger and hatred and forgive those who harm us. Forgiveness is seen as a divine virtue that helps us purify our hearts and minds, allowing us to move closer to self-realisation.

Forgiveness is also linked to the concept of *ahimsa* (non-violence) in *Yoga*. It is through forgiveness that we let go of the mental and emotional burdens that cause suffering. By forgiving, we release ourselves from the chains of the past and create space for healing and peace. Forgiveness is an act of self-liberation and a tool to cultivate compassion, both for others and ourselves.

STANZA-WISE INTERPRETATION

- **Stanza 1:** This stanza introduces Forgiveness as the key to peace. It is a healing force that releases negative emotions and brings tranquility to the heart.
- **Stanza 2:** Forgiveness allows us to release the emotional baggage of the past. It clears the mind of anger and resentment, allowing us to embrace peace.
- **Stanza 3:** The poem emphasises that forgiveness is not about the other person but about freeing ourselves

from the burden of holding onto hurt and pain. It is an act of self-love.

- **Stanza 4:** Forgiveness is a transformative practice that leads to peace. It allows us to break free from blame and the cycle of suffering.
- **Stanza 5:** The act of forgiveness releases us from the past and enables us to move forward in life. It frees us from the chains that hold us back.
- **Stanza 6:** This stanza shows that Forgiveness is an act of love. It opens the heart and allows us to rise above negativity and resentment.
- **Stanza 7:** The poem concludes by emphasising that Forgiveness heals the soul and restores our sense of wholeness. It brings strength and allows us to embrace life fully.

PHILOSOPHICAL INSIGHTS

This topic explores Forgiveness as a powerful spiritual tool. In Indian philosophy, forgiveness is seen as an act of grace that brings peace and healing. It is through forgiveness that we release the past and move forward with lightness in our hearts. The Bhagavad Gita and other Vedic scriptures teach that forgiving others is essential for spiritual growth, as it allows us to transcend anger and suffering. The poem illustrates how forgiveness frees us from the chains of the past and helps us embrace life with love and compassion.

PRACTICAL GUIDANCE

What grudges or resentment are you holding onto? Are you ready to forgive and release the emotional burden?

Start by reflecting on the people or situations you need to forgive. Practice forgiving yourself first, releasing any guilt or regret. Meditate on the power of forgiveness, using it to free your heart from negative emotions. Each day, practice small acts of forgiveness, letting go of anger and choosing peace instead. Use affirmations like "I forgive myself," "I release the past," and "I choose peace." Let forgiveness become a healing force in your life, transforming your emotional landscape and bringing you peace.

15

The Power of Self-Love

Self-love is the root of all things,
It is the strength that allows us to sing.
It is the foundation, the light we seek,
The courage to stand, humble and meek.

Through self-love, we heal the soul,
We accept ourselves, and we feel whole.
It is the power to forgive and grow,
To embrace our flaws and let them show.

Self-love is the act of trust,
In ourselves, in what we must.
It is the acceptance of who we are,
And knowing we're already a star.

In self-love, we find our strength,
The courage to go any length.
It is the fuel for the heart's fire,
And the foundation for all we desire.

When we love ourselves, we rise,
We open our hearts and reach the skies.
Through self-love, we begin to see,
The truth of who we're meant to be.

Self-love is not pride or vanity,
It is the key to our true humanity.
It is the recognition of our worth,
And the acceptance of our true birth.

Through self-love, we are whole and free,
Living in love and harmony.
It is the foundation on which we build,
A life of joy, fulfilled.

INTERPRETATION

Self-love is the foundation of all spiritual and personal growth

In Indian philosophy, self-love is not seen as selfishness or vanity but as an essential practice for emotional well-being and spiritual growth. *Krishna* in the Bhagavad Gita teaches that self-love is fundamental to loving others. By recognizing our own worth and treating ourselves with kindness, we are able to extend that love to others. Self-love is connected to the concept of *Atman*, the true self, and *Ahimsa* (non-violence), where we treat ourselves with compassion and care.

Through self-love, we align with the divine within us, recognizing that we are worthy of love and happiness. This internal peace allows us to interact with the world with confidence and compassion. Self-love is not about ego or pride, but about honouring our divine nature and understanding our true value.

STANZA-WISE INTERPRETATION

- **Stanza 1:** This stanza introduces self-love as the foundation of our strength. It is the source from which all positive actions and emotions flow.
- **Stanza 2:** Self-love heals the soul and brings a sense of completeness. By accepting ourselves fully, we can embrace our imperfections and grow.
- **Stanza 3:** This stanza shows that self-love is an act of trust and acceptance. It is about recognizing our

inherent worth and understanding that we are worthy of love.

- **Stanza 4:** Self-love gives us the strength and courage to pursue our desires. It fuels our inner fire and provides the foundation for all that we seek.
- **Stanza 5:** Through self-love, we unlock our true potential. We rise to become the best version of ourselves, confident and at peace with who we are.
- **Stanza 6:** Self-love is not about pride but about recognizing our true humanity. It is about honouring our worth and embracing our divine nature.
- **Stanza 7:** The poem concludes by reinforcing that self-love is the foundation for a fulfilling life. It leads to joy, harmony, and fulfilment.

PHILOSOPHICAL INSIGHTS

This topic emphasises self-love as the cornerstone of a balanced and fulfilled life. Indian spiritual practices teach that loving oneself is essential for spiritual growth and harmony. Self-love is not egotism but a recognition of our divine nature. The poem illustrates that through self-love, we heal, grow, and align with our true purpose. It encourages the reader to cultivate self-compassion and treat themselves with the love and respect they deserve.

PRACTICAL GUIDANCE

How often do you show love and compassion to yourself? Are you ready to embrace your true worth?

Start by practising self-compassion. Speak kindly to yourself, and treat yourself with the same love and respect you offer others. Meditate on your inner worth and recognise the divinity within you. Practice affirmations such as "I love and accept myself," "I am worthy of love," and "I am enough." Each day, engage in activities that nurture your body, mind, and spirit. By cultivating self-love, you lay the foundation for a life filled with joy, peace, and purpose.

16

The Power of Surrender

Surrender is not giving up the fight,
It is trusting the darkness, seeking the light.
It's letting go, and yet standing tall,
Opening the heart to the divine call.

In surrender, there is strength, not defeat,
It is the power to accept life's beat.
It is the courage to release control,
And let go of the ego, to make us whole.

Surrender is the freedom to be,
To accept life as it is, and see,
That in letting go, we find our way,
And in trust, we live each day.

Through surrender, the heart becomes light,
Free from fear, and free from might.
It is in surrender that we are free,
To live in harmony with eternity.

Surrender is the art of letting go,
Of trusting the flow, letting it grow.
It's knowing that all will unfold,
As the divine plan is quietly told.

In surrender, we find our grace,
We release the past, we embrace our place.
It is the highest form of trust,
In surrender, our hearts adjust.

To surrender is to find true power,
It is the bloom of the lotus flower.
In the stillness of surrender's flow,
We find our strength, and let it grow.

INTERPRETATION

Surrender is the ultimate act of trust

In Indian spirituality, surrender (*prapatti*) is considered a powerful practice that leads to spiritual liberation. It is not about weakness, but about yielding the personal ego to a higher divine purpose. *Krishna*, in the Bhagavad Gita, advises *Arjuna* to surrender his will to the divine, as true freedom and peace come from surrendering the ego and aligning with the divine will. Through surrender, we accept that we are not in control of everything and release the need for domination.

Surrender opens the door to divine grace, where we trust the flow of life and align ourselves with the greater cosmic plan. It is through surrender that we achieve inner peace, emotional release, and spiritual growth, letting go of the fear and uncertainty that stem from the ego.

STANZA-WISE INTERPRETATION

- **Stanza 1:** This stanza explains that surrender is not about giving up but about trusting the divine. It is the act of letting go of control and opening up to divine guidance.
- **Stanza 2:** The poem highlights that surrender brings strength and acceptance. It is through releasing control that we experience freedom.
- **Stanza 3:** Surrender allows us to see life clearly, without the filter of ego or control. It brings clarity and aligns us with the flow of life.

- **Stanza 4:** In surrender, we release fear and embrace trust. This helps us align with the eternal flow of life, finding peace and contentment.
- **Stanza 5:** Surrender is shown as an art that involves trust and acceptance. It is the process of letting go and allowing life to unfold naturally.
- **Stanza 6:** The act of surrender brings grace and balance into our lives. We stop resisting life and accept our place in the grand design.
- **Stanza 7:** The final stanza portrays surrender as the ultimate form of strength. It is through surrender that we tap into the divine power and experience growth.

PHILOSOPHICAL INSIGHTS

This topic emphasises surrender as the ultimate spiritual practice. In Indian spirituality, surrender is not about giving up or weakness, but about letting go of the ego and trusting the divine. The Bhagavad Gita teaches that surrendering to the divine will is the path to true peace and spiritual enlightenment. The poem highlights that through surrender, we release control, trust the flow of life, and experience divine grace. Surrender is the highest act of strength and trust that allows us to align with the greater cosmic plan.

PRACTICAL GUIDANCE

Are you ready to surrender your need for control and trust the divine process? Can you embrace life as it comes without resistance?

Start by practising small acts of surrender each day. Let go of the need to control every situation, and instead, trust the flow of life. When challenges arise, take a deep breath, and remind yourself that surrendering to the divine plan brings peace. Use meditation and prayer to connect with the divine presence and ask for guidance in trusting the process of life. Affirmations like "I trust the divine plan," "I surrender to the flow of life," and "I am at peace with life" will help you align with the energy of surrender.

17

The Energy of Compassion

Compassion is the light that shines,
A gentle force that intertwines.
It opens the heart, it heals the soul,
It is the energy that makes us whole.

In compassion, we see the truth,
In every being, in every youth.
It is the bond that ties us all,
Compassion is the answer to life's call.

Through compassion, we heal the world,
Every wound, every flag unfurled.
It is the energy that fuels the heart,
And helps us all play our part.

In compassion, there is no fear,
Only love, and the path is clear.
It is the power to heal and mend,
To bring together, to transcend.

Compassion is the gift we give,
To others and ourselves to live.
In every act, in every thought,
We sow compassion, what we've sought.

Through compassion, we see the divine,
In every face, in every sign.
It is the force that unites us all,
Compassion is the answer to the call.

To live with compassion is to be free,
It is the energy of harmony.
When compassion flows, we understand,
That all are one, hand in hand.

INTERPRETATION

Compassion is the energy that connects us all

In Indian spiritual teachings, compassion is seen as a divine virtue that transcends personal desires and aligns us with the universal consciousness. *Ahimsa* (non-violence) is the foundation of compassion, and it teaches us to act with love and kindness toward all beings. The Bhagavad Gita emphasises the importance of compassion as it helps us align with divine truth and strengthen our connection with the divine. Compassion is not just an emotion but a powerful force that heals and transforms.

When we cultivate compassion, we move beyond our ego and become attuned to the suffering of others, offering love and understanding in response. Compassion allows us to transcend our individual selves and see the divine in all beings. It is through compassion that we create a world of peace, understanding, and unity.

STANZA-WISE INTERPRETATION

- **Stanza 1:** This stanza introduces compassion as a transformative force. It is the energy that heals and makes us whole, allowing us to live in harmony with others.
- **Stanza 2:** The poem emphasises that compassion helps us see the truth in others. It is the bond that unites all beings, making us one in spirit.
- **Stanza 3:** Compassion is the healing force of the world. It helps us overcome suffering and create a positive impact in the world.

- **Stanza 4:** The poem shows that compassion transcends fear and allows us to heal and unite. It is the force that brings peace and understanding.
- **Stanza 5:** Compassion is depicted as a gift we offer to others and ourselves. It brings us closer to love, understanding, and peace.
- **Stanza 6:** This stanza reveals that compassion helps us recognise the divine in every being. It unites us in love and understanding.
- **Stanza 7:** The final stanza encourages the reader to live with compassion, as it is through this energy that we find freedom, peace, and unity.

PHILOSOPHICAL INSIGHTS

This topic explores compassion as a divine energy that connects all beings. In Indian spiritual traditions, compassion is a central virtue that aligns us with the universal consciousness. The Bhagavad Gita teaches that compassion transcends ego and helps us see the divine in others. Through compassion, we create a peaceful, harmonious world where all beings are respected and loved. This poem illustrates that compassion is the force that unites us, heals us, and allows us to live with love and understanding.

PRACTICAL GUIDANCE

How often do you practice compassion in your daily life? Can you extend compassion to yourself and others?

Start by practising compassion toward yourself. Be gentle with yourself, recognizing your own struggles and offering kindness. Extend that compassion to others, especially those who may be suffering. In moments of conflict, try to see the situation from the other person's perspective and respond with love and understanding. Use affirmations like "I am compassionate," "I embrace all with love," and "I act with kindness." By cultivating compassion, you align with the divine and create a world of peace and understanding.

CHAPTER 2

The Inner Journey

18

The Journey of Self-Discovery

The path within is vast and wide,
A journey that no one can hide.
It calls us to explore, to seek,
The truth inside, both strong and meek.

Self-discovery is not a race,
But a journey to find your space.
It's a walk through valleys deep,
Where secrets of the soul we keep.

In the depths of your heart, you find,
The mysteries of your own mind.
With every step, you learn to see,
The boundless truth of who you can be.

Self-discovery is the art of knowing,
The self within, the seed that's growing.
It is a journey of peeling away,
The layers that hide the light of day.

In moments of silence, the truth is clear,
It whispers softly, calm and near.
The voice inside will always guide,
When we let go of ego and pride.

Self-discovery is the power to be,
The person you were meant to see.
It's finding the truth that lies within,
And embracing it without, free from sin.

To discover the self is to truly live,
It's to learn to forgive and give.
The journey leads us home again,
To the place where we begin.

INTERPRETATION

Self-discovery is the process of uncovering your true nature

In Indian philosophy, the journey of self-discovery is central to spiritual growth. The concept of *Atman* (the true self) is key to understanding that the self is not just the body or the mind, but the soul, which is eternal and connected with the divine. The Upanishads emphasise that self-realisation is the highest goal of life, and it is through this journey of discovery that we understand our connection to the universe and the divine.

Self-discovery involves peeling away layers of ego and illusion to reveal the truth of who we really are. The process is gradual and requires patience, as the journey inward can be both challenging and transformative. In *Yoga*, *dhyana* (*meditation*) is the tool used to quiet the mind and listen to the deeper truth that lies within. The more we connect with our true self, the more we experience peace, wisdom, and a sense of unity with the universe.

STANZA-WISE INTERPRETATION

- **Stanza 1:** This stanza introduces the idea that self-discovery is a vast journey that requires exploration. It emphasises that this path is personal and unique for each individual.
- **Stanza 2:** Self-discovery is described as a process of self-exploration, not a race or competition. It involves diving deep into the self and uncovering hidden truths.

- **Stanza 3:** The stanza highlights that self-discovery involves getting in touch with our inner selves. By examining our thoughts and emotions, we begin to understand who we truly are.
- **Stanza 4:** The poem emphasises that self-discovery is an ongoing process of peeling back the layers of the ego. With every step, we uncover more of our authentic selves.
- **Stanza 5:** In silence, the truth of who we are becomes clear. The voice of the inner self speaks in quiet moments, guiding us to deeper understanding.
- **Stanza 6:** Self-discovery leads us to our true power. By embracing our authentic selves, we align with our higher purpose and become who we are meant to be.
- **Stanza 7:** The poem concludes by stating that self-discovery is essential for living a fulfilled life. It is a process of learning, growing, and ultimately returning to our true essence.

PHILOSOPHICAL INSIGHTS

This topic delves into the journey of self-discovery, which is an essential part of spiritual growth in Indian philosophy. Through practices like *dhyana* (meditation) and introspection, we begin to uncover the truth of who we really are. The poem emphasises that self-discovery is not a quick process but a gradual unfolding of the layers of the ego to reveal the soul's true essence. By embracing this journey, we come to realize our true potential and our connection to the divine.

PRACTICAL GUIDANCE

Are you ready to embark on the journey of self-discovery? What truths about yourself have you yet to uncover?

Begin by setting aside time each day for reflection and meditation. Use this time to quiet your mind and listen to the inner voice of your soul. Reflect on your experiences, both joyful and challenging, to understand the lessons they offer. Journaling can help you uncover patterns and deeper truths about yourself. Be patient with the process, and trust that with each step, you are uncovering more of your authentic self. Let go of the need for external validation and allow your inner truth to guide you.

19

Embracing Vulnerability

Vulnerability is the gift we hold,
A strength that cannot be bought or sold.
It opens us up, both soft and raw,
Revealing our hearts, without a flaw.

To be vulnerable is to be free,
To let go of the walls that bind you and me.
In vulnerability, we find our grace,
Opening our hearts to a warm embrace.

The shield we carry, we must let fall,
For in our vulnerability, we stand tall.
It is in our fragility we find strength,
That transcends the limits of earthly length.

Vulnerability is the courage to feel,
To experience life, and let it heal.
In embracing our deepest fears,
We clear the path, we wipe the tears.

When we are vulnerable, we allow the light,
To shine through the darkness, burning bright.
It is through our openness we find,
The courage to heal the wounds of the mind.

Vulnerability is the bridge we build,
To connect with others, hearts fulfilled.
Through our openness, we see the truth,
That we are all connected, in our youth.

Embrace your vulnerability, let it shine,
For in its truth, we are divine.
It is through the cracks that the light flows,
Allowing us to live, to love, and to grow.

INTERPRETATION

Vulnerability is the strength that enables transformation

In Indian spiritual teachings, vulnerability is seen as an essential aspect of growth and connection. It is not weakness, as often perceived, but a powerful and courageous act of being open to life. The practice of *bhakti* (devotion) and surrender both require vulnerability — the willingness to open oneself to divine grace. In the Bhagavad Gita, Lord *Krishna* teaches *Arjuna* that only through the surrender of the ego can one truly experience the divine power within.

Vulnerability is about releasing the need for control, and it opens the door to deep healing and connection. It allows us to embrace our true nature and acknowledge our imperfections without shame. It is through vulnerability that we experience empathy, deepen relationships, and ultimately evolve into our highest selves.

STANZA-WISE INTERPRETATION

- **Stanza 1:** This stanza introduces vulnerability as a strength, emphasising that embracing our true selves without defense or guard allows us to connect deeply with life.
- **Stanza 2:** The poem highlights that being vulnerable is an act of freedom, where we release barriers and open ourselves to genuine emotional experiences.

- **Stanza 3:** Vulnerability is presented as the courage to let go of protective walls. The poem suggests that our true power is found in our openness.
- **Stanza 4:** Here, vulnerability is portrayed as a path to healing. By embracing vulnerability, we let go of fear and create space for personal growth.
- **Stanza 5:** The stanza illustrates that vulnerability allows us to embrace our fears and transform them into a source of strength. It helps us heal from past wounds and become whole.
- **Stanza 6:** Vulnerability is portrayed as a way to connect with others. By being open and transparent, we create bonds of trust with others.
- **Stanza 7:** The final stanza encourages the reader to embrace their vulnerability, as it is through our openness that we allow divine light to enter and guide us toward growth.

PHILOSOPHICAL INSIGHTS

This topic focuses on the transformative power of vulnerability in our lives. In Indian philosophy, vulnerability is not seen as weakness but as an essential aspect of spiritual evolution. Through vulnerability, we open ourselves to divine grace, allowing the ego to dissolve and our true nature to emerge. *Krishna's* teachings in the Bhagavad Gita show that by surrendering to vulnerability, we create deep connections with ourselves, others, and the divine. This poem emphasises that vulnerability is a strength that enables us to heal, grow, and embrace life fully.

PRACTICAL GUIDANCE

How do you respond to your vulnerabilities? Are you ready to embrace them as sources of strength?

Start by accepting your own imperfections and letting go of the need to appear perfect to others. Practice being open and authentic in your interactions, sharing your true thoughts and feelings. In moments of fear or doubt, remind yourself that vulnerability is a strength, not a weakness. Through meditation, reflect on your fears and allow yourself to feel them without judgment. Embrace vulnerability as the gateway to greater emotional connection, personal growth, and spiritual evolution.

20

Embracing the Shadow Self

The shadow lurks within the light,
A part of us that hides from sight.
Yet it is not to be feared or cast,
For in embracing it, we are made vast.

The shadow holds the pain we deny,
The fears, the doubts that make us shy.
It is the part we try to outrun,
But in facing it, the journey's begun.

Embrace the darkness, let it in,
For in it, you will find your win.
The shadow teaches us to grow,
To understand what we don't know.

When we face the shadow with grace,
We find the light in every place.
It is the path to self-realisation,
A journey of deep transformation.

The shadow is not your enemy,
But a part of your soul, wild and free.
Through acceptance, we heal and grow,
And let our true light glow.

In the shadow, we see our fears,
We embrace them, wipe the tears.
For when we walk through the night,
We emerge with newfound light.

To embrace the shadow is to be whole,
It is the key to healing the soul.
Through acceptance, we find the way,
To live in peace, every day.

INTERPRETATION

Embracing the shadow self is the key to spiritual integration

In Indian philosophy, the concept of the shadow self relates to the parts of ourselves that we reject or hide from, often driven by ego and societal expectations. These are the traits or desires that we perceive as negative or shameful, yet they are part of our whole being. The Bhagavad Gita teaches that the ego often blocks us from accepting our true nature. By integrating the shadow, we learn to accept and embrace all parts of ourselves.

The Upanishads and *Yoga* philosophy speak of self-realization — understanding all aspects of the self, both light and dark. The process of confronting our shadow self requires courage and patience but leads to spiritual enlightenment and inner peace. It is through self-acceptance and the integration of the shadow that we achieve wholeness.

STANZA-WISE INTERPRETATION

- **Stanza 1:** This stanza introduces the shadow self as a part of us that we often ignore or fear. However, it emphasises that we should not fear it but embrace it to become whole.
- **Stanza 2:** The poem explains that the shadow represents the pain, doubts, and fears we hide from others and ourselves. Acknowledging these aspects is the first step to healing.

- **Stanza 3:** Embracing the shadow is shown as a transformative act. By facing what we hide, we begin a journey of growth and self-understanding.
- **Stanza 4:** The stanza emphasises that through facing the shadow, we uncover light and wisdom. Accepting it is the path to spiritual transformation.
- **Stanza 5:** The shadow is not an enemy but a part of the soul. By accepting it, we heal and release the negativity that it carries.
- **Stanza 6:** This stanza shows that by embracing the **shadow**, we confront our fears, find emotional release, and grow in strength.
- **Stanza 7:** The final stanza reinforces that embracing the shadow self leads to wholeness. It is through accepting both light and dark that we find inner peace.

PHILOSOPHICAL INSIGHTS

This topic discusses embracing the shadow self as a path to self-realization and spiritual integration. In Indian philosophy, the shadow represents the parts of ourselves that we often deny or repress. By confronting and integrating these aspects, we achieve a deeper understanding of who we truly are. This process, while challenging, leads to spiritual growth and peace. The poem emphasises that embracing the shadow self is necessary for personal transformation and achieving a balanced, harmonious life.

PRACTICAL GUIDANCE

What parts of yourself have you been hiding or rejecting? Are you ready to embrace the shadow within you?

Start by reflecting on the parts of yourself you find difficult to accept. Through meditation and self-reflection, allow yourself to explore these aspects of your personality. Practice self-compassion and acceptance as you confront these parts of yourself. Use journaling to explore your fears and vulnerabilities, and affirm that you are whole, even in your imperfections. Self-inquiry and mindfulness practices will help you understand and integrate the shadow, leading to greater spiritual growth and inner peace.

21

Resilience and the Will to Rise

In every fall, there is a rise,
A strength that breaks through all disguise.
Resilience is the heart's true song,
It carries us, we move along.

Through hardship, we find our might,
Like the flame that burns so bright.
Resilience helps us find our way,
To stand tall, come what may.

It is the will to rise once more,
To open each and every door.
No matter how many times we fall,
Resilience lifts us above it all.

Resilience is the power within,
To rise again and yet again.
It is the force that lets us stand,
Firmly grounded, yet hand in hand.

In the face of loss, in the face of pain,
Resilience helps us break the chain.
It gives us strength to carry on,
And find the light before the dawn.

Resilience is not the absence of grief,
But the courage to find relief.
It is the strength to hold on tight,
And keep moving forward in the night.

Resilience is the soul's great power,
It blooms in the darkest hour.
With resilience, we stand tall,
Rising again, no matter how small.

INTERPRETATION

Resilience is the strength to overcome adversity

In Indian philosophy, resilience is a key trait that connects to the concept of *dharma* (righteous living) and *karma* (action). Life's challenges are inevitable, but resilience teaches us to face them with courage and grace. The Bhagavad Gita emphasises that *Krishna*'s teachings encourage *Arjuna* to rise above his doubts and fears and fulfil his dharma, regardless of the obstacles.

Resilience is not the absence of struggle, but the ability to endure and rise after facing setbacks. It is the inner strength that sustains us through life's trials. In *Yoga*, resilience is linked to the practice of *pranayama* (breathing exercises) and *dhyana* (meditation), which help build mental strength and emotional fortitude. Through these practices, we cultivate the resilience needed to face life's challenges and maintain peace and balance.

STANZA-WISE INTERPRETATION

- **Stanza 1:** This stanza introduces resilience as the strength to rise after each fall. It emphasises that resilience is what helps us overcome obstacles and move forward.
- **Stanza 2:** The poem highlights that resilience shines in difficult times, and it is the driving force that helps us continue our journey despite adversity.
- **Stanza 3:** Resilience is portrayed as the ability to rise after each fall, no matter how many setbacks we face. It empowers us to keep moving forward.

- **Stanza 4:** Resilience is presented as a force within us. It gives us the strength to stand firm, even when life presents challenges.
- **Stanza 5:** The poem shows that resilience helps us navigate pain and loss. It is the strength that allows us to find light after dark times.
- **Stanza 6:** Resilience is not about avoiding grief, but about embracing it with courage. It helps us move forward, even when the journey feels difficult.
- **Stanza 7:** The final stanza emphasises that resilience is the soul's strength. It enables us to rise again and keep going, no matter the circumstances.

PHILOSOPHICAL INSIGHTS

This topic highlights the power of resilience as the strength to overcome adversity and continue on the path of life. In Indian philosophy, resilience is deeply connected to *dharma* and *karma* — the ability to continue fulfilling our purpose, no matter the challenges. The poem illustrates that resilience is not the absence of difficulties but the courage to face them and rise again. It encourages us to keep moving forward, to rise with strength after every setback, and to trust that we have the inner power to overcome life's challenges.

PRACTICAL GUIDANCE

How do you respond to adversity in your life? Are you ready to cultivate the strength of resilience?

Begin by acknowledging the challenges you face and accepting that they are part of your growth. Reflect on past experiences where you overcame obstacles, and remind yourself of your inner strength. Use meditation to build mental and emotional resilience, focusing on deep breathing and calming the mind. Practice affirmations like "I am resilient," "I rise above challenges," and "I have the strength to overcome any obstacle." With every trial, allow resilience to guide you forward, knowing that you are capable of overcoming anything.

22

The Courage to Begin Again

To start again is to be free,
From the chains of what used to be.
It takes courage to leave behind,
The past that haunts the heart and mind.

In every ending, a new beginning lies,
Like the sunrise in the morning skies.
It's the courage to embrace the unknown,
And trust that we are never alone.

To begin again is to shed the old,
To step forward, brave and bold.
It's the leap of faith, the chance to grow,
And trust that we are capable of what we don't know.

Every new start brings a fresh view,
A chance to start again, to renew.
It's the wisdom that comes from within,
To rise once more and begin again.

The courage to begin again is the spark,
That lights the way through the dark.
It's the willingness to embrace change,
And let go of what feels strange.

With every step, we heal and learn,
For every ending, there's a return.
To begin again is to be free,
To start afresh, to simply be.

So take the leap, start anew,
Embrace the change, let it through.
The courage to begin again, you'll find,
Is the key to peace of heart and mind.

INTERPRETATION

The courage to begin again is the path to renewal

In Indian spiritual teachings, the idea of starting afresh and beginning again is linked to the concept of *samsara*, the cycle of birth, death, and rebirth. Life is in constant flux, and each moment offers us a chance for a new beginning. The Bhagavad Gita teaches that life's true purpose is fulfilled through constant growth, learning, and adapting to the flow of the universe.

In *Yoga* and Meditation, we learn to shed past attachments, fears, and regrets in order to embrace a new moment. The practice of letting go and beginning again allows us to heal from past wounds and step into the present with courage and purpose. The Upanishads emphasise that liberation (moksha) comes from detaching from the past and moving forward in the eternal present.

STANZA-WISE INTERPRETATION

- **Stanza 1:** This stanza introduces the idea that to begin again requires the courage to let go of the past. The poem highlights that this act of starting afresh is liberating.
- **Stanza 2:** The poem emphasises that with every ending, there is a new opportunity for a fresh start. It takes courage to embrace the unknown and trust in the process.

- **Stanza 3:** Beginning again is portrayed as a personal choice to step forward, embracing the unknown. It requires courage and trust in one's ability to grow.
- **Stanza 4:** Each new beginning offers us a new perspective. It is an opportunity for renewal and growth, allowing us to shed old limitations and see the world in a new light.
- **Stanza 5:** The poem speaks of courage as the inner strength that guides us through uncertain times. It encourages us to embrace change and trust that new beginnings lead to growth.
- **Stanza 6:** The poem suggests that with every new start, we find healing and wisdom. Every ending brings with it the opportunity for a return to a new beginning.
- **Stanza 7:** The final stanza reinforces the idea that **courage** to start again is the key to inner peace. It encourages the reader to embrace the opportunity for renewal.

PHILOSOPHICAL INSIGHTS

This topic focuses on the courage to begin again. In Indian philosophy, starting anew is a vital part of the spiritual journey. The Bhagavad Gita teaches that true peace and fulfilment come when we are able to detach from past experiences and embrace each moment as an opportunity for growth and renewal. The poem illustrates that courage to begin again allows us to shed past fears, embrace change, and step into the future with a sense of hope and possibility.

PRACTICAL GUIDANCE

How do you respond when faced with new beginnings? Are you ready to embrace change and start fresh?

Reflect on past experiences where you had to begin again. What did you learn from them? Use meditation to center yourself and let go of any fear or resistance to change. Embrace each new opportunity with an open heart and trust that it will bring growth. Begin each day with a sense of renewal, affirming, "I am open to new beginnings," "I embrace change," and "I am courageous." Step forward with confidence, knowing that each new start is a step toward your highest potential.

23

Healing the Inner Child

The inner child lies deep within,
A part of us that feels the wind.
It is the purest, untainted soul,
The part that makes us whole and whole.

Healing the child is to return,
To innocence, to love, to learn.
It's nurturing the wounds of the past,
And helping the heart to heal at last.

The inner child is a voice so pure,
It calls for love, to feel secure.
It's the laughter, the joy, the spark,
That resides within, deep in the dark.

To heal the inner child is to care,
To offer love and be aware.
It's accepting the wounds we've carried,
And forgiving the past that we've buried.

Healing the inner child is to be,
In the moment, full and free.
It's letting go of old grief,
And offering the heart relief.

The inner child seeks the truth,
To be loved, to feel the proof,
That it is worthy, it is enough,
And that healing can be gentle, not tough.

In healing the child, we heal the soul,
We return to innocence, we become whole.
It is the key to peace and grace,
To heal the inner child, find your place.

INTERPRETATION

Healing the inner child is a transformative process of self-acceptance and love

In Indian spirituality, the concept of the inner child represents the pure, untainted essence of the self before societal conditioning and ego took hold. *Yoga* and meditation often focus on reconnecting with the heart and healing past emotional wounds. The inner child symbolizes innocence, vulnerability, and creativity, and its healing is central to emotional and spiritual well-being.

The Bhagavad Gita teaches us to return to a state of innocence and purity, shedding the ego and reconnecting with the divine essence within. The Upanishads emphasise that true wisdom is gained through self-realization, which often involves healing the past, forgiving old wounds, and restoring the inner harmony that allows us to reconnect with our divine self.

STANZA-WISE INTERPRETATION

- **Stanza 1:** This stanza introduces the inner child as the purest aspect of the self, highlighting its innocence and connection to the true self.
- **Stanza 2:** Healing the inner child is depicted as a return to innocence. It involves addressing past wounds and offering love and nurturing to the vulnerable parts of ourselves.
- **Stanza 3:** The poem describes the inner child as a voice that longs for love and security. It is a source of joy and creativity that resides deep within.

- **Stanza 4:** Healing the inner child involves self-care, acceptance, and forgiveness. It is about nurturing the wounds that have been carried for too long.
- **Stanza 5:** The poem emphasises that healing the inner child brings relief and freedom. It is a process of letting go of old pain and offering the heart comfort.
- **Stanza 6:** The inner child seeks love and affirmation. It reminds us that we are worthy of love and healing, and that the process can be gentle and nurturing.
- **Stanza 7:** The final stanza highlights that healing the inner child brings peace and wholeness. It is a crucial part of the spiritual journey toward self-realisation and balance.

PHILOSOPHICAL INSIGHTS

This topic focuses on healing the inner child as an essential process for emotional and spiritual growth. In Indian philosophy, the inner child represents our original, pure self before the external influences shaped us. Healing the inner child involves addressing past emotional wounds, practising self-love, and accepting ourselves as we are. The poem illustrates that by healing the inner child, we reconnect with our true essence and experience inner peace and fulfilment.

PRACTICAL GUIDANCE

How often do you acknowledge and care for your inner child? Are you ready to heal the wounds of the past?

Begin by acknowledging the emotional wounds of your past, and approach them with compassion. Practice mindfulness and meditation to connect with the inner child within you, offering love and care. Reflect on moments of childhood that shaped you and forgive yourself for any past mistakes. Use affirmations like "I love my inner child," "I am whole and complete," and "I am worthy of healing." Through self-care and nurturing, you can heal the inner child and reconnect with the joy, innocence, and creativity within.

24

The Inner Compass of Intuition

Intuition is the voice that speaks,
In whispers soft, it gently seeks.
It guides us through the dark unknown,
And leads us back to our true home.

It's the knowing without the mind,
The subtle force that we can't find.
It doesn't speak in words or sound,
But in stillness, its voice is profound.

Intuition is the heart's true call,
It shows us the way through it all.
It leads us down the path of light,
And helps us see beyond the night.

In intuition, there is trust,
A knowing that we must adjust.
It guides us to make the right choice,
And silences the mind's loud voice.

Through intuition, we learn to see,
The hidden truths that set us free.
It is the wisdom of the soul,
That makes us complete and whole.

When we listen to intuition's song,
We find our way, where we belong.
It is the quiet force inside,
That helps us navigate with pride.

The inner compass that guides our soul,
Is intuition, making us whole.
By listening to its subtle voice,
We find our truth, we make the choice.

INTERPRETATION

Intuition is the guiding force within us

In Indian philosophy, intuition (*buddhi*) is considered a key aspect of spiritual awakening. The teachings of the Bhagavad Gita emphasise that true wisdom comes not from intellectual knowledge but from the inner guidance of the heart and soul. Intuition is the subtle voice of the higher self, guiding us towards truth and self-realisation. The Upanishads speak of *jnana* (knowledge) as a higher wisdom that transcends the material world and comes through direct, intuitive perception of reality.

Intuition is not bound by logic or reason, but is a divine gift that allows us to perceive the truth of situations without external evidence. It is through listening to our inner voice that we align ourselves with our higher purpose and the divine plan.

STANZA-WISE INTERPRETATION

- **Stanza 1:** This stanza introduces intuition as a guiding force. It speaks to us softly, helping us navigate through uncertainty and leading us to our true path.
- **Stanza 2:** Intuition is presented as a knowing that transcends the intellect. It is a deeper, silent wisdom that cannot be found through logic alone.
- **Stanza 3:** The poem emphasises that intuition provides guidance during difficult times, leading us through challenges with clarity and light.

- **Stanza 4:** Intuition is portrayed as a quiet force that requires trust. It helps us make the right choices and quiets the loud, distracting voice of the ego.
- **Stanza 5:** Intuition is the source of wisdom that frees us from limitations. It reveals hidden truths, helping us connect with our soul's purpose.
- **Stanza 6:** By listening to intuition, we are guided toward our true selves. It empowers us to navigate life with confidence and purpose.
- **Stanza 7:** The final stanza emphasises that intuition is our inner compass. It is through listening to this divine voice that we find our truth and make aligned choices.

PHILOSOPHICAL INSIGHTS

This topic explores intuition as the inner compass that guides us toward spiritual growth and self-realisation. In Indian spirituality, intuition is seen as the voice of the higher self, providing direct access to wisdom and truth. The Bhagavad Gita and the Upanishads emphasise that true knowledge comes from intuitive perception, which transcends logical thinking. The poem encourages the reader to trust their inner voice and use intuition as a guiding force in life.

PRACTICAL GUIDANCE

Do you listen to your intuition? How often do you trust the inner voice that guides you?

Begin by tuning in to your inner voice. Practice mindfulness and meditation to quiet the distractions of the mind and connect with your deeper self. When making decisions, take a moment to listen to your heart's guidance before acting. Reflect on past moments when you followed your intuition and experienced clarity. Trust that the more you listen to this inner compass, the more aligned you will feel with your true path. Use affirmations like "I trust my intuition," "I am guided by my inner wisdom," and "I am aligned with my higher purpose."

25

The Dance of Balance

Balance is the rhythm of life's song,
It helps us move, it keeps us strong.
In the dance of life, we find our way,
In balance, we move through night and day.

It's not the absence of struggle or strife,
But the harmony of body and life.
Balance is the gentle sway,
That guides us through each passing day.

In balance, we find peace of mind,
We leave the chaos behind.
It's the stillness in the storm,
The calm that keeps us warm.

Balance is the art of giving and take,
Of knowing when to bend, when to break.
It's the quiet strength that helps us cope,
The thread of wisdom, the rope of hope.

Through balance, we learn to grow,
To live with grace, to let go.
In balance, we find our center,
A place of peace, a soul's mentor.

Balance is not perfection or ease,
But the ability to bend with the breeze.
It's the dance between light and dark,
That leaves its mark, a sacred spark.

In balance, we are free to live,
To take, to love, to forgive.
It is the dance of life we share,
In balance, we find love everywhere.

INTERPRETATION

Balance is the foundation of a harmonious life

In Indian philosophy, balance is the key to spiritual and emotional well-being. *Krishna*, in the Bhagavad Gita, teaches *Arjuna* about the importance of equanimity — the ability to maintain balance in the face of life's ups and downs. *Yoga* also emphasises balance, both physically and mentally, to achieve harmony within oneself and the world.

Balance is not about avoiding challenges but about responding to them with grace and understanding. The Upanishads speak of balance as the alignment of the body, mind, and soul. Achieving balance allows us to live in harmony with ourselves and the universe, guiding us toward peace and spiritual fulfilment.

STANZA-WISE INTERPRETATION

- **Stanza 1:** The poem introduces balance as the core of life's rhythm. It helps us navigate life's challenges, maintaining our strength through the ups and downs.
- **Stanza 2:** Balance is shown as a process of harmonizing our internal and external worlds. It is not the absence of struggle but the ability to handle it with grace.
- **Stanza 3:** In balance, we find peace and stillness. It is through balance that we can remain calm amidst life's storms.
- **Stanza 4:** The poem emphasises that balance involves knowing when to act and when to pause. It is about finding the right moments to give and receive.

- **Stanza 5:** Balance allows us to grow and evolve. It helps us stay grounded while embracing change and letting go of attachments.
- **Stanza 6:** The poem shows that balance is not about perfection but about moving with life's natural flow. It is about accepting both light and dark in life.
- **Stanza 7:** The final stanza encourages the reader to live in balance, embracing both the challenges and joys of life. It is through balance that we experience peace and love.

PHILOSOPHICAL INSIGHTS

This topic emphasises the importance of balance in life. In Indian spiritual teachings, balance is key to emotional and spiritual well-being. By maintaining balance, we harmonize our actions, thoughts, and emotions, enabling us to live a peaceful and purposeful life. The poem illustrates that balance is not about avoiding life's challenges but about navigating them with grace, understanding, and inner peace. It reminds us that true balance brings peace, growth, and fulfilment.

PRACTICAL GUIDANCE

How do you maintain balance in your life? Are there areas where you feel out of balance?

Start by identifying areas of your life where you feel imbalance. Reflect on how you can bring more harmony to these areas, whether it's through work, relationships, or personal health. Use mindfulness and meditation to center yourself, focusing on your breath and being present. Practice *pranayama* (breath control) to calm your mind and body. Use affirmations like "I am balanced," "I flow with life's rhythm," and "I embrace both light and dark." Embrace the dance of balance as it helps you move through life with grace and peace.

26

The Power of Curiosity

Curiosity is the spark of the mind,
A quest for answers, a desire to find.
It opens the doors to worlds unknown,
And lets us see what's yet to be shown.

In curiosity, we seek the truth,
A hunger for knowledge, a thirst for youth.
It pushes us to question, to learn,
And opens our hearts with each turn.

Curiosity is the fire that burns,
That leads us to places where wisdom churns.
It's the spark that fuels the mind,
And leaves no mystery behind.

With curiosity, we break the mold,
We seek beyond what we are told.
It's the path of the seeker's soul,
A journey that makes us whole.

Curiosity is the lens through which we see,
A way to experience life fully and free.
It brings new perspectives, new sights,
And guides us to greater heights.

In curiosity, we are never still,
We ask, we explore, we seek to fulfil.
It's the strength that keeps us moving,
And pushes us towards our proving.

So embrace curiosity, let it grow,
Let your mind and spirit glow.
Through curiosity, we find our way,
And live fully each and every day.

INTERPRETATION

Curiosity is the driving force behind learning and growth

In Indian philosophy, curiosity (*jijnasa*) is considered the starting point of knowledge. The Bhagavad Gita teaches that true wisdom arises from questioning, introspection, and seeking to understand the deeper truths of existence. *Krishna* encourages *Arjuna* to look beyond his initial understanding and embrace the path of self-inquiry and self-realisation.

Curiosity is the foundation of spiritual and intellectual exploration. It is the force that propels us to seek answers to life's greatest questions. The Upanishads teach that questioning the nature of reality and the self is essential for attaining *moksha* (liberation). In *Yoga*, curiosity fuels the practice of self-awareness and spiritual growth, enabling us to continuously evolve.

STANZA-WISE INTERPRETATION

- **Stanza 1:** This stanza introduces curiosity as the spark that ignites the desire to explore and learn, helping us discover new truths and experiences.
- **Stanza 2:** The poem emphasises that curiosity drives us to seek knowledge and truth. It encourages us to question and open our hearts to new discoveries.
- **Stanza 3:** Curiosity is portrayed as the flame that drives our intellectual and spiritual journeys, constantly seeking wisdom and understanding.

- **Stanza 4:** The stanza highlights that curiosity leads us beyond conventional knowledge, pushing us to seek deeper truths and understand our soul's path.
- **Stanza 5:** Curiosity allows us to see life in new ways, providing fresh perspectives and enabling us to grow intellectually and spiritually.
- **Stanza 6:** The poem illustrates that curiosity is an active force that keeps us engaged in the world, continually moving toward growth and fulfilment.
- **Stanza 7:** The final stanza calls for the reader to embrace curiosity, as it is the path to discovering new truths, enhancing our lives, and expanding our consciousness.

PHILOSOPHICAL INSIGHTS

This topic explores curiosity as a powerful force for self-growth and spiritual evolution. In Indian spirituality, curiosity is seen as the desire to understand the world and the self. The Bhagavad Gita encourages us to seek knowledge and truth, which leads to self-realization and liberation. Curiosity is not just an intellectual pursuit but a spiritual journey, helping us uncover deeper wisdom and connect more fully with the divine. The poem emphasises that curiosity is the key to discovering new perspectives and living a fulfilled life.

PRACTICAL GUIDANCE

What is your deepest curiosity about life? Are you actively exploring and seeking new knowledge?

Start by asking yourself questions about the world and your place in it. Engage in activities that stimulate your intellectual and spiritual curiosity, such as reading, journaling, or discussions. Practice meditation to quiet the mind and listen to your inner questions. Allow yourself to explore new ideas, practices, and philosophies. Use affirmations like "I am open to new knowledge," "Curiosity guides my journey," and "I embrace the unknown with open arms." Let curiosity be the driving force behind your personal growth and spiritual evolution.

27

The Strength of Self-Awareness

Self-awareness is the mirror of the soul,
Reflecting the truth that makes us whole.
It's the light that shines within,
Revealing the self beneath the skin.

In self-awareness, we see our mind,
The thoughts and patterns we try to hide.
It helps us break free from the past,
And create a future that will last.

Self-awareness is the path to know,
The essence of the self, to let it show.
It brings clarity and peace within,
A strength that lies beneath the skin.

Through self-awareness, we see our flaws,
And embrace them without pause.
It is the courage to face our truth,
And transform our wounds into proof.

Self-awareness is the power to grow,
To see the self, and let it flow.
It is the wisdom to know our place,
And accept ourselves with grace.

In self-awareness, we find our strength,
The power to go any length.
It's the force that leads us to be,
The highest version of what we can see.

To be self-aware is to be free,
To understand who we are meant to be.
It is the key to inner peace,
Where the journey of the soul will never cease.

INTERPRETATION

Self-awareness is the foundation of personal transformation

In Indian spirituality, self-awareness (*swarupa-jnana*) is the key to understanding the true self. The Bhagavad Gita emphasises the importance of self-awareness as a way to overcome the influence of the ego and align with the divine. *Krishna* encourages *Arjuna* to recognise his true nature beyond his external identity and illusions.

Self-awareness involves understanding our thoughts, emotions, and behaviours in order to align with our highest potential. The Upanishads speak of the importance of *Atman* (the true self) and *jnana* (knowledge), which can only be realized through deep self-awareness and reflection. In *Yoga*, self-awareness is developed through mindfulness, meditation, and *pranayama* (breathing exercises).

STANZA-WISE INTERPRETATION

- **Stanza 1:** This stanza introduces self-awareness as the key to self-understanding. It is the light that illuminates the truth of who we are.
- **Stanza 2:** Self-awareness allows us to observe our thoughts and behaviours. It gives us the opportunity to break free from past conditioning and create a new future.
- **Stanza 3:** Self-awareness is the path to knowing our true self. It brings clarity and peace, allowing us to see ourselves for who we really are.

- **Stanza 4:** The poem emphasises that self-awareness requires courage to face our flaws and imperfections. Through this acceptance, we transform and grow.
- **Stanza 5:** Self-awareness is presented as a powerful force that enables us to grow and evolve. It is through this awareness that we reach our highest potential.
- **Stanza 6:** This stanza highlights that self-awareness empowers us to be the best version of ourselves. It is the wisdom that guides us toward a purposeful life.
- **Stanza 7:** The final stanza states that self-awareness is the path to inner peace. It is through self-awareness that we find harmony within and align with our soul's purpose.

PHILOSOPHICAL INSIGHTS

This topic focuses on self-awareness as the foundation for personal and spiritual growth. In Indian philosophy, self-awareness is key to realizing our true self, which is beyond the ego and illusions. Through practices like meditation and self-inquiry, we develop the ability to observe our thoughts and behaviours, leading to a deeper understanding of ourselves. The poem illustrates that self-awareness brings clarity, acceptance, and inner peace, allowing us to live in alignment with our highest potential.

PRACTICAL GUIDANCE

How well do you know yourself? Are you aware of the thoughts, emotions, and behaviours that shape your life?

Start by taking time each day for self-reflection. Observe your thoughts without judgment and ask yourself what they reveal about your inner state. Practice mindfulness and meditation to increase your awareness of your emotions and reactions. Keep a journal to record your observations and insights. Use affirmations like "I am aware of my thoughts and feelings," "I embrace my true self," and "I am aligned with my highest potential." Through self-awareness, you will begin to understand yourself more deeply and live a life of peace and purpose.

28

Mastery over the Mind

The mind is a tempest, wild and free,
A river that flows, but cannot see.
It pulls us here, it pushes there,
A force that's beyond compare.

But in the depths, we find our way,
Mastery begins with the light of day.
To control the mind is not to bind,
But to calm the storm within the mind.

Mastery is the stillness of the heart,
It's the wisdom to know where to start.
It's the power to tame the raging sea,
And let the mind become calm and free.

Through meditation, we find the peace,
In the silence, our thoughts cease.
It's the practice of awareness deep,
That makes the restless mind sleep.

Mastery is the art of control,
It's the power to stay whole.
To direct the mind with grace and ease,
And find the peace we seek to seize.

The mind can be a powerful friend,
But without control, it can offend.
Through mastery, we rise above,
And direct the mind with peace and love.

To master the mind is to be free,
It's the key to living in harmony.
With the mind at rest, the soul takes flight,
And we live in truth, in pure light.

INTERPRETATION

Mastery over the mind is essential for spiritual and emotional balance

In Indian philosophy, the mind is often seen as the greatest obstacle to spiritual growth. The Bhagavad Gita teaches that the mind can be both a source of liberation and bondage, depending on how it is controlled. *Krishna* advises *Arjuna* to learn to master the mind, as it is through the mind's discipline that one can achieve inner peace and wisdom.

The practice of meditation (*dhyana*) is one of the most effective methods for gaining mastery over the mind. *Yoga* and *pranayama* (breathing exercises) also help calm the mind, allowing us to cultivate focus, awareness, and clarity. When the mind is disciplined, we are able to transcend distractions and achieve mental stillness, which is the key to self-realisation and spiritual freedom.

STANZA-WISE INTERPRETATION

- **Stanza 1:** The poem begins by describing the restless nature of the mind. It is often uncontrollable and unpredictable, like a tempest or a river flowing without direction.
- **Stanza 2:** Mastery over the mind begins with stillness and inner peace. The stanza emphasises that control is not about suppression but about calming the mind and guiding it to a peaceful state.

- **Stanza 3:** Mastery is shown as a practice of discipline and wisdom. It involves learning to tame the mind's constant fluctuations and finding inner peace.
- **Stanza 4:** Meditation is presented as the tool for achieving mastery over the mind. It is through mindfulness and silence that we can quiet the mind and experience true peace.
- **Stanza 5:** The poem suggests that mastery over the mind requires constant practice. It is the ability to direct our thoughts with ease and grace, leading to inner balance.
- **Stanza 6:** The mind can be a valuable ally when it is controlled, but left unchecked, it can lead to confusion and turmoil. The poem reinforces the importance of discipline.
- **Stanza 7:** The final stanza affirms that mastery over the mind brings freedom. It is through controlling the mind that we unlock the potential for true spiritual growth and inner harmony.

PHILOSOPHICAL INSIGHTS

This topic emphasises the importance of mastery over the mind for spiritual and personal growth. In Indian spirituality, the mind is seen as a powerful force that can either bind us or liberate us. Through practices like meditation, *pranayama*, and *yoga*, we can gain control over the mind, calming its fluctuations and achieving mental stillness. Mastery over the mind is the key to inner peace, self-realisation, and spiritual freedom, allowing us to live in harmony with our true self.

PRACTICAL GUIDANCE

How often do you let your mind control your actions? Are you ready to take control of your thoughts and emotions?

Start by practising meditation to quiet the mind. Focus on your breath and allow your thoughts to come and go without attachment. Practice mindfulness throughout the day, being present in each moment and observing your thoughts without judgment. Use affirmations like "I am the master of my mind," "I am calm and centered," and "I direct my thoughts with clarity." With regular practice, you will gain greater control over your mind and experience inner peace and harmony.

29

The Path to Emotional Resilience

Emotional resilience is the strength to rise,
To face the storm and look to the skies.
It's the power to endure, to stand tall,
And rise above life's deepest fall.

In resilience, there is quiet power,
The ability to grow in every hour.
It's the courage to move through pain,
And find the joy through the strain.

Resilience is not about never falling,
But the strength to keep on calling.
It's the will to get back on track,
And rise again, never looking back.

Through resilience, we find our way,
Through the darkness to the light of day.
It's the strength to stand when all seems lost,
And trust that peace will come, no matter the cost.

Resilience is the power to bend,
To grow through each hardship and trend.
It is the gift that life bestows,
To help us heal and let go.

With resilience, we build our core,
A strength that will never ignore.
It's the fire within that keeps us warm,
Guiding us through life's storm.

To be resilient is to know your worth,
To trust yourself, to heal and birth.
It's the strength to carry on,
And rise again with each new dawn.

INTERPRETATION

Emotional resilience is the ability to recover from difficulties

In Indian spirituality, resilience is closely linked to the concept of *dharma* (righteous duty) and *karma* (action). Life presents challenges and obstacles, but emotional resilience teaches us to face them with strength and grace. The teachings in the Bhagavad Gita emphasise that no matter how difficult life becomes, we must perform our duties with equanimity and trust the process of life. By developing emotional resilience, we can rise above adversity and grow stronger in the face of hardship.

In *Yoga*, emotional resilience is developed through the practice of *pranayama* (breath control) and meditation, which help us build mental and emotional strength. Resilience is not about avoiding pain or difficulties but about learning to navigate them with wisdom and composure. It is the power to endure and transform, emerging stronger and more connected to the divine.

STANZA-WISE INTERPRETATION

- **Stanza 1:** The poem introduces emotional resilience as the strength to overcome difficulties and rise above life's challenges, standing tall in the face of adversity.
- **Stanza 2:** Resilience is described as the inner strength that helps us endure and grow. It allows us to navigate pain and find joy despite life's struggles.

- **Stanza 3:** The poem emphasises that resilience is not about never failing but about having the strength to rise again after each fall and continue moving forward.
- **Stanza 4:** Resilience is the ability to remain hopeful and trust that peace and light will come, even when facing the darkest times.
- **Stanza 5:** Resilience is the power to adapt to life's hardships. It is the ability to grow through pain and challenges, learning from each experience.
- **Stanza 6:** The poem reinforces that resilience is a core strength that helps us navigate life's storms. It is the internal fire that keeps us going.
- **Stanza 7:** The final stanza emphasises that emotional resilience allows us to know our worth and continue forward, rising again with each new opportunity.

PHILOSOPHICAL INSIGHTS

This topic explores emotional resilience as the strength to overcome life's challenges and continue moving forward. In Indian philosophy, resilience is seen as an essential trait for living a fulfilling life. Resilience is not the absence of hardship but the ability to navigate through it with grace and wisdom. The Bhagavad Gita teaches that by fulfilling our *dharma* and trusting in the process of life, we can endure any hardship. This poem illustrates that through emotional resilience, we find our inner strength, rise above adversity, and transform ourselves into stronger, more compassionate beings.

PRACTICAL GUIDANCE

How do you respond to emotional challenges? Are you ready to build resilience in the face of adversity?

Begin by acknowledging your feelings without judgment. Practice mindfulness and meditation to calm your mind and connect with your inner strength. Reflect on past experiences where you showed resilience and find the lessons they offer. Use affirmations like "I am emotionally strong," "I rise above challenges," and "I trust the process of life." Each day, practice small acts of resilience by facing difficulties with courage and a positive mindset. Through regular practice, you will cultivate emotional resilience and experience inner peace.

CHAPTER 3

Navigating Challenges with Grace

30

Resilience to Change

Change is the only constant, they say,
It sweeps through life, day by day.
To resist it is to fight the tide,
But in embracing it, we find our stride.

Resilience to change is the power to grow,
To adapt with grace, to let go.
It's the courage to move through the storm,
And find the strength to be reborn.

In every change, there's a lesson to learn,
A chance for the heart to discern.
Through change, we shed the old and the worn,
And make space for what's newly born.

Resilience to change means not to fear,
But to trust that transformation is near.
It's the strength to bend and not to break,
And to rise again, no matter the stake.

Through change, we grow and evolve,
With each challenge, a problem to solve.
It's the power to embrace the unknown,
And trust that it leads us to be whole.

To face change with resilience is to see,
That through every shift, we are free.
It's the courage to move forward with grace,
And trust that we'll find our rightful place.

Resilience to change is the key to peace,
It is through it that suffering will cease.
In embracing the flow, we find our way,
To live fully, come what may.

INTERPRETATION

Resilience to change is the ability to embrace transformation with strength and grace

In Indian philosophy, change (*parinama*) is an essential aspect of the universe. Everything is in a constant state of flux, and resisting change only leads to suffering. The Bhagavad Gita teaches that *Krishna* advises *Arjuna* to accept the impermanence of life and to embrace the opportunities that change brings. *Krishna* tells us that true peace comes from adapting to change, rather than resisting it.

Resilience in the face of change allows us to grow, evolve, and learn. The practice of detachment (*vairagya*) is often associated with resilience. When we are not overly attached to a specific outcome or situation, we can navigate life's transformations with ease. Through spiritual practices such as meditation, *yoga*, and *pranayama*, we build the mental flexibility needed to adapt to life's changes with grace and wisdom.

STANZA-WISE INTERPRETATION

- **Stanza 1:** This stanza introduces resilience to change as the strength to move with the flow of life. The poem suggests that resisting change only leads to struggle, while embracing it helps us grow.
- **Stanza 2:** Resilience to change is depicted as the ability to adapt with grace. The poem emphasises the importance of courage and trust when navigating life's inevitable shifts.

- **Stanza 3:** The poem suggests that change brings valuable lessons. Through each transformation, we shed old limitations and create space for new growth.
- **Stanza 4:** This stanza emphasises that resilience to change is about trust and adaptability. It is about bending without breaking and facing challenges with strength.
- **Stanza 5:** Change is presented as an opportunity for personal growth and evolution. Through each challenge, we learn to embrace the unknown and move forward with confidence.
- **Stanza 6:** The poem reinforces that resilience to change brings freedom. By embracing change with resilience, we align ourselves with the flow of life and discover peace.
- **Stanza 7:** The final stanza emphasises that resilience to change is the key to a peaceful and fulfilling life. It encourages us to embrace life's transformations with openness and trust.

PHILOSOPHICAL INSIGHTS

This topic explores resilience to change as the ability to adapt and grow through life's constant transformations. In Indian philosophy, change is inevitable, and true peace comes from embracing it with strength and grace. The Bhagavad Gita teaches us to accept change and perform our duties with equanimity. The poem illustrates that by developing resilience to change, we are able to navigate life's challenges, learn from them, and grow into our highest potential.

PRACTICAL GUIDANCE

How do you respond when faced with change? Are you willing to embrace it with strength and grace?

Start by reflecting on past changes in your life. How did you adapt? What did you learn from those experiences? Practice meditation to connect with the present moment, and let go of any fears or attachments that hinder your ability to embrace change. Use affirmations like "I am resilient in the face of change," "I trust the flow of life," and "Change brings growth and transformation." With each change, trust that it is leading you toward your highest good.

31

The Interplay of Chaos and Order

In the midst of chaos, there is a plan,
A divine rhythm, a cosmic span.
Chaos is the dance of creation,
While order is its foundation.

In the chaos, we find our truth,
The spark of life, the force of youth.
It's the clash of light and dark,
That forms the universe, a sacred spark.

Order is the calm that follows the storm,
It's the silence, the gentle norm.
It is the structure beneath the flow,
The hidden force that makes life grow.

In every storm, there's a reason why,
A lesson in the winds that fly.
Chaos leads to a path unknown,
And through it, the seeds of truth are sown.

In the interplay of chaos and order, we see,
The divine design unfolding, wild and free.
Chaos gives birth to creation's flow,
While order ensures the seeds we sow.

Through the dance of opposites, we rise,
To see beyond the earth and skies.
It is in the tension between the two,
That life's true meaning comes into view.

The interplay of chaos and order is the key,
To understanding life's mystery.
Through both, we learn to navigate,
And in their balance, we find our fate.

INTERPRETATION

The interplay of chaos and order is the divine rhythm that governs the universe

In Indian philosophy, the dualities of chaos and order are seen as complementary forces that create balance and harmony in the universe. *Krishna* in the Bhagavad Gita speaks of the eternal dance between creation and destruction, where the universe is in constant flux, yet held together by a divine order. This cycle of chaos and order reflects the cyclical nature of existence itself — from birth to death, from creation to dissolution.

The Upanishads teach that through the tension between opposing forces, the deeper truths of the universe unfold. In *Yoga*, this balance is mirrored in the practice of balancing effort and surrender. Order provides structure and stability, while chaos allows for growth, change, and transformation. The balance between these two forces is essential for spiritual growth, as it teaches us to navigate life's complexities with grace and wisdom.

STANZA-WISE INTERPRETATION

- **Stanza 1:** This stanza introduces the relationship between chaos and order. It presents chaos as a necessary force for creation, while order provides the foundation for stability.
- **Stanza 2:** The poem emphasises that within chaos, we find truth and vitality. It is through the interplay of light and dark that the universe forms.

- **Stanza 3:** Order is shown as the calm that follows chaos. It is the structure that sustains life and allows growth to occur.
- **Stanza 4:** The poem suggests that every chaotic event carries purpose and meaning. Chaos is the vehicle for growth, guiding us to new understanding.
- **Stanza 5:** Chaos and order are presented as complementary forces. The poem highlights that both are necessary for creation and the unfolding of divine purpose.
- **Stanza 6:** The poem suggests that through the balance of chaos and order, we rise to greater wisdom and understanding, seeing the greater picture of life.
- **Stanza 7:** The final stanza reinforces that understanding the interplay of chaos and order helps us navigate life. By finding balance between these forces, we understand the true meaning of existence.

PHILOSOPHICAL INSIGHTS

This topic explores the interplay of chaos and order as a divine rhythm that governs the universe. In Indian spirituality, chaos and order are not opposing forces but complementary ones. *Krishna* teaches that through the dance of creation and destruction, the universe continues to evolve. The poem illustrates that the balance between chaos and order is essential for spiritual growth. Through both forces, we learn to navigate life's challenges, embrace transformation, and find harmony.

PRACTICAL GUIDANCE

How do you respond when life feels chaotic? Are you able to see the order within the chaos?

Begin by reflecting on moments in your life when chaos led to growth or transformation. Practice meditation to quiet your mind and find peace within life's fluctuations. Observe the balance between effort and surrender in your daily life, and recognise when chaos is necessary for change. Use affirmations like "I embrace the chaos," "I trust the process of life," and "I find balance in all things." By understanding the interplay of chaos and order, you will navigate life with grace and clarity.

32

The Ripple Effect of Kindness

A single act can change the flow,
Like a pebble tossed, the ripples grow.
Kindness spreads from heart to heart,
A simple gesture, a work of art.

In kindness, there's a power untold,
It warms the heart, it heals the cold.
A smile, a word, a gentle touch,
Can heal the soul, it means so much.

Kindness is the seed we sow,
It spreads like a river's flow.
One act of love, one small deed,
Can plant the root for others' need.

Through kindness, we break the chain,
Of anger, sorrow, grief, and pain.
It has the power to transform,
To heal, to soothe, to calm the storm.

Kindness is the light we share,
In moments of darkness, it's always there.
It is the bond that ties us all,
A strength we find when we stand tall.

The ripple effect of kindness grows,
Touching lives wherever it goes.
In every act, we see the truth,
That kindness is the key to youth.

To live with kindness is to be free,
It's the energy that brings unity.
Through kindness, we heal and grow,
And let the light of love forever flow.

INTERPRETATION

Kindness is a transformative power that creates a ripple effect of positive change

In Indian philosophy, kindness (*daya*) is a divine virtue that has the power to heal and transform. The Bhagavad Gita teaches that kindness is an expression of *ahimsa* (non-violence), where we act with compassion and love toward all beings. *Krishna* encourages *Arjuna* to perform acts of kindness and compassion, as they align with the divine path. The Upanishads also emphasise that true spiritual growth involves developing kindness toward others, as it strengthens the heart and nurtures the soul.

In *Yoga*, kindness is seen as a path to inner peace, allowing us to break free from the cycles of ego and attachment. The practice of *karuna* (compassionate action) is essential in creating harmony in both our inner and outer worlds.

STANZA-WISE INTERPRETATION

- **Stanza 1:** The poem begins by describing how a small act of kindness creates ripples that grow, touching many lives. The impact of kindness is far-reaching and transformative.
- **Stanza 2:** Kindness is portrayed as a healing force. Even the smallest gestures have the power to warm the heart and alleviate pain.
- **Stanza 3:** The stanza shows how kindness spreads. One act of kindness plants the seed for more love and compassion, creating a cycle of goodness.

- **Stanza 4:** Kindness has the power to break the chains of negativity. It transforms anger, sorrow, and pain, replacing them with healing and peace.
- **Stanza 5:** Kindness is depicted as a light that illuminates the darkness. It brings people together, fostering unity and understanding.
- **Stanza 6:** The ripple effect of kindness continues to grow, spreading from one person to another, touching lives and creating a legacy of goodwill.
- **Stanza 7:** The final stanza encourages the reader to live with kindness, as it is through kindness that we heal, grow, and experience the fullness of life.

PHILOSOPHICAL INSIGHTS

This topic emphasises that kindness has a powerful ripple effect. In Indian spirituality, kindness is a divine virtue that creates healing and transformation. The Bhagavad Gita and Upanishads teach that through acts of kindness and compassion, we align with the divine and contribute to the well-being of the world. The poem illustrates how kindness spreads, touching lives and creating a positive impact that ripples outward. It encourages us to live with kindness, knowing that even the smallest act can lead to profound change.

PRACTICAL GUIDANCE

How often do you engage in acts of kindness? Are you ready to create a ripple effect of love and compassion in the world?

Start by practising small acts of kindness each day. Smile at someone, help a neighbour, or offer a word of encouragement to a friend. Reflect on the power of these small actions to bring about larger changes. Practice compassion toward yourself as well, acknowledging your worth and treating yourself with kindness. Use affirmations like "I am kind," "Kindness is my strength," and "I spread love and compassion." By living with kindness, you create a wave of positivity that touches the hearts of others.

33

The Strength Found in Weakness

In weakness, there's a hidden might,
A strength that shines through darkest night.
It's the power to endure and stand,
To rise again, to take command.

Weakness is not something to fear,
It's the place where strength draws near.
It's in our fragility we find grace,
And the courage to face life's race.

In weakness, we learn to bend,
To accept that we must transcend.
It's the strength to be vulnerable,
To heal and become lovable.

Weakness is the soil where growth begins,
Where we face our faults, our losses, our sins.
It is in the cracks that light comes through,
And reveals the strength we never knew.

Through weakness, we find our true power,
The ability to rise, to bloom, to flower.
It is the force that helps us rise,
When we let go of pride and disguise.

Weakness is not defeat or shame,
It's the doorway to the soul's true name.
It is the invitation to be real,
To face our fears and start to heal.

In weakness, we find the strength to be,
True to ourselves, wild and free.
For it's through weakness we grow strong,
And find the courage to carry on.

INTERPRETATION

Strength is often found in moments of weakness

In Indian philosophy, the concept of weakness is not seen as a negative attribute, but rather as an essential part of the human experience. *Krishna* in the Bhagavad Gita teaches that true strength arises from surrender and vulnerability. In *Yoga*, it is through moments of weakness that we learn to let go of the ego and embrace our true self. Weakness is the space where transformation happens, where we face our limitations and, in doing so, transcend them.

The teachings of Vedanta and the Upanishads emphasise that true strength comes not from pride or arrogance, but from humility and the ability to embrace our fragility. Weakness allows us to tap into deeper reservoirs of strength, resilience, and wisdom. It is through accepting our vulnerabilities that we are able to grow and evolve spiritually.

STANZA-WISE INTERPRETATION

- **Stanza 1:** The poem begins by introducing the paradox that weakness holds a hidden strength. It suggests that within moments of weakness, we find the power to endure and rise.
- **Stanza 2:** Weakness is presented as an opportunity for growth. It is the place where true strength begins to emerge.
- **Stanza 3:** The poem highlights that weakness allows us to accept vulnerability. It is through this acceptance that we find grace and courage to face life's challenges.

- **Stanza 4:** Weakness is shown as the fertile ground where growth begins. It is in our vulnerability that we discover strength and wisdom.
- **Stanza 5:** The poem emphasises that through weakness, we find the true power to rise. By letting go of pride, we embrace our authentic self and tap into our inner strength.
- **Stanza 6:** Weakness is reframed as an invitation to be real. It is through embracing our vulnerabilities that we heal and grow.
- **Stanza 7:** The final stanza reinforces the idea that through weakness, we become stronger. It is through facing our limitations and fears that we grow in strength and courage.

PHILOSOPHICAL INSIGHTS

This topic explores the concept that strength is found in weakness. In Indian spirituality, weakness is seen not as a flaw but as an opportunity for growth and transformation. *Krishna* teaches that true strength comes from surrendering the ego and embracing our vulnerabilities. The poem illustrates that through weakness, we tap into deeper strength and wisdom. It encourages us to embrace our limitations, knowing that they are the gateway to true strength, resilience, and growth.

PRACTICAL GUIDANCE

How do you perceive your weaknesses? Are you ready to embrace them as pathways to strength?

Start by acknowledging your vulnerabilities and embracing them with compassion. Practice meditation to connect with your true self and observe your thoughts without judgment. Reflect on past experiences where your weaknesses led to personal growth or wisdom. Use affirmations like "I embrace my vulnerabilities," "I am strong in my weakness," and "I learn and grow through challenges." Allow weakness to become a source of strength and transformation in your life.

34

The Power of Non-Attachment

Non-attachment is not the absence of love,
But the freedom to rise above.
It's the strength to let go of the grip,
And allow life to freely slip.

In non-attachment, we find peace,
A release from the mind's tight leash.
It's the art of holding things lightly,
Without fear, without pride, or might.

Non-attachment frees the heart,
It gives us the strength to depart.
From desires, from expectations,
It clears the path for true liberation.

To be unattached is to be free,
From the burden of ownership, you see.
It's the ability to enjoy without clinging,
To experience life without stinging.

In non-attachment, there's balance and grace,
The wisdom to accept life's pace.
It's knowing when to hold and when to release,
And finding peace in every piece.

Non-attachment is not to detach,
But to live without an emotional match.
It's the freedom to love without control,
To let life flow and nurture the soul.

Through non-attachment, we find our way,
To walk through life with ease each day.
It is the path to true freedom,
And to living fully in the moment.

INTERPRETATION

Non-attachment is the path to spiritual freedom

In Indian philosophy, non-attachment (*vairagya*) is considered one of the key practices on the path to self-realisation. The Bhagavad Gita teaches that attachment to the material world and to desires is a source of suffering. *Krishna* advises *Arjuna* to perform his duties without attachment to the results, emphasising that true freedom comes from detaching from the fruits of action.

Non-attachment does not mean renouncing love or relationships but refers to releasing the emotional grip on outcomes. *Yoga* and meditation help us cultivate this state of detachment by focusing on the present moment and letting go of past and future attachments. In doing so, we experience peace, clarity, and spiritual growth. The Upanishads also emphasise that freedom comes when we relinquish attachment to the material world and align with the higher self.

STANZA-WISE INTERPRETATION

- **Stanza 1:** The poem introduces non-attachment as the freedom to rise above attachments. It emphasises that detachment is not about abandoning love but about releasing the grip on life.
- **Stanza 2:** Non-attachment brings peace by freeing us from the mind's constant desire for control. It helps us live lightly, without fear or pride.

- **Stanza 3:** The poem highlights that non-attachment helps us release desires and expectations. It is a practice that leads to true liberation and freedom.
- **Stanza 4:** Non-attachment is presented as the ability to enjoy life without clinging to outcomes. It is the freedom to experience life without being attached to its results.
- **Stanza 5:** The poem emphasises that non-attachment brings balance and grace. It teaches us when to hold on and when to let go, creating a peaceful flow in life.
- **Stanza 6:** Non-attachment is the freedom to love without control. It is the ability to be emotionally free while remaining connected to the world.
- **Stanza 7:** The final stanza affirms that non-attachment leads to spiritual freedom. It encourages us to live fully in the moment, free from the weight of attachment.

PHILOSOPHICAL INSIGHTS

This topic explores non-attachment as the key to spiritual freedom and peace. In Indian philosophy, non-attachment is not about renouncing the world but about releasing emotional clinging to outcomes, people, and possessions. *Krishna* teaches in the Bhagavad Gita that performing duties without attachment leads to true liberation. The poem illustrates that by practising non-attachment, we experience emotional freedom, peace, and a deeper connection with the divine.

PRACTICAL GUIDANCE

How often do you find yourself clinging to outcomes or desires? Are you ready to embrace the freedom of non-attachment?

Start by observing your attachments and how they affect your peace. Practice meditation to center yourself and let go of any clinging to past or future outcomes. Reflect on the impermanence of life, and remind yourself that true freedom comes from detachment. Use affirmations like "I release attachment," "I am free from the grip of desire," and "I live fully in the present moment." Through non-attachment, you will experience greater peace, clarity, and spiritual growth.

35

Facing Life's Struggles with Wisdom

Life's struggles are not here to break,
But to help us grow, to bend, not shake.
With wisdom, we face what comes our way,
And find the strength to live each day.

In struggle, there's a lesson we learn,
A path of growth at every turn.
It's through adversity we grow strong,
And find our place where we belong.

Wisdom teaches us to see,
That struggles are part of the journey.
It's not in avoiding, but in embracing,
That we find the strength for overcoming.

Through struggles, we gain insight,
Into the truth of what is right.
We learn to see beyond the pain,
And rise above, again and again.

Wisdom shows us how to cope,
How to turn our trials into hope.
It helps us see the purpose in pain,
And find the strength to rise again.

Struggles are not obstacles to flee,
But opportunities to be free.
With wisdom, we navigate life's maze,
And find peace through every phase.

Facing life's struggles with wisdom is key,
It is the path to being truly free.
Through each challenge, we grow wise,
And rise above, reaching the skies.

INTERPRETATION

Facing life's struggles with wisdom is the path to spiritual growth

In Indian philosophy, struggles are seen as opportunities for growth and transformation. The Bhagavad Gita teaches that challenges are part of the divine plan, and we must face them with courage, wisdom, and equanimity. *Krishna* advises *Arjuna* to perform his duties with wisdom, recognizing that adversity is a natural part of life's journey.

Yoga and meditation help us develop the wisdom needed to navigate life's struggles with clarity and peace. By cultivating viveka (discernment) and vairagya (detachment), we learn to respond to challenges with wisdom, turning them into opportunities for spiritual evolution. The Upanishads also emphasise that true wisdom comes from understanding the deeper meaning of life's experiences and seeing them as part of our path to liberation.

STANZA-WISE INTERPRETATION

- **Stanza 1:** The poem begins by emphasising that life's struggles are not meant to break us but to help us grow. Wisdom allows us to face challenges with strength and resilience.
- **Stanza 2:** The poem highlights that struggles bring valuable lessons. Through each difficulty, we grow stronger and find our true path.

- **Stanza 3:** Wisdom is presented as the ability to embrace challenges rather than avoid them. It teaches us that overcoming struggles is a path to spiritual growth.
- **Stanza 4:** Through wisdom, we gain insight into life's struggles. It helps us see beyond pain and find deeper meaning in our experiences.
- **Stanza 5:** Wisdom helps us cope with difficulties by seeing the purpose behind pain and transforming it into strength and hope.
- **Stanza 6:** The poem reframes struggles as opportunities for freedom. Through wisdom, we learn to navigate life's challenges with peace and clarity.
- **Stanza 7:** The final stanza emphasises that facing struggles with wisdom is the key to spiritual freedom. Through each challenge, we grow wiser and rise above adversity.

PHILOSOPHICAL INSIGHTS

This topic emphasises that facing life's struggles with wisdom is the path to spiritual growth. In Indian spirituality, challenges are seen as essential parts of our journey toward self-realisation. The Bhagavad Gita teaches us to face adversity with wisdom, recognizing that it is an opportunity for growth. The poem illustrates that through wisdom, we transform struggles into opportunities for personal and spiritual evolution, leading to peace and fulfilment.

PRACTICAL GUIDANCE

How do you react when faced with struggles? Are you able to see the deeper meaning in them?

Start by reflecting on past struggles and the lessons you've learned from them. Practice meditation to develop viveka (discernment) and gain clarity in times of difficulty. When challenges arise, remind yourself that they are opportunities for growth. Use affirmations like "I embrace life's challenges with wisdom," "I grow stronger through adversity," and "I find peace in every struggle." By facing struggles with wisdom, you will navigate life's challenges with grace and grow spiritually.

36

The Gift of Perspective

Perspective is the lens through which we see,
It shapes our thoughts, it sets us free.
What once seemed dark may now be bright,
When viewed through a different light.

In every challenge, there's a gift,
A new way to see, a chance to lift.
When we shift our view, we find,
A world of peace within the mind.

Perspective teaches us to grow,
To see beyond what we know.
It's the wisdom that comes from change,
That helps us find a wider range.

Through perspective, we learn to see,
The beauty in all things that be.
It's the ability to shift and sway,
To view the world in a brighter way.

In every moment, we have a choice,
To see through the mind or hear the voice.
Perspective is the gift we own,
The power to make the unknown known.

The gift of perspective helps us see,
That life is not what it seems to be.
It's through a shift, a turn, a glance,
That we find joy in the dance.

So embrace the gift of perspective,
And see the world in ways reflective.
For in changing how we look and feel,
We find that life becomes more real.

INTERPRETATION

The gift of perspective is the ability to see beyond the surface

In Indian philosophy, perspective is deeply linked to the concept of *maya* (illusion) and the understanding that the world we perceive is not the ultimate reality. The Bhagavad Gita encourages us to see the world not through the ego but through the wisdom of the self, recognizing that our perception is shaped by our thoughts and attachments. By shifting our perspective, we move closer to spiritual truth and understanding.

In *Yoga*, perspective is cultivated through mindfulness and meditation. These practices help us detach from our habitual ways of thinking and open us up to a broader understanding of the world around us. The Upanishads teach that by expanding our perspective, we align ourselves with the cosmic consciousness and gain deeper insight into the nature of reality.

STANZA-WISE INTERPRETATION

- **Stanza 1:** This stanza introduces perspective as a powerful tool that shapes how we see and experience life. It emphasises that our perception can transform challenges into opportunities when viewed from a different angle.
- **Stanza 2:** The poem highlights that every challenge contains a hidden gift. By shifting our perspective, we

can find peace and understanding in the most difficult situations.

- **Stanza 3:** Perspective is presented as the ability to see beyond what we know. It is the wisdom that arises from being open to new ways of thinking and experiencing the world.
- **Stanza 4:** The poem emphasises that through **perspective**, we can see the beauty in all things. It is the ability to shift our point of view that allows us to appreciate life more fully.
- **Stanza 5:** Perspective is shown as a choice we make every day. It is the ability to choose how we see the world and how we respond to it.
- **Stanza 6:** The poem reinforces that the gift of perspective is the ability to understand that life is not always what it seems. By shifting our view, we can discover hidden beauty and meaning.
- **Stanza 7:** The final stanza encourages us to embrace **perspective** as a tool for personal growth. By changing how we see the world, we can unlock deeper levels of understanding and connection.

PHILOSOPHICAL INSIGHTS

This topic focuses on the gift of perspective, which allows us to transform how we see the world and respond to life's challenges. In Indian philosophy, perspective is linked to the concept of maya, the illusion of the material world. The poem emphasises that by shifting our perception, we can unlock deeper truths and find peace. Through practices like meditation and self-inquiry, we learn to expand our perspective and align with the higher self, experiencing life in a more profound and meaningful way.

PRACTICAL GUIDANCE

How do you currently perceive the challenges in your life? Are you ready to shift your perspective to see them as opportunities for growth?

Start by reflecting on the challenges you are currently facing. Ask yourself how changing your perspective might help you see these challenges differently. Practice mindfulness to observe your thoughts and emotions without attachment. Try to see life from a broader view, recognizing that there is more to every situation than meets the eye. Use affirmations like "I see with clarity and understanding," "I embrace life's challenges with an open heart," and "I choose to see the beauty in every moment." By shifting your perspective, you will experience life in a more fulfilling and harmonious way.

37

The Strength of Empathy

Empathy is the power to feel,
To understand, to deeply heal.
It is the bond that ties us all,
And helps us answer to life's call.

In empathy, we see the soul,
Not the body, not the goal.
It is the wisdom that binds us tight,
In the dark, it's our guiding light.

Empathy is the heart's true voice,
It helps us make the loving choice.
It teaches us to feel the pain,
And find the joy, despite the strain.

Through empathy, we learn to see,
The struggles of others, just like me.
It helps us bridge the gap so wide,
And walk with others by our side.

Empathy is the light we share,
It's the compassion that we wear.
Through it, we heal, we grow, we give,
Empathy is the way we live.

In empathy, we rise above,
The selfish ways that lack real love.
It teaches us to give with grace,
And make the world a kinder place.

To live with empathy is to be whole,
It's the key to healing the soul.
Through empathy, we understand,
And extend a loving, helping hand.

INTERPRETATION

Empathy is the ability to deeply understand and connect with others' feelings

In Indian philosophy, empathy (*karuna*) is a central virtue that allows us to recognise the divinity in all beings. The Bhagavad Gita teaches that we must act with compassion and love toward others, seeing them as extensions of the divine. *Krishna* encourages *Arjuna* to perform his duties with a loving heart and to empathize with those who are suffering.

Empathy helps us understand the pain and joy of others, creating connections that transcend the ego. The Upanishads speak of *atman* (the soul), which connects all living beings. In *Yoga*, empathy is cultivated through practices that encourage compassion, such as selfless service (*seva*) and mindfulness. Through empathy, we are able to heal not only others but also ourselves.

STANZA-WISE INTERPRETATION

- **Stanza 1:** The poem begins by introducing empathy as the ability to feel deeply for others. It is the bond that connects us to all living beings and helps us respond to the needs of others.
- **Stanza 2:** Empathy is portrayed as the wisdom that allows us to see beyond the surface. It connects us to the soul of others and guides us toward compassion.
- **Stanza 3:** The poem emphasises that empathy helps us make loving choices. It teaches us to understand

the pain of others and find joy even in difficult circumstances.

- **Stanza 4:** Empathy is presented as the ability to connect with the struggles of others. It bridges the gap between individuals, helping us walk alongside others in their journey.
- **Stanza 5:** Empathy is the light that we share with others. Through it, we give, heal, and grow together, creating a more compassionate world.
- **Stanza 6:** The poem highlights that empathy helps us rise above selfishness and teaches us to give with grace and kindness.
- **Stanza 7:** The final stanza affirms that to live with empathy is to live with a compassionate heart. It is the key to healing and creating deeper connections with others.

PHILOSOPHICAL INSIGHTS

This topic emphasises empathy as a transformative force that connects us to others. In Indian philosophy, empathy is seen as a divine virtue that helps us see the suffering and joy of others and respond with compassion. *Krishna* teaches in the Bhagavad Gita that empathy is essential for performing our duties with love and kindness. The poem illustrates that through empathy, we heal, grow, and create meaningful connections that foster compassion and understanding in the world.

PRACTICAL GUIDANCE

How often do you practice empathy in your daily life? Are you ready to connect more deeply with others' feelings and experiences?

Start by practising active listening. When someone speaks to you, listen deeply without judgment or interruption. Reflect on their words and try to understand their emotions. Practice compassion, both toward yourself and others. Use meditation to cultivate a compassionate heart, focusing on sending love and kindness to those around you. Use affirmations like "I am compassionate," "I connect deeply with others," and "I extend empathy to all beings." By living with empathy, you create a ripple effect of kindness and understanding that can transform your relationships and the world.

38

The Power of Inner Strength

Within each of us lies a well,
Of strength untapped, a force to quell.
It's the power to rise, to stand,
The silent force that guides the hand.

Inner strength is the will to endure,
The courage to heal, to be pure.
It's the voice that rises within,
That whispers softly, "You will win."

In times of trial, it shows its face,
A quiet power, filled with grace.
It is the light in the darkest hour,
The flame that rises from the flower.

Inner strength is not in might,
But in standing tall despite the fight.
It's the wisdom to bend and sway,
And still rise again, come what may.

Through inner strength, we find our way,
It keeps us grounded, day by day.
It's the strength to speak, to act, to be,
The core of who we are, to see.

Inner strength is a gift we own,
It's the power that helps us atone.
It is the silent force inside,
That lifts us up, that helps us guide.

To tap into inner strength is to see,
That all we need is found within thee.
With this strength, we walk in grace,
And find our peace in every space.

INTERPRETATION

Inner strength is the deep, unwavering power within us that guides us through life's challenges

In Indian philosophy, inner strength (*sahas*) is considered a vital attribute for personal growth and spiritual progress. The Bhagavad Gita speaks of the importance of mental fortitude and inner resolve, as *Krishna* encourages *Arjuna* to recognise his strength within and rise above external challenges. True inner strength comes from the ability to remain steadfast in the face of adversity and maintain equanimity in all situations.

The practice of *Yoga*, particularly *pranayama* (breathing techniques) and *dhyana* (meditation), helps cultivate inner strength by developing focus and emotional resilience. The Upanishads emphasise the importance of *tapas* (spiritual discipline) and inner courage as the foundation of self-realization. Inner strength is not about external power but about drawing from an inner well of peace, courage, and wisdom.

STANZA-WISE INTERPRETATION

- **Stanza 1:** This stanza introduces inner strength as a powerful, untapped force within each person. It emphasises that this strength guides us silently through life's challenges.
- **Stanza 2:** Inner strength is portrayed as the ability to endure trials and keep moving forward. It is a quiet, resilient force that encourages us to persevere.

- **Stanza 3:** The poem highlights that inner strength shows up in times of difficulty, offering grace and light when we need it most.
- **Stanza 4:** Inner strength is not about force or dominance but about resilience and the wisdom to adapt and continue, even in the face of adversity.
- **Stanza 5:** This stanza emphasises that inner strength helps us stay grounded and true to ourselves. It provides us with the strength to act and express ourselves fully.
- **Stanza 6:** The poem suggests that inner strength is a divine gift. It helps us overcome obstacles and remain true to our highest self.
- **Stanza 7:** The final stanza reinforces that inner strength is the key to spiritual peace. It allows us to navigate life's challenges with grace and find balance in all situations.

PHILOSOPHICAL INSIGHTS

This topic emphasises inner strength as the ability to face life's challenges with courage and wisdom. In Indian spirituality, inner strength is developed through practices like *Yoga*, meditation, and self-discipline (*tapas*). It is not about external power but about cultivating peace, focus, and resilience within. The Bhagavad Gita teaches that the true source of strength is within, and by tapping into it, we can overcome any adversity. The poem illustrates that inner strength empowers us to navigate difficulties, maintain our true path, and live with grace.

PRACTICAL GUIDANCE

How do you respond when faced with challenges? Are you tapping into your inner strength to rise above them?

Start by reflecting on past challenges and the inner strength you have called upon to overcome them. Practice mindfulness and meditation to connect with your inner self and strengthen your emotional resilience. Use affirmations like “I am strong,” “I am resilient,” and “I trust in my inner strength.” Engage in *pranayama* to calm your mind and center yourself, allowing your inner strength to flow. With each challenge, trust that you have the power within to rise above and continue on your path.

39

Living with Patience

Patience is the quiet art of waiting,
The calm in times of hesitating.
It is the wisdom to slow the pace,
And trust that life will find its place.

In patience, we find peace within,
The strength to wait, to breathe, to begin.
It is not about idle delay,
But the grace to wait for the right day.

Patience is the courage to endure,
Through moments that seem unclear.
It's the stillness in the rush of life,
The calm in the midst of strife.

Through patience, we learn to see,
That not everything happens instantly.
It teaches us to trust the flow,
And let the seeds of wisdom grow.

Patience is the art of balance,
Of waiting without the fear of silence.
It is knowing that time will unfold,
And in that time, we will be whole.

In patience, we find our pace,
The rhythm of life, the sacred space.
It is the strength to persevere,
And the courage to remain clear.

Living with patience is the key,
To peace, to love, to being free.
For in patience, we find the truth,
That life reveals itself, uncouth.

INTERPRETATION

Patience is the ability to wait without frustration or anxiety

In Indian philosophy, patience (*kshama*) is seen as an essential virtue for spiritual growth. The Bhagavad Gita teaches that we must perform our duties with patience and without attachment to outcomes. *Krishna* tells *Arjuna* to be patient and trust in the divine timing of life. True patience allows us to accept what is unfolding in the moment, trusting that everything is part of a larger, divine plan.

The Upanishads speak of time as an illusion, and that true wisdom comes from recognizing the perfect flow of life. In *Yoga*, patience is cultivated through practices that develop mindfulness and the ability to be present in the moment. Patience allows us to trust the process of life, knowing that growth and change take time.

STANZA-WISE INTERPRETATION

- **Stanza 1:** The poem begins by describing patience as the ability to remain calm while waiting. It is about trusting that life will unfold at the right time.
- **Stanza 2:** Patience is shown as an inner peace that helps us wait without anxiety. It is the wisdom to recognise that everything has its time.
- **Stanza 3:** The poem emphasises that patience is not about being idle, but about waiting with grace for the right moment to act.

- **Stanza 4:** Patience teaches us that not everything happens immediately. It helps us trust in the natural flow of life and gives us the space to grow.
- **Stanza 5:** Patience is presented as the art of balance. It is the ability to wait without fear or frustration, knowing that time will reveal the answers.
- **Stanza 6:** The poem emphasises that patience brings clarity and strength. It is the ability to persevere while maintaining peace and focus.
- **Stanza 7:** The final stanza reinforces that living with patience is the key to peace and freedom. It is through patience that we learn to trust life's journey.

PHILOSOPHICAL INSIGHTS

This topic explores patience as the key to peace and spiritual growth. In Indian spirituality, patience is considered a powerful tool for cultivating wisdom and emotional resilience. *Krishna* teaches in the Bhagavad Gita that patience is necessary for fulfilling our duties and trusting the divine plan. The poem illustrates that through patience, we align ourselves with the natural flow of life, allowing things to unfold at their own pace. By living with patience, we experience inner peace and spiritual fulfilment.

PRACTICAL GUIDANCE

How do you practice patience in your life? Are you able to wait without frustration or anxiety?

Start by observing areas of your life where impatience arises. Reflect on the reasons for your impatience and explore how you can approach these moments with greater calm. Practice mindfulness and meditation to help cultivate inner peace and the ability to remain present in the moment. Use affirmations like "I am patient," "I trust in divine timing," and "I embrace life's flow." Through patience, you will experience greater peace and alignment with the natural rhythms of life.

CHAPTER 4

Growth and Expansion

40

The Journey of Continuous Growth

Growth is not just a fleeting thing,
But a journey that's eternal, a song to sing.
It's the path we walk with every breath,
Through every trial, through life, through death.

Growth is not in a single leap,
But in the small steps, in what we keep.
It's in the wisdom that we gain,
Through joy and sorrow, through pleasure and pain.

In every moment, there's something to learn,
A lesson in each twist and turn.
Growth is the seed that takes its time,
To break through the earth, to reach for the climb.

The journey of growth is never done,
It continues long after the setting sun.
It's in the choices we make each day,
To move forward, to live and play.

Growth is not about perfection,
But about learning from each reflection.
It's the ability to rise each time we fall,
To keep going, no matter how small.

Through growth, we find our true self,
A deeper peace, a higher wealth.
It's the power to evolve and become,
To be all that we were meant to overcome.

The journey of growth is one of grace,
It's the ability to embrace each space.
Through growth, we reach for the sky,
And continue to soar, and never ask why.

INTERPRETATION

The journey of continuous growth is a lifelong process of learning and evolving

In Indian philosophy, growth is considered an integral part of life's purpose. The Bhagavad Gita teaches that we are constantly evolving as individuals and that each experience, whether positive or negative, offers opportunities for growth and transformation. *Krishna* advises *Arjuna* to see growth not as a destination but as a continuous journey, filled with learning, discipline, and reflection.

Growth is closely linked to self-realization in *Yoga*, where practitioners strive to grow spiritually, mentally, and emotionally. The Upanishads speak of the importance of continuous self-discovery and inner development. Self-discipline (*tapas*) and meditation (*dhyana*) are essential tools for cultivating growth, as they allow us to understand our true nature and continue evolving toward higher states of being.

STANZA-WISE INTERPRETATION

- **Stanza 1:** The poem introduces growth as a continuous and eternal journey. It's a path that unfolds with each step and each experience in life.
- **Stanza 2:** The poem emphasises that growth is not a single event but a collection of small steps that accumulate over time. It's shaped by both positive and negative experiences.

- **Stanza 3:** Growth is presented as a process of learning from every experience. It's the quiet unfolding of potential, like a seed breaking through the earth.
- **Stanza 4:** The poem shows that growth continues throughout life, never ending. Each day is an opportunity for us to make choices that contribute to our growth.
- **Stanza 5:** Growth is portrayed as a journey that requires humility and self-reflection. We grow not by being perfect but by learning from each experience.
- **Stanza 6:** The poem highlights that through growth, we find a deeper connection with our true self. Growth leads to inner peace and a greater understanding of who we are.
- **Stanza 7:** The final stanza emphasises that growth is a journey of grace. As we continue to grow, we expand our potential and soar toward our highest purpose.

PHILOSOPHICAL INSIGHTS

This topic emphasises that growth is a continuous journey of learning, evolving, and self-discovery. In Indian spirituality, growth is seen as an integral aspect of life, where each experience contributes to our development. *Krishna* teaches in the Bhagavad Gita that growth is a never-ending process that requires self-discipline, introspection, and reflection. The poem illustrates that growth is not about perfection but about embracing each step of the journey and learning from both successes and failures.

PRACTICAL GUIDANCE

How do you view your growth in life? Are you open to learning from every experience?

Start by reflecting on your current journey. What areas of your life do you feel are stagnant or in need of growth? Use meditation and mindfulness to connect with your inner self and explore where growth is needed. Practice gratitude for the lessons life has taught you, and approach challenges as opportunities for growth. Use affirmations like "I am always growing," "I embrace change with open arms," and "Each experience teaches me valuable lessons." Trust that growth is a continual process, and allow yourself the grace to evolve at your own pace.

41

The Resilience of Dreams

Dreams are the whispers of the soul,
A vision, a purpose, a distant goal.
They carry us through the darkest night,
Guiding us with their inner light.

In dreams, we see what can be,
A future that is waiting, wild and free.
It is the courage to chase what we desire,
And let our hearts burn with fire.

The resilience of dreams is the will to persist,
To keep moving forward through every twist.
Even when the path is unclear,
We follow our dreams, casting off fear.

Dreams are the force that keeps us alive,
They give us the strength to strive and thrive.
In them, we find our deepest desire,
A spark that sets our hearts on fire.

The resilience of dreams teaches us to rise,
To reach for the stars, to touch the skies.
It's the strength to continue, no matter the cost,
And to never give up, no matter what is lost.

Dreams are the wings that help us soar,
To break free from what holds us to the floor.
They lift us above, they carry us high,
And help us see beyond the sky.

The resilience of dreams is the key to life,
It helps us overcome, it helps us fight.
Through dreams, we find our path and guide,
And live our truth with nothing to hide.

INTERPRETATION

The resilience of dreams is the determination to pursue one's purpose despite obstacles

In Indian philosophy, dreams (*svapna*) are seen as reflections of our higher aspirations and desires. The Bhagavad Gita teaches that our dreams and desires, when aligned with our higher self, lead us toward self-realisation. *Krishna* encourages *Arjuna* to pursue his dharma (righteous duty) and remain steadfast in his quest for truth, even when faced with obstacles.

Dreams are not just fleeting desires but a manifestation of our deepest purpose. *Yoga* and meditation help us connect with our inner vision and allow us to remain resilient in the face of challenges. The Upanishads emphasise that true fulfilment comes when we align our dreams with the divine will and the greater cosmic plan.

STANZA-WISE INTERPRETATION

- **Stanza 1:** The poem begins by presenting dreams as the whispers of the soul, guiding us toward our purpose. They provide us with direction, even in difficult times.
- **Stanza 2:** Dreams are shown as a vision of the future. They give us the courage to chase what we truly desire and ignite a passionate drive within us.
- **Stanza 3:** The poem emphasises the resilience needed to pursue dreams. Despite obstacles and uncertainties, we continue to follow our dreams, trusting that they will lead us forward.

- **Stanza 4:** Dreams are portrayed as the force that keeps us moving. They fuel our ambitions and give us the strength to persevere through life's challenges.
- **Stanza 5:** The poem highlights that dreams give us the strength to rise and reach for greatness. They inspire us to push beyond our limitations and never give up.
- **Stanza 6:** Dreams are presented as the wings that lift us up. They help us break free from limitations and reach for higher goals.
- **Stanza 7:** The final stanza reinforces that dreams are the key to living a fulfilled life. They guide us on our path and help us live our truth with confidence and determination.

PHILOSOPHICAL INSIGHTS

This topic emphasises that the resilience of dreams is the force that propels us forward in life. In Indian philosophy, dreams represent our higher aspirations and purpose. The Bhagavad Gita teaches us to pursue our dreams with determination, even when faced with obstacles. The poem illustrates that resilience in following our dreams is the key to living a purposeful life. By remaining steadfast in our pursuit, we align with our true self and find fulfilment.

PRACTICAL GUIDANCE

What are your dreams, and how often do you pursue them with resilience? Are you willing to face the challenges that come with them?

Start by reflecting on your dreams and the obstacles that may be holding you back. Practice meditation to connect with your deeper aspirations and align your actions with your higher purpose. Use affirmations like "I am resilient in pursuing my dreams," "I trust in my journey," and "My dreams guide me toward my true path." Take small steps every day toward your dreams, and trust that the resilience to overcome challenges will be within you as you continue on your journey.

42

The Power of Visualization

Visualization is the art of seeing,
The unseen world, the future's being.
It's the power to shape what's not yet there,
To bring to life the dreams we dare.

In the mind's eye, we plant the seed,
Of hopes and dreams, of every need.
With clarity, we create the path,
To manifest our future's wrath.

Visualization gives form to the formless,
It brings our desires into fullness.
With each thought, we build the frame,
For the life we choose, we claim the name.

Through visualization, we see the end,
Before the journey has even begun, my friend.
It's the blueprint of the life we dream,
A picture of hope, a radiant beam.

Visualization is the power of focus,
It makes us feel what's yet to be noticed.
We draw from within and make it real,
Creating what we cannot feel.

Through visualization, we see with the heart,
A world that's waiting for us to start.
It's the force that helps us believe,
And manifest what we perceive.

The power of visualization is the key,
To unlock the world of possibility.
In our mind, we plant the seed,
And through belief, it is freed.

INTERPRETATION

The power of visualization is the ability to create our reality through focused thought

In Indian philosophy, the concept of visualization is rooted in the understanding that the mind is the creator of reality. The Bhagavad Gita teaches that the mind has the power to shape our actions and perceptions, and thus, by focusing the mind on a particular vision or goal, we can bring it into manifestation. *Krishna* advises *Arjuna* to concentrate on his purpose and vision, and to detach from the results, trusting the process of creation.

Visualization is not just an intellectual exercise but a deeply spiritual practice. The Upanishads emphasise that the mind and consciousness are powerful forces capable of bringing thoughts into being. *Yoga* teaches that visualization is a tool for manifesting desires and cultivating the life we want. By focusing on positive, empowering images, we align ourselves with the universal flow of energy, and manifest our deepest desires into reality.

STANZA-WISE INTERPRETATION

- **Stanza 1:** The poem introduces visualization as the power to see what is not yet real. It emphasises that visualization helps us create the life we dream of by focusing on our desires.
- **Stanza 2:** Visualization is shown as a practice of planting seeds of hope and desire in the mind. By

creating a clear vision, we set the course for the future we wish to manifest.

- **Stanza 3:** The poem highlights that visualization brings intangible desires into reality. By focusing on our goals, we create the framework for our dreams to come true.
- **Stanza 4:** Visualization is presented as the ability to see the end result before taking action. It allows us to create a mental blueprint for the life we aspire to live.
- **Stanza 5:** The poem emphasises the focus required in visualization. It is not just about imagining but feeling the reality of what we desire, creating a connection to our future success.
- **Stanza 6:** Visualization is the practice of seeing with the heart, creating a vision that resonates deeply with our soul. It is a practice of belief and trust in the unseen.
- **Stanza 7:** The final stanza reinforces that visualization is the key to manifesting our desires. It is through focusing on positive images and trusting the process that we bring our dreams into reality.

PHILOSOPHICAL INSIGHTS

This topic explores visualization as a powerful tool for manifestation and creation. In Indian spirituality, the mind and consciousness are seen as potent forces capable of shaping our reality. The Bhagavad Gita teaches that by focusing on our vision and trusting the process, we can bring our desires into being. The poem illustrates that visualization helps us align with the universal energy, creating the life we desire. It emphasises the importance of clarity, focus, and belief in manifesting our dreams.

PRACTICAL GUIDANCE

How clear is your vision for the future? Are you able to focus on what you truly desire?

Start by creating a clear mental picture of your goals. Visualize them daily, with all the details that excite you. Feel the emotions associated with achieving those goals, and embrace the sense of fulfilment it brings. Practice meditation to quiet the mind and strengthen your ability to focus. Use affirmations like "I am creating the life I desire," "I trust in the process of manifestation," and "My vision is becoming reality." With consistent focus and belief, you will bring your desires into existence.

43

Nurturing the Seeds of Creativity

Creativity is a spark deep inside,
A force that flows, that cannot hide.
It's the gift we all have within,
To create, to explore, to begin.

Creativity is the seed we plant,
In our hearts, it grows, we chant.
It starts small, but soon it grows,
Into something new, something that glows.

To nurture creativity, we must be free,
To think beyond what we can see.
It's in the quiet moments we find,
The spark that comes from an open mind.

Creativity is the force that leads,
It takes the form of words and deeds.
It's the power to bring dreams to life,
To turn our ideas into life's strife.

In creativity, we find our truth,
It helps us see the world in youth.
It's the force that fuels our soul,
It's the fire that makes us whole.

To nurture creativity is to trust,
In the process, in the rise, in the must.
It is the courage to try and fail,
And the strength to rise with the gale.

Creativity is the path to follow,
A journey of hope, a road to hollow.
In nurturing it, we create anew,
A life that's true, a life that's you.

INTERPRETATION

Creativity is the divine force that allows us to express our inner self and transform the world

In Indian philosophy, creativity (*srishti*) is regarded as a divine expression of the soul. The Bhagavad Gita teaches that creation is not only an external act but a spiritual process that aligns us with the divine. *Krishna* encourages *Arjuna* to be creative in fulfilling his duty, knowing that creativity is the force that drives life and evolution.

The Upanishads emphasise that the universe itself is a manifestation of divine creativity. The practice of *Yoga* helps unlock this inner creative potential by quieting the mind and allowing the flow of ideas. Creativity is nurtured when we align with the divine essence and trust in the process of creation. By embracing creativity, we can transform our lives and bring new ideas into the world.

STANZA-WISE INTERPRETATION

- **Stanza 1:** The poem begins by introducing creativity as an innate force that lies deep within each of us. It is a spark that drives us to create and explore.
- **Stanza 2:** Creativity is presented as a seed that we plant in our hearts. It begins small but grows into something powerful and transformative.
- **Stanza 3:** The poem emphasises that to nurture creativity, we must free ourselves from limitations. By opening our minds, we allow creative ideas to flow.

- **Stanza 4:** Creativity is the force that brings our dreams and ideas into reality. It gives us the power to manifest our vision and make an impact.
- **Stanza 5:** Creativity helps us see the world with new eyes. It fuels our soul and inspires us to live fully, embracing the transformative power of creation.
- **Stanza 6:** The poem highlights that nurturing creativity requires trust in the process, as well as the courage to face failure and rise again.
- **Stanza 7:** The final stanza affirms that creativity is a path of personal growth. By nurturing it, we create a life that is authentic and aligned with our true self.

PHILOSOPHICAL INSIGHTS

This topic explores creativity as the divine force that allows us to express our true self and transform the world. In Indian spirituality, creativity is viewed as an expression of the soul, connecting us to the divine essence of life. The Bhagavad Gita teaches that creativity is a key element of fulfilling our duties and creating the world around us. The poem emphasises that nurturing creativity requires trust, courage, and a willingness to embrace both success and failure.

PRACTICAL GUIDANCE

How often do you allow yourself to create freely? Are you ready to embrace your inner creativity?

Start by giving yourself permission to create without limitations. Practice meditation to quiet your mind and connect with your inner creative source. Reflect on past creative projects and the lessons they brought. Use affirmations like "I am a creative being," "I trust the process of creation," and "My creativity flows freely." Nurture your creativity through daily practice, and allow it to guide you toward new ideas and projects. By embracing your creative potential, you will unlock new possibilities in your life.

44

The Rhythm of Universal Flow

The universe moves with silent grace,
A rhythm that flows in every space.
From the stars to the sea, from the earth to the sky,
Everything moves in harmony, as time passes by.

The rhythm of the universe is the beat of life,
It moves through joy and pain, through calm and strife.
It flows through the air, it moves through the trees,
It carries us forward, like a dance with the breeze.

In every heartbeat, we feel the flow,
The rhythm of life, the ebb and the glow.
It's the pulse of creation, the source of all,
Guiding us gently, answering the call.

The rhythm is constant, yet it changes with time,
A melody that's played, sublime and divine.
It whispers softly in the quiet of night,
A reminder of the world's sacred light.

In the rhythm, we find our place,
A part of the dance, in time and space.
We are not separate, but part of the whole,
Connected to the rhythm that flows in our soul.

The rhythm of life is the flow of the heart,
It's the song that unites us, every part.
It's the force that moves the stars above,
It is the embodiment of love.

To align with the rhythm is to live in peace,
To feel the flow that will never cease.
It is the key to being whole,
And living a life that's in tune with the soul.

INTERPRETATION

The rhythm of the universal flow connects all beings, guiding us through life's ebbs and flows

In Indian philosophy, the concept of universal flow is closely tied to the idea of *Prakriti* (nature) and *Brahman* (the ultimate reality). The Bhagavad Gita teaches that the universe operates in harmony, and everything within it, including human life, is a reflection of this flow. *Krishna* speaks of the divine rhythm that permeates the universe, reminding us that we are part of a greater whole. By aligning with this universal flow, we find peace and spiritual fulfilment.

The Upanishads also emphasise that the entire universe is in constant motion, from the smallest particles to the grand cosmic order. In *Yoga*, practitioners seek to align their actions with this rhythm, allowing them to live harmoniously with the world around them. This alignment leads to inner peace, spiritual growth, and a deeper connection with the divine.

STANZA-WISE INTERPRETATION

- **Stanza 1:** The poem begins by describing the universal **flow** as a graceful rhythm that moves through everything in the universe. It shows that this flow is constant, connecting all things.
- **Stanza 2:** The rhythm of the universe is introduced as a force that moves through both joy and sorrow. It is present in all experiences and flows through nature, guiding our journey.

- **Stanza 3:** The poem emphasises that we feel the flow of life in every heartbeat. It is the pulse of creation, an ever-present force guiding us toward our destiny.
- **Stanza 4:** The rhythm is portrayed as both constant and dynamic. It changes over time but remains a fundamental part of the universe. The quiet moments remind us of the divine light that guides us.
- **Stanza 5:** The poem encourages us to find our place in the rhythm of life, showing that we are all part of a greater, unified whole. We are not separate but connected to the flow of existence.
- **Stanza 6:** Rhythm is depicted as the force that unites all beings. It moves through everything, from the stars to our hearts, creating harmony in the universe.
- **Stanza 7:** The final stanza emphasises that to align with the universal flow is to find peace and harmony. By living in tune with this rhythm, we live a life that is fulfilling and in harmony with our soul.

PHILOSOPHICAL INSIGHTS

This topic explores the rhythm of the universal flow as a guiding force that permeates all of existence. In Indian philosophy, this rhythm is seen as the fundamental pulse of the universe, which connects everything and everyone. The Bhagavad Gita teaches us that when we align ourselves with this flow, we experience peace and harmony. The poem illustrates that the universal rhythm is the source of life, creation, and love, and by aligning with it, we live in harmony with the world and our inner selves.

PRACTICAL GUIDANCE

How well do you feel aligned with the flow of life? Are you able to sense the natural rhythm that guides your journey?

Start by practising mindfulness to become more aware of the rhythms around you, whether in nature or in your daily life. Take time each day to reflect on the flow of your experiences, both the highs and the lows. Practice *yoga* and meditation to center yourself and align with the universal flow. Use affirmations like "I am in harmony with the universe," "I trust the rhythm of life," and "I am connected to the flow of creation." Through alignment with the universal rhythm, you will find peace and fulfilment.

45

The Power of Self-Discovery

Self-discovery is the path to truth,
A journey that begins in our youth.
It's the quest to understand the soul,
And find the pieces that make us whole.

In self-discovery, we find our way,
Through life's challenges, we sway.
It's the courage to look within,
And uncover the truth where it begins.

Self-discovery is the art of seeing,
The hidden truths that have been fleeing.
It's the wisdom that comes with time,
And the patience to trust the climb.

Through self-discovery, we break free,
From the chains that bind us, you and me.
It's the courage to face the unknown,
And embrace the seeds that are sown.

Self-discovery is the force that leads,
It's the spark that ignites our needs.
It guides us on the journey within,
To find the peace that lies beneath the skin.

Through self-discovery, we see the light,
That shines through darkness, clear and bright.
It's the power to align with truth,
And to embrace the wisdom of youth.

The power of self-discovery is the key,
To understanding the self, to being free.
It's the path to peace, to joy, to bliss,
The power to live in eternal bliss.

INTERPRETATION

Self-discovery is the journey to uncover our true essence

In Indian philosophy, self-discovery (*atman-jnana*) is considered the highest path to wisdom and enlightenment. The Bhagavad Gita teaches that true understanding comes from knowing the self, and that all external knowledge is secondary to the knowledge of the *atman* (the soul). *Krishna* guides *Arjuna* toward self-realization, showing that only by discovering our true nature can we experience lasting peace and freedom.

In *Yoga*, self-discovery is a continuous practice that involves introspection, meditation, and mindfulness. The Upanishads describe self-discovery as the process of peeling away the layers of ego and illusion to reveal the divine truth within. By connecting with our true self, we align with the universal consciousness and unlock the potential for spiritual awakening.

STANZA-WISE INTERPRETATION

- **Stanza 1:** The poem introduces self-discovery as the journey to uncover our true self. It is a quest that begins with a deep inner search for meaning.
- **Stanza 2:** Self-discovery is described as the ability to face life's challenges while seeking truth. It requires courage to look within and understand the deeper aspects of ourselves.

- **Stanza 3:** The poem emphasises that self-discovery involves uncovering hidden truths. It is a process that takes time, patience, and introspection.
- **Stanza 4:** Through self-discovery, we break free from the constraints that hold us back. It is the courage to confront the unknown and embrace personal growth.
- **Stanza 5:** Self-discovery is presented as a force that guides us toward our true path. It ignites the spark of transformation and helps us align with our highest purpose.
- **Stanza 6:** The poem highlights that through self-discovery, we find light in darkness. It is the power to see the truth clearly and align with our authentic self.
- **Stanza 7:** The final stanza emphasises that self-discovery is the key to inner peace and spiritual fulfilment. It is the path to joy, bliss, and a deeper connection with the universe.

PHILOSOPHICAL INSIGHTS

This topic explores self-discovery as the path to understanding our true self and realizing our divine nature. In Indian spirituality, self-discovery is seen as the most important journey, as it leads to freedom from ego and suffering. *Krishna* teaches that by knowing the self, we unlock the ultimate wisdom and achieve spiritual liberation. The poem illustrates that self-discovery requires introspection, patience, and courage, and that it leads us to peace, joy, and alignment with the universal truth.

PRACTICAL GUIDANCE

How often do you take time to look inward and explore your true self? Are you ready to embark on the journey of self-discovery?

Start by setting aside time for self-reflection. Practice meditation and mindfulness to connect with your true self and quiet the distractions of the world. Reflect on your inner values, passions, and purpose. Use affirmations like "I am discovering my true self," "I trust the process of self-discovery," and "I align with my highest purpose." Through self-discovery, you will unlock deeper understanding, inner peace, and spiritual growth.

46

Finding Freedom in Discipline

Discipline is the strength to steer,
The focus to persevere and clear.
It's the structure that leads us forward,
A foundation that keeps us grounded, toward.

In discipline, there is a quiet power,
That shapes our day, each waking hour.
It's the habit that becomes our guide,
Through every challenge, we stride with pride.

Discipline is the key to progress,
The strength to move beyond the stress.
It teaches us patience and control,
And keeps our actions in line with our soul.

Through discipline, we find our way,
One step at a time, each passing day.
It is the order that sets us free,
To act with purpose and clarity.

Discipline is not restraint, but choice,
A power that gives us a clear voice.
It is the wisdom to stay on track,
And the courage to never look back.

Through discipline, we grow and evolve,
We overcome the obstacles that revolve.
It is the key to mastery and peace,
A path that leads to inner release.

Finding freedom in discipline is the way,
To live with purpose each day.
In discipline, we rise and soar,
And unlock the life we're meant for.

INTERPRETATION

Discipline is the path that leads to true freedom

In Indian philosophy, discipline (*tapas*) is considered essential for spiritual and personal growth. The Bhagavad Gita teaches that self-discipline is a necessary part of fulfilling one's dharma (duty). *Krishna* advises *Arjuna* to control his impulses and maintain focus on his higher purpose, showing that discipline is not about restriction but about aligning with one's true path.

The Upanishads speak of *tapas* as the process of purifying the mind and body, making them receptive to spiritual wisdom. In *Yoga*, discipline is not only about physical practices but also about cultivating mental and emotional focus. It is through discipline that we learn to control our desires and impulses, freeing us from distractions and aligning ourselves with the divine will.

STANZA-WISE INTERPRETATION

- **Stanza 1:** The poem introduces discipline as the strength that guides us through life's journey. It is the foundation that keeps us grounded and moving forward with purpose.
- **Stanza 2:** Discipline is depicted as a quiet power that shapes our daily actions. It is the habit that becomes a guide, helping us navigate life's challenges.
- **Stanza 3:** The poem emphasises that discipline is the key to progress. It brings patience and control, aligning our actions with our higher goals.

- **Stanza 4:** Discipline is presented as a methodical path. It helps us stay on track and act with clarity and purpose.
- **Stanza 5:** Discipline is described as the power of choice. It gives us the wisdom to stay focused and the courage to move forward without looking back.
- **Stanza 6:** Discipline is shown as a path of growth and evolution. Through it, we overcome obstacles and continue to evolve toward our higher selves.
- **Stanza 7:** The final stanza emphasises that freedom is found in discipline. It is through consistent effort and focus that we unlock the life we are meant to live.

PHILOSOPHICAL INSIGHTS

This topic highlights the idea that discipline is the path to freedom. In Indian spirituality, discipline (*tapas*) is essential for achieving spiritual growth and self-realisation. The Bhagavad Gita teaches that through self-discipline, we align ourselves with our higher purpose and fulfil our duties with clarity and focus. The poem illustrates that discipline is not about restriction but about choosing to live with intention and purpose, freeing ourselves from distractions and guiding us toward inner peace and fulfilment.

PRACTICAL GUIDANCE

How do you approach discipline in your life? Do you see it as a tool for freedom?

Start by identifying areas where discipline can improve your life. Whether it's your physical, mental, or emotional well-being, establish small daily practices that support your goals. Practice meditation and *yoga* to strengthen your focus and self-control. Use affirmations like "I am disciplined and focused," "I am in control of my actions," and "Discipline leads me to freedom." By incorporating discipline into your life, you will create a path to personal and spiritual growth.

47

The Timeless Wisdom of Nature

Nature speaks in whispers loud,
In winds that blow, in thundercloud.
It teaches us in silent ways,
The timeless wisdom of the days.

In every leaf, in every tree,
Nature shows us how to be free.
It flows with grace and harmony,
A reflection of the divine we see.

The mountains stand with strength and might,
While rivers flow with gentle light.
Each creature moves with purpose true,
Teaching us to trust and renew.

In nature's rhythm, there's a plan,
A divine order, a cosmic span.
The sun rises, the moon takes its turn,
A cycle of wisdom we must learn.

The wisdom of nature is in the earth,
In every seed, in every birth.
It teaches us to stay grounded and true,
And to trust the flow that carries through.

Nature's wisdom is the light that shines,
Through every storm, through all times.
It teaches us patience, it teaches us grace,
To move with love, at life's own pace.

In the wisdom of nature, we find our way,
A path to peace, a path to stay.
To honour the earth and all it gives,
Is to live in truth, and to truly live.

INTERPRETATION

The timeless wisdom of nature offers profound teachings about life, growth, and harmony

In Indian philosophy, nature (*prakriti*) is seen as a manifestation of the divine. The Bhagavad Gita teaches that *Krishna* resides in all aspects of nature, and by observing the natural world, we can gain insight into the divine order of existence. The rhythm of nature reflects the divine harmony that governs the universe, and by aligning ourselves with it, we live in peace and balance.

The Upanishads describe nature as a teacher, offering wisdom about the cycles of life, death, and rebirth. In *Yoga*, practitioners learn to connect with the natural world, recognizing that nature's wisdom is mirrored within us. Through mindfulness and meditation, we align ourselves with nature's cycles, finding peace, patience, and understanding. Nature teaches us to stay grounded and trust the flow of life, knowing that all things unfold in their right time.

STANZA-WISE INTERPRETATION

- **Stanza 1:** The poem introduces nature as a teacher that speaks in whispers. It shows that nature's wisdom is often subtle but powerful, teaching us important lessons through its beauty and simplicity.
- **Stanza 2:** Nature is depicted as a reflection of the divine, teaching us to live with grace and harmony. Through observing nature, we can learn how to live more freely and in tune with the universe.

- **Stanza 3:** The poem highlights the wisdom found in the natural world, from the strength of the mountains to the flow of the rivers. Nature teaches us to trust and renew ourselves as we move through life.
- **Stanza 4:** The poem emphasises that nature follows a divine order, a rhythm that teaches us patience and trust. Nature's cycles offer profound wisdom about life's flow.
- **Stanza 5:** Nature's wisdom is described as the wisdom of the earth itself. It teaches us to stay grounded and to trust in the natural flow of life, knowing that everything has its place.
- **Stanza 6:** Nature's wisdom provides light in times of darkness. It teaches us to move with love and grace, understanding that everything has its time and purpose.
- **Stanza 7:** The final stanza affirms that by honouring nature and its wisdom, we align ourselves with truth and live fully. It encourages us to embrace nature's teachings for a peaceful and harmonious life.

PHILOSOPHICAL INSIGHTS

This topic emphasises the timeless wisdom of nature, which offers profound teachings about life, growth, and balance. In Indian spirituality, nature is viewed as a manifestation of the divine, and by aligning ourselves with its rhythms, we find peace and understanding. The Bhagavad Gita and Upanishads teach that nature reflects the divine order of the universe, and by connecting with it, we live in harmony with our true selves. The poem illustrates that nature's wisdom helps us stay grounded, patient, and graceful, guiding us through life's challenges.

PRACTICAL GUIDANCE

How often do you connect with nature? Are you open to learning from its timeless wisdom?

Start by spending time in nature. Observe the rhythms and cycles of the world around you, whether it's the changing seasons, the flow of a river, or the stillness of the trees. Practice mindfulness to connect with nature's energy and allow it to guide you. Reflect on how nature's wisdom can help you find balance in your own life. Use affirmations like "I am grounded in nature's wisdom," "I trust the flow of life," and "I live in harmony with the world." By embracing nature's teachings, you will align yourself with peace, patience, and spiritual growth.

48

The Strength of Willpower

Willpower is the force inside,
That helps us conquer, helps us glide.
It's the strength to rise and stand,
To overcome, to take command.

In willpower, there's an inner might,
It fuels our dreams, ignites our fight.
It's the power to push through doubt,
And the courage to let fear out.

Willpower is the will to endure,
The force that helps us find a cure.
It's the strength to stay the course,
To remain steadfast with no remorse.

In every challenge, willpower grows,
It's the power that everyone knows.
It's the fire that burns deep within,
That helps us rise again and begin.

Willpower teaches us to stay true,
To trust in ourselves and what we do.
It's the energy to make it right,
And the strength to keep up the fight.

Through willpower, we find our way,
To keep moving, come what may.
It's the power to change and rise,
To see the truth beyond the lies.

The strength of willpower is the key,
To unlocking all that we can be.
It gives us the courage to strive,
And to live fully, to thrive and survive.

INTERPRETATION

Willpower is the inner strength that enables us to persist and achieve our goals

In Indian philosophy, willpower (*iccha-shakti*) is seen as a vital force that helps us overcome obstacles and fulfil our higher purpose. The Bhagavad Gita teaches that willpower is necessary for self-discipline (*tapas*) and for overcoming the distractions of the mind. *Krishna* emphasises that through unwavering determination, we can stay focused on our dharma (duty) and transcend the challenges that life presents.

In *Yoga*, willpower is developed through meditation, (*pranayama*), and mental discipline. It is the inner force that helps us stay grounded in the face of adversity and pursue our goals with determination. The Upanishads highlight the importance of aligning willpower with the divine will, recognizing that true strength lies in aligning our desires with the higher consciousness.

STANZA-WISE INTERPRETATION

- **Stanza 1:** The poem introduces willpower as an inner force that helps us rise above challenges and take control of our destiny. It is the strength that empowers us to act with determination.
- **Stanza 2:** Willpower is depicted as the energy that helps us overcome doubt and fear. It ignites our passion and drives us forward.

- **Stanza 3:** The poem emphasises that willpower enables us to stay on course despite obstacles. It teaches us to remain steadfast and unshaken in our pursuit.
- **Stanza 4:** Willpower is shown as the force that grows with each challenge. It is the fire that fuels us to continue, no matter how difficult the journey may be.
- **Stanza 5:** The poem emphasises that willpower requires self-trust and determination. It is the strength to make the right choices and persevere through hardship.
- **Stanza 6:** Willpower is portrayed as the inner strength that guides us toward our purpose. It helps us see the truth and stay true to ourselves.
- **Stanza 7:** The final stanza reinforces that willpower is the key to unlocking our potential. It is the force that enables us to live fully and achieve our highest goals.

PHILOSOPHICAL INSIGHTS

This topic emphasises willpower as the inner strength that drives us to overcome challenges and achieve our goals. In Indian spirituality, willpower (*iccha-shakti*) is viewed as a vital force that helps us stay disciplined and focused on our higher purpose. *Krishna* teaches in the Bhagavad Gita that through willpower, we can overcome distractions and stay aligned with our duty. The poem illustrates that willpower empowers us to persist in the face of adversity, remain true to our values, and unlock our fullest potential.

PRACTICAL GUIDANCE

How do you use your willpower to overcome challenges? Are you fully committed to your goals?

Start by reflecting on areas of your life where you need more willpower. Set small, achievable goals and commit to them with determination. Practice meditation to strengthen your focus and align your will with your higher purpose. Use affirmations like "I am strong and determined," "I trust in my willpower," and "I stay focused on my goals." By cultivating willpower, you will develop the strength to navigate challenges and fulfil your dreams.

49

The Law of Attraction and Manifestation

The Law of Attraction is the force we call,
It brings to us what we think most of all.
Our thoughts, our desires, our deepest dreams,
Are drawn to us, like the flowing streams.

In manifestation, we see our truth,
What we focus on becomes the proof.
It's the power to shape what we see,
To bring into life all that can be.

The Law of Attraction works with intent,
It's the power that we give, the energy sent.
Through our thoughts, we create our space,
Attracting the life we embrace.

In manifestation, we set the stage,
We ignite the spark and turn the page.
Through belief and vision, we see it unfold,
A life of abundance, a story told.

The Law of Attraction is the power we wield,
It manifests through the energy we yield.
What we focus on becomes our way,
It's the force that shapes our day.

To manifest, we must align,
With our deepest desires, our goals divine.
Through visualization, we bring to life,
The dreams that end all worldly strife.

The Law of Attraction is the key,
To manifest the life we long to see.
Through the power of belief and trust,
We bring to life what's pure and just.

INTERPRETATION

The Law of Attraction and manifestation is the principle that our thoughts and intentions shape our reality

In Indian philosophy, the idea of manifestation (*sankalpa*) is rooted in the understanding that the mind is the creator of our world. The Bhagavad Gita teaches that our thoughts and intentions have the power to shape our actions and the world around us. *Krishna* emphasises that by focusing on our purpose with clarity and devotion, we can manifest our desires and fulfil our duties.

The Upanishads speak of the mind's power to create reality, and the concept of *Brahman* (the ultimate reality) as the source of all manifestations. Through *Yoga* and meditation, we learn to focus our thoughts, align our intentions with the divine will, and manifest our deepest desires. The Law of Attraction is based on the principle that like attracts like, and by aligning with positive energy, we draw similar energies into our lives.

STANZA-WISE INTERPRETATION

- **Stanza 1:** The poem introduces the Law of Attraction as the force that draws our desires to us. It highlights that our thoughts shape our reality and attract what we focus on.
- **Stanza 2:** Manifestation is presented as the process of bringing our desires into reality. By focusing on what we want, we create the life we desire.

- **Stanza 3:** The poem emphasises that the Law of Attraction works through intent and focus. By directing our energy toward our goals, we create the space for them to manifest.
- **Stanza 4:** Manifestation is presented as a process of vision and belief. By visualizing our desires and believing in their realisation, we bring them into being.
- **Stanza 5:** The Law of Attraction is depicted as the force that shapes our lives. Through our thoughts and energy, we attract the circumstances and opportunities we need.
- **Stanza 6:** The poem highlights that to manifest our desires, we must align with them deeply. By focusing on our goals with intention and visualization, we bring them into existence.
- **Stanza 7:** The final stanza emphasises that the Law of Attraction is the key to manifesting a fulfilling life. By believing and trusting in the process, we create the reality we desire.

PHILOSOPHICAL INSIGHTS

This topic explores the Law of Attraction and manifestation as the principle that our thoughts, intentions, and energy shape our reality. In Indian philosophy, manifestation is seen as the ability to bring our desires into being through focused thought and alignment with the divine will. The Bhagavad Gita teaches that by focusing on our *dharma* (purpose) with clarity and devotion, we can manifest our highest potential. The poem illustrates that the Law of

Attraction works when we align our thoughts with our desires and trust in the process of creation.

PRACTICAL GUIDANCE

What are you focusing on in your life right now? Are you attracting the life you desire?

Start by reflecting on the thoughts and desires that dominate your mind. Are they positive and aligned with your goals? Practice visualization and affirmations to focus on the life you want to manifest. Meditate regularly to clear your mind of distractions and connect with your deepest desires. Use affirmations like "I attract abundance and positivity," "I trust in the Law of Attraction," and "I am manifesting my dreams into reality." By focusing on what you truly want and aligning your energy with it, you will manifest the life you desire.

50

The Role of Passion in Personal Growth

Passion is the fire that lights the way,
A spark that ignites the brightest day.
It's the strength that pushes us through,
The power to create, to dream, to renew.

With passion, we rise, we stand tall,
It's the drive that answers life's call.
It fuels our actions, it guides our stride,
With passion, there's nothing to hide.

Passion is the heart's true song,
It gives us the strength to move along.
It's the energy that drives the soul,
And fills our lives with a sacred goal.

Through passion, we find our place,
A journey of purpose, a life of grace.
It leads us to discover what's true,
And inspires us to be who we are, anew.

Passion is the light we follow,
It's the force that makes us whole.
It transforms our pain, it heals our heart,
And gives us the courage to start.

In passion, we find the will to grow,
The strength to push past what we know.
It fuels our dreams, it opens the door,
To the life we long to explore.

The role of passion is to ignite,
To fill our hearts with pure delight.
It's the power that leads us forward,
To a life of meaning, rich and inward.

INTERPRETATION

Passion is the driving force that propels us toward personal growth and self-realization

In Indian philosophy, passion (*rāga*) is seen as both a motivator and a challenge on the path to self-mastery. The Bhagavad Gita teaches that passion, when aligned with *dharma* (righteous duty), can be a powerful force for good. *Krishna* encourages *Arjuna* to perform his duties with passion, yet without attachment to the results. This kind of passion leads to personal growth and the fulfilment of life's purpose.

In *Yoga*, passion is balanced with detachment (*vairagya*), helping us channel energy constructively without being overwhelmed by desires. The Upanishads highlight that true personal growth occurs when we cultivate a passion for truth and self-realisation, allowing us to transcend worldly distractions.

STANZA-WISE INTERPRETATION

- **Stanza 1:** The poem introduces passion as a guiding force that illuminates our path. It empowers us to take action and move forward with purpose.
- **Stanza 2:** Passion is portrayed as the strength that drives us to achieve our goals. It fuels our actions and keeps us focused on our dreams.
- **Stanza 3:** The poem emphasises that passion connects with the heart and soul, guiding us toward meaningful

pursuits. It is a source of energy that fills our lives with purpose.

- **Stanza 4:** Passion is shown as a force that leads us to discover our true self. It inspires us to pursue our authentic path and live with grace.
- **Stanza 5:** Passion is depicted as the light that transforms our challenges. It helps us heal and gives us the courage to overcome obstacles.
- **Stanza 6:** The poem highlights that passion is the energy that pushes us to grow and explore. It motivates us to reach beyond our comfort zones.
- **Stanza 7:** The final stanza reinforces that passion is the key to a meaningful life. It leads us forward on a journey of self-discovery and fulfilment.

PHILOSOPHICAL INSIGHTS

This topic emphasises that passion is essential for personal growth and transformation. In Indian philosophy, passion (*rāga*) can be both a force for good and a potential distraction. When aligned with *dharma*, it becomes a driving force that propels us toward self-realisation. *Krishna* teaches that passion, when detached from selfish desires, leads to meaningful action and personal fulfilment. The poem illustrates that passion fuels our pursuit of purpose and helps us overcome obstacles, guiding us toward a life of inner peace and growth.

PRACTICAL GUIDANCE

How often do you tap into your passion to guide your life? Are you aligned with your true purpose?

Start by reflecting on your passions. What excites you? What inspires you to move forward? Practice mindfulness to connect with your true desires and use meditation to focus your energy on what truly matters. Use affirmations like "I am passionate about my life's purpose," "My passion guides me," and "I channel my passion into meaningful action." Embrace your passions and let them lead you toward personal growth and fulfilment.

51

Nurturing Inner Creativity

Creativity is the voice of the soul,
It speaks in colors, in words, in whole.
It flows like rivers, wild and free,
A wellspring of boundless energy.

To nurture creativity, we must let go,
Of doubts and fears that stop the flow.
It's the courage to express, to create,
And bring forth something truly great.

In creativity, there is freedom found,
A space where we can truly be unbound.
It's the joy in creating, the bliss of form,
The spark of life in its creative storm.

To nurture creativity, we must believe,
That we are worthy, that we can achieve.
It's the strength to trust in the process,
And the courage to never second guess.

Creativity is the energy of life,
It cuts through silence, it ends all strife.
It's the power to transform, to renew,
To turn visions into something true.

In creativity, we find our voice,
We give expression to what we rejoice.
It is the force that helps us create,
A life of meaning, of love, of fate.

To nurture creativity is to embrace,
The beauty of life, the sacred space.
It is to honour the spark within,
And trust that creativity will always win.

INTERPRETATION

Creativity is the divine force that allows us to express our deepest selves

In Indian philosophy, creativity (*srishti*) is seen as a divine gift that flows from the *Atman* (soul). The Bhagavad Gita teaches that our creative energies should be channeled into fulfilling our *dharma* (purpose) and contributing to the greater good. *Krishna* encourages *Arjuna* to perform his duties with devotion, seeing every act as a form of creation.

The Upanishads describe the universe itself as a manifestation of divine creativity, with all beings and things originating from the *Brahman* (the ultimate reality). In *Yoga*, creativity is cultivated by silencing the mind through practices like meditation and *pranayama* (breathing exercises), allowing the inner creative potential to flow. By embracing our creativity, we align ourselves with the divine source of all creation.

STANZA-WISE INTERPRETATION

- **Stanza 1:** The poem begins by introducing creativity as the voice of the soul. It expresses itself in various forms, from art to action, and is a limitless force within us.
- **Stanza 2:** Creativity requires us to let go of fears and doubts that block its flow. It is the courage to express ourselves fully and bring new ideas into being.

- **Stanza 3:** Creativity is shown as a source of freedom. It gives us the space to create joyfully and express the beauty of life.
- **Stanza 4:** Creativity requires belief in ourselves. It is the strength to trust the creative process and have confidence in our ideas.
- **Stanza 5:** Creativity is portrayed as a powerful energy that transforms life. It turns visions into reality and helps us create something meaningful.
- **Stanza 6:** The poem emphasises that creativity is the way we express our deepest truths and joys. It is the force that helps us bring purpose and love into our lives.
- **Stanza 7:** The final stanza affirms that nurturing creativity allows us to honour the spark within us. It is through creativity that we find meaning and connection with the world.

PHILOSOPHICAL INSIGHTS

This topic emphasises creativity as a divine force that allows us to express our true selves and transform the world around us. In Indian spirituality, creativity (*srishti*) is a reflection of the divine source, and by nurturing it, we align with the greater cosmic flow. The Bhagavad Gita teaches that every action, when performed with devotion and creativity, contributes to the divine order. The poem illustrates that creativity is the force that helps us express our soul's purpose, bringing joy, love, and meaning into our lives.

PRACTICAL GUIDANCE

How often do you give yourself the space to create freely? Are you nurturing your creative potential?

Start by creating a routine that supports your creativity. Set aside time each day for creative expression, whether through writing, painting, or any other form of art. Practice meditation to clear your mind and connect with your inner creative source. Use affirmations like "I am a creative being," "I trust my creativity," and "I express my true self through creation." Embrace the creative process without fear or judgment, and trust that your creativity will guide you to new possibilities.

CHAPTER 5

Universal Connection

52

Quantum Physics and the Web of Connected Consciousness

At the heart of the universe's core,
Lies a truth we cannot ignore.
Quantum physics unveils the veil,
Revealing the web where all truths sail.

Every particle, every wave,
Connected in a cosmic crave.
The quantum field, where all things meet,
In the web of consciousness, we are complete.

What is within us, we can't see,
But in the depths, we find unity.
The dance of atoms, the dance of soul,
The web of life, making us whole.

Quantum physics reveals the truth,
That consciousness is the ultimate proof.
Through it, we see the interconnectedness,
Of all things in the universe, boundless and blessed.

Every thought, every feeling we send,
Is woven into the cosmic blend.
The web of consciousness, vast and wide,
Is the force where we all reside.

In this quantum field, we find our place,
In every breath, in every space.
We are all part of a greater whole,
Connected through consciousness, mind, and soul.

Through the lens of quantum's grace,
We find that all things share a space.
The web of connected consciousness is the key,
To understanding our unity and divinity.

INTERPRETATION

Quantum physics and the web of connected consciousness reveal the interconnectedness of all things

In Indian philosophy, the concept of interconnectedness is foundational, as it teaches that all living beings are part of a unified whole. *Brahman*, the ultimate reality, is the source of all things, and *atman* (the soul) is intimately connected with it. The Bhagavad Gita emphasises that everything in the universe is connected, and our actions and thoughts have an impact on the world around us.

Quantum physics has confirmed this ancient wisdom by showing that on the subatomic level, everything is connected through quantum fields. The interconnectedness revealed by quantum mechanics mirrors the Upanishads, which describe the universe as a dynamic, interconnected system where the self and the divine are inseparable. By understanding this connection, we can align ourselves with the flow of the universe, creating harmony and balance in our lives.

STANZA-WISE INTERPRETATION

- **Stanza 1:** The poem introduces quantum physics as a gateway to understanding the interconnectedness of the universe. It emphasises the unveiling of a truth that reveals the web of connected consciousness.
- **Stanza 2:** Quantum physics is portrayed as revealing the interconnection of all things at the atomic level. It

shows how every particle and wave is part of a vast web of unity.

- **Stanza 3:** The poem highlights that the unseen world within us reflects the unity of all things. It is through the quantum field that we find our wholeness, where mind and soul are interconnected.
- **Stanza 4:** The quantum field is described as proof of the interconnectedness of all things. Our consciousness, thoughts, and actions are all part of this divine flow.
- **Stanza 5:** Quantum physics reveals that our thoughts and feelings are woven into the universal web. Every action we take affects the larger cosmic system, creating a ripple effect of interconnected energy.
- **Stanza 6:** The poem emphasises that the quantum field provides the space where all things are interconnected. We find our true place in the greater whole, understanding that we are part of an infinite web of life.
- **Stanza 7:** The final stanza affirms that the web of connected consciousness is the key to understanding unity and divinity. By seeing life through the lens of quantum physics, we recognise the inherent interconnectedness of all existence.

PHILOSOPHICAL INSIGHTS

This topic explores how quantum physics reveals the underlying interconnectedness of all things, mirroring ancient Indian philosophy. The Bhagavad Gita and the Upanishads teach that the universe is a web of interconnected energy, where the *atman* (soul) is intimately connected with *Brahman* (the divine). Quantum mechanics has confirmed this understanding by showing that at the subatomic level, everything is interconnected. The poem illustrates that by recognizing this interconnection, we align ourselves with the cosmic flow and achieve unity and peace.

PRACTICAL GUIDANCE

How do you perceive the interconnectedness of all things? Are you aware of the impact your thoughts and actions have on the world around you?

Start by practising mindfulness to observe your thoughts and feelings. Reflect on the interconnectedness of life and the ripple effect of your actions. Engage in meditation to connect with the quantum field of consciousness and align yourself with the universal flow. Use affirmations like "I am part of the universal web of life," "My thoughts and actions are interconnected with the divine," and "I am in harmony with the flow of the universe." Through this awareness, you will begin to experience a deeper connection with the world around you and the divine within you.

53

The Synergy of Collective Consciousness

Collective consciousness is the power of we,
A force that moves beyond you and me.
It's the energy of all, the unity of the mind,
A collective force that's intertwined.

In collective consciousness, we find our strength,
A power that spans any distance or length.
It's the shared wisdom that guides our way,
And the energy that builds each new day.

Through collective consciousness, we heal,
It's the wisdom to understand, to feel.
In the unity of many, we find our power,
A force that grows stronger with every hour.

Collective consciousness is the voice of the whole,
It speaks to the heart, it guides the soul.
It is the energy of all that exists,
A divine force that cannot resist.

Through collective consciousness, we transcend,
The boundaries of ego, and our minds extend.
It's the wisdom that comes when we are one,
A force that rises with the sun.

In the synergy of many, we see the light,
It is the power to make wrongs right.
Through unity, we create the change,
And transform the world, rearrange.

The synergy of collective consciousness is the key,
To healing the world and setting us free.
Together we rise, together we stand,
In the power of unity, hand in hand.

INTERPRETATION

The synergy of collective consciousness is the recognition that we are all part of a shared, interconnected energy

In Indian philosophy, collective consciousness (*samasta-chit*) reflects the understanding that all beings are part of a greater universal mind. The Bhagavad Gita teaches that when individuals act in harmony with their higher selves and each other, they contribute to the collective good. *Krishna* speaks of performing one's duty for the welfare of all, emphasising the power of collective effort.

The Upanishads describe the idea of the *Atman* (individual soul) and *Brahman* (universal consciousness) being one. *Yoga* encourages the practitioner to connect with the collective consciousness through practices that unify the individual mind with the divine, contributing to the well-being of all. The collective consciousness represents the energy that transcends individual egos and fosters unity, peace, and shared wisdom.

STANZA-WISE INTERPRETATION

- **Stanza 1:** The poem introduces collective consciousness as the power of unity. It is the energy that connects all beings and transcends individual boundaries.
- **Stanza 2:** Collective consciousness is depicted as a force that strengthens through shared wisdom and intention. It is the energy that guides the collective journey of humanity.

- **Stanza 3:** Collective consciousness is portrayed as a healing force. It helps individuals connect with each other's feelings and wisdom, creating unity and understanding.
- **Stanza 4:** Collective consciousness is presented as the voice of the collective. It guides the soul and offers wisdom that benefits all beings, creating harmony and balance.
- **Stanza 5:** Collective consciousness helps us transcend the ego. It extends our minds and hearts, uniting us with the greater divine consciousness.
- **Stanza 6:** The poem emphasises that unity is the power that creates positive change. Through collective consciousness, we have the ability to transform the world.
- **Stanza 7:** The final stanza reinforces that the synergy of collective consciousness is the key to healing and transformation. When we unite in purpose, we rise together and create a better world.

PHILOSOPHICAL INSIGHTS

This topic explores the synergy of collective consciousness, which is the recognition that all individuals are connected through a shared, divine energy. In Indian philosophy, collective consciousness (*samasta-chit*) emphasises the interconnectedness of all beings and the importance of unity for spiritual growth. *Krishna* teaches in the Bhagavad Gita that when individuals act for the collective good, they contribute to the well-being of all. The poem illustrates that by uniting in purpose and action, we can create positive change and transform the world.

PRACTICAL GUIDANCE

How can you contribute to the collective consciousness around you? Are you aware of the impact your thoughts and actions have on others?

Start by reflecting on how your actions and thoughts affect the world around you. Practice mindfulness and meditation to align with the collective energy. Recognise that every thought and action contributes to the collective good. Use affirmations like "I am part of the collective consciousness," "I contribute to the well-being of all," and "Together, we create positive change." Through unity and shared intention, we can heal the world and create a better future for all.

54

The Dance Between Faith and Action

Faith is the seed, action the tree,
One without the other cannot be.
Faith is the vision, action the stride,
Together they take us far and wide.

Faith is the trust that fuels the soul,
Action is the way that makes us whole.
It's the belief that guides the hand,
And the work that helps us understand.

Through faith, we see the path unfold,
Through action, we make the journey bold.
Faith gives us purpose, action gives us pace,
Together they lead us to a sacred space.

Faith without action is a dream in the air,
Action without faith leads nowhere.
Together they form the perfect blend,
The path that leads to the highest end.

In every step, faith gives us light,
Action gives us strength, takes us to new height.
The dance between the two is divine,
A rhythm that flows and intertwines.

Through faith, we act with devotion,
Through action, we fulfil the emotion.
It is the perfect union, the two as one,
Leading us toward all that is done.

The dance between faith and action is the key,
To creating the life we wish to see.
With faith as our guide and action as our tool,
We move forward, creating our world with every rule.

INTERPRETATION

The dance between faith and action is the balance required to manifest our desires

In Indian philosophy, faith (*shraddha*) is seen as the foundation of spiritual growth, while action (*karma*) is the means through which we fulfil our *dharma* (righteous duty). The Bhagavad Gita teaches that one must have faith in the divine will while performing one's duties with devotion and discipline. *Krishna* emphasises that it is not enough to just believe; we must also act with sincerity, knowing that our actions are aligned with the divine purpose.

The Upanishads describe faith as the deep trust in the ultimate reality, while action is the vehicle through which we realize our true nature. *Yoga* teaches us that through disciplined action and unwavering faith, we align ourselves with the higher self and the divine. Faith and action must work in harmony to achieve spiritual and material success, creating a balance between belief and manifestation.

STANZA-WISE INTERPRETATION

- **Stanza 1:** The poem introduces the concept of faith and action as complementary forces. Faith is the vision, while action is the manifestation of that vision. Together, they create movement and progress.
- **Stanza 2:** Faith is depicted as the trust that fuels the soul, while action is what brings that trust into reality.

Without action, faith remains a mere dream, and without faith, action lacks purpose.

- **Stanza 3:** The poem emphasises that faith helps us see the path forward, while action gives us the ability to walk it. Faith provides the direction, and action provides the momentum.
- **Stanza 4:** Faith without action is like a dream without realisation, and action without faith lacks foundation. Only when the two are combined can we achieve true success.
- **Stanza 5:** The poem highlights that faith illuminates the path, while action provides the strength to overcome obstacles and move forward. The balance of both leads to growth and transformation.
- **Stanza 6:** Faith and action are shown as a divine union. They are the forces that work together to fulfil our desires and bring our goals into reality.
- **Stanza 7:** The final stanza emphasises that the dance between faith and action is the key to creating the life we want. By aligning both, we can manifest our dreams and move toward our highest purpose.

PHILOSOPHICAL INSIGHTS

This topic explores the dance between faith and action as the balance required to create the life we desire. In Indian philosophy, faith (*shraddha*) is the foundation of our beliefs and purpose, while action (*karma*) is the vehicle through which we fulfil our duties and manifest our desires. The Bhagavad Gita teaches that we must act with faith, knowing that our actions are aligned with the divine will. The poem illustrates that faith and action must work together in harmony to manifest our goals, creating a life of purpose, peace, and fulfilment.

PRACTICAL GUIDANCE

How can you align your actions with your deepest beliefs? Are you willing to trust in the process and take action toward your goals?

Start by reflecting on the beliefs and values that guide your life. How can you take action that aligns with those principles? Practice mindfulness to stay focused on your intentions and keep your actions aligned with your higher self. Use affirmations like "I trust in the process of creation," "My actions align with my deepest beliefs," and "I move forward with purpose and faith." By combining faith and action, you will manifest your goals and move closer to your higher purpose.

55

The Path of Unity and Wholeness

The path of unity is the way to peace,
A journey where all struggles cease.
It's the path where all are one,
In unity, we shine like the sun.

Through unity, we find our strength,
It is the force that goes to great length.
It binds us together, heart and soul,
Making us feel completely whole.

Unity is the force that heals the pain,
It removes the darkness, breaks the chain.
It is the bond that ties us all,
A force that answers humanity's call.

In unity, we see the divine,
It reflects in each face, in each line.
Through unity, we find our place,
In the vast, eternal cosmic space.

Unity is the force that leads us on,
It is the strength that makes us strong.
It gives us purpose, it gives us peace,
And helps us find a sweet release.

Through unity, we rise above,
The separation that divides in love.
It is the oneness that we seek,
A world where all are strong and meek.

The path of unity is the way to go,
It leads to wholeness, it helps us grow.
Through unity, we find our grace,
And walk together, in the same space.

INTERPRETATION

The path of unity and wholeness leads to peace, connection, and fulfilment

In Indian philosophy, unity (*ekatva*) is seen as the highest ideal, as all beings are interconnected through the *Atman* (soul) and *Brahman* (the divine). The Bhagavad Gita teaches that when we act with the awareness of unity, we transcend the ego and act in harmony with the divine will. *Krishna* emphasises that unity is the foundation of true strength, and only through unity can we experience lasting peace.

The Upanishads describe the ultimate reality as the unity of all things. By recognizing the oneness of all life, we align ourselves with the divine consciousness. *Yoga* teaches that through practices like meditation and self-inquiry, we cultivate the awareness of unity, breaking the boundaries of ego and experiencing the fullness of life. The path of unity is the path to wholeness, where we transcend separation and connect with the divine in all things.

STANZA-WISE INTERPRETATION

- **Stanza 1:** The poem introduces unity as the path to peace. It emphasises that when we come together in unity, all struggles cease and we become one.
- **Stanza 2:** Unity is presented as the strength that binds us together. It brings wholeness and connection, creating a sense of purpose and strength.

- **Stanza 3:** The poem shows that unity is a healing force. It removes pain and division, creating a bond that unites humanity in a shared vision.
- **Stanza 4:** Unity is described as the reflection of the divine. It is through unity that we experience our place in the vast cosmic order and recognise the divine in all beings.
- **Stanza 5:** Unity is depicted as the strength that guides us forward. It provides us with purpose and peace, helping us live harmoniously with ourselves and others.
- **Stanza 6:** The poem highlights that unity helps us rise above division and separation. It is the oneness that transcends love and conflict.
- **Stanza 7:** The final stanza emphasises that the path of **unity** leads to wholeness. By embracing unity, we walk together in peace, grace, and shared purpose.

PHILOSOPHICAL INSIGHTS

This topic explores the path of unity and wholeness as the way to peace, fulfilment, and spiritual growth. In Indian spirituality, unity (*ekatva*) is the highest ideal, representing the interconnectedness of all beings. The Bhagavad Gita teaches that when we act with the awareness of unity, we transcend ego and align with the divine. The poem illustrates that unity is the force that heals, empowers, and connects us to our highest purpose. By walking the path of unity, we experience peace and fulfilment.

PRACTICAL GUIDANCE

How often do you embrace unity in your daily life? Are you willing to connect with others and transcend the boundaries of separation?

Start by reflecting on how you can cultivate unity in your interactions. Practice mindfulness and meditation to connect with the divine within yourself and others. Recognise the interconnectedness of all beings and embrace the oneness of life. Use affirmations like "I am one with all," "Unity brings me peace and strength," and "I act in harmony with the divine will." Through embracing unity, you will find peace, wholeness, and connection with the world around you.

56

The Mirror of Relationships

Relationships are the mirror of the soul,
Reflecting our truth, making us whole.
In the eyes of others, we see our light,
Our flaws, our strengths, both dark and bright.

Through relationships, we find our way,
The lessons they bring, the words they say.
They mirror the parts we fail to see,
And in them, we learn who we can be.

In each connection, there's a reflection true,
A reminder of what we must pursue.
What we give is what we receive,
In the mirror of others, we believe.

Relationships are the heart's true test,
They challenge us, put us to rest.
Through love and conflict, we grow and evolve,
The mirror of relationships helps us solve.

What we see in others is what we must face,
The parts of ourselves we often erase.
Relationships show us what's hidden deep,
And in their reflection, we leap.

The mirror of relationships reveals the truth,
It helps us grow, it restores our youth.
It's the force that challenges the mind,
Helping us leave the past behind.

In the mirror of relationships, we see,
The reflection of the self, wild and free.
Through each connection, we understand,
That love and growth go hand in hand.

INTERPRETATION

The mirror of relationships is a tool for self-reflection and growth

In Indian philosophy, relationships (*sambandha*) are viewed as sacred and transformative, providing opportunities for personal development and self-realisation. The Bhagavad Gita teaches that our interactions with others reveal our inner nature, and through relationships, we learn about ourselves and the world around us. *Krishna* encourages *Arjuna* to see the divinity in all beings, teaching that every relationship is an opportunity to reflect on our own soul.

The Upanishads highlight the importance of relationships in the journey of self-discovery. By connecting with others, we recognise the interconnectedness of all beings and deepen our understanding of our true self. In *Yoga*, relationships are seen as mirrors that reflect the ego and help us transcend our attachments, leading to greater spiritual growth. Relationships challenge us to confront our shadows and embrace the divine nature within ourselves and others.

STANZA-WISE INTERPRETATION

- **Stanza 1:** The poem introduces relationships as mirrors that reflect our inner truth. They show us both our strengths and weaknesses, helping us understand who we truly are.
- **Stanza 2:** Relationships are depicted as guiding us on our journey. They provide lessons that help us see parts of ourselves we may otherwise ignore or hide.

- **Stanza 3:** The poem emphasises that what we give in relationships is what we receive. It's a reminder that relationships reflect our actions and intentions.
- **Stanza 4:** Relationships are shown as tests of the heart. They challenge us to grow and evolve, offering opportunities to confront our limitations and transcend them.
- **Stanza 5:** The poem explains that relationships reveal aspects of ourselves we may not want to face. Through them, we learn to confront our shadows and embrace our true self.
- **Stanza 6:** Relationships are described as forces that help us grow and renew ourselves. They reflect the divine truth within us, guiding us toward spiritual awakening.
- **Stanza 7:** The final stanza affirms that relationships help us understand the deeper connection between love and growth. They challenge and transform us, allowing us to evolve and experience greater peace.

PHILOSOPHICAL INSIGHTS

This topic explores relationships as mirrors that reflect our true selves. In Indian philosophy, relationships are seen as sacred opportunities for growth, self-discovery, and spiritual realisation. The Bhagavad Gita teaches that our interactions with others reveal the divinity within, and by reflecting on these connections, we gain insight into our own soul. The poem illustrates that relationships provide the space for self-reflection, healing, and transformation, allowing us to confront our limitations and embrace the divine truth within.

PRACTICAL GUIDANCE

How do your relationships reflect your inner truth? What do you learn from the people around you?

Start by reflecting on the relationships in your life. What do they teach you about yourself? Practice mindfulness to observe your reactions in different interactions. Use meditation to connect with the deeper meaning of your relationships and how they reflect your spiritual growth. Use affirmations like "I learn and grow through my relationships," "I see the divine in others," and "I embrace the lessons that relationships bring." By recognizing the lessons and reflections in your relationships, you can transform them into powerful tools for personal growth.

57

The Ripple of Shared Intentions

Intentions are the seeds we sow,
They grow in ways we may not know.
When shared, their power multiplies,
And touches the world beneath the skies.

A shared intention is a force so strong,
It propels us forward, where we belong.
Together we create, together we rise,
Guided by the stars in the endless skies.

Shared intentions unite the hearts,
They bind us together, no matter how far apart.
In the unity of purpose, we find our strength,
And together we go to any length.

The ripple of shared intentions is vast,
It echoes forward, it spans the past.
It's the power of unity, the strength of will,
The energy to create, the force to fulfil.

In shared intention, we find our way,
We create the world anew each day.
With every thought, with every act,
We form the future, we make the pact.

The ripple of intention flows in time,
It carries our energy, sublime.
It connects us all in a common thread,
Guiding us forward, where we're led.

The ripple of shared intentions is the key,
To shaping the future, to setting us free.
Together we rise, together we move,
In the power of shared intentions, we prove.

INTERPRETATION

The ripple of shared intentions demonstrates the collective power of aligned thoughts and actions

In Indian philosophy, the concept of intention (*sankalpa*) is central to creating change, both individually and collectively. The Bhagavad Gita teaches that the mind's focused intention directs energy toward a specific goal, and when individuals unite in purpose, their collective intentions become a powerful force for change. *Krishna* encourages *Arjuna* to act with a pure heart and unwavering intention, knowing that the collective will can shape the future.

The Upanishads describe the interconnectedness of all beings, and the idea that every action, thought, and intention is woven into the fabric of the universe. *Yoga* teaches that when we align our personal intentions with the greater divine will, we manifest collective goals and create harmony in the world. The ripple effect of shared intentions shows how unity of purpose can influence not just individuals but the world around them, creating a harmonious flow of energy.

STANZA-WISE INTERPRETATION

- **Stanza 1:** The poem introduces intentions as seeds that, when planted, grow into powerful forces. When shared by many, they multiply, creating a ripple effect.
- **Stanza 2:** Shared intentions are shown as a collective force that unites people. They propel us forward, guiding us toward our collective goals and purpose.

- **Stanza 3:** The poem emphasises that shared intentions bring people together, creating strength and unity. When people unite in purpose, they can overcome any obstacle.
- **Stanza 4:** Shared intentions create a ripple effect that spans time. The poem highlights that collective energy can shape the future and transform the world.
- **Stanza 5:** The poem underscores that shared intentions are the key to manifesting our collective goals. With each thought and action, we shape the future together.
- **Stanza 6:** Shared intentions are portrayed as a force that flows through time, connecting all beings in a common purpose. They guide us toward unity and harmony.
- **Stanza 7:** The final stanza affirms that the ripple of shared intentions is the key to shaping the future. By uniting in purpose, we create a world of peace and possibility.

PHILOSOPHICAL INSIGHTS

This topic explores the ripple of shared intentions as the collective power of aligned thoughts and actions. In Indian spirituality, *sankalpa* (intention) is a powerful force that shapes reality. The Bhagavad Gita teaches that when individuals act with pure intention, their collective energy can create lasting change. The poem illustrates that when we unite in purpose, we can shape the future and create a world of harmony, peace, and shared wisdom.

PRACTICAL GUIDANCE

What intentions are you setting in your life? Are you willing to align your purpose with those around you?

Start by reflecting on the intentions you have for your life. Are they aligned with your higher purpose and the collective good? Practice meditation and mindfulness to align your intentions with your soul's mission. Use affirmations like "I set powerful and positive intentions," "My intentions are aligned with the divine will," and "Together, we create a harmonious world." By aligning your intentions with others, you contribute to the greater collective energy and manifest positive change.

58

The Compassion of a Global Heart

Compassion is the heart's true call,
It transcends borders, unites us all.
It speaks in silence, it moves the soul,
Filling us with love, making us whole.

Through compassion, we learn to care,
For all beings, everywhere.
It's the strength to stand, the will to help,
To ease the pain, to heal the yelp.

Compassion is the bond that ties,
It breaks through walls, it heals the ties.
It flows beyond race and creed,
To meet the world's most basic need.

In the heart of compassion, we find peace,
A power that makes all struggles cease.
It is the strength to rise above,
And offer others, a life of love.

Compassion gives us the eyes to see,
The pain of others, the misery.
It's the ability to feel the cries,
And answer with kindness, without disguise.

Through compassion, we connect the world,
A force of love, unfurled.
It is the light in the darkest night,
Guiding us toward what is right.

The compassion of a global heart is the key,
To healing the world, to setting us free.
Through love and kindness, we find our way,
And create a world where we all can stay.

INTERPRETATION

Compassion is the force that binds us all, transcending borders and divisions

In Indian philosophy, compassion (*karuṇā*) is seen as one of the highest virtues, essential for spiritual growth and social harmony. The Bhagavad Gita teaches that compassion is a manifestation of divine love, and *Krishna* encourages *Arjuna* to act with kindness and empathy toward all beings, regardless of their background. *Krishna's* teachings show that true strength comes not from power but from compassion, which binds us together and heals the world.

In *Yoga*, compassion is cultivated through practices like *ahimsa* (non-violence), which teaches us to act with kindness and respect for all life. The Upanishads emphasise the interconnectedness of all beings, and compassion is the natural result of recognizing the oneness of existence. By embracing compassion, we can heal not only ourselves but also the world around us, creating a harmonious, peaceful society.

STANZA-WISE INTERPRETATION

- **Stanza 1:** The poem introduces compassion as a universal force that transcends borders and unites all beings. It is the essence of the heart, making us whole and connected.
- **Stanza 2:** Compassion is portrayed as the strength that drives us to care for others. It is the will to help alleviate suffering and provide comfort to those in need.

- **Stanza 3:** The poem emphasises that compassion is not limited by race, religion, or creed. It is a universal bond that addresses the world's most basic needs.
- **Stanza 4:** Compassion is shown as a healing force that brings peace to the world. It is the ability to rise above challenges and offer love and support to others.
- **Stanza 5:** The poem highlights that compassion enables us to empathize with others' suffering. It teaches us to respond to pain with kindness and understanding.
- **Stanza 6:** Compassion is presented as the light that connects us to others. It is the force that guides us toward kindness and righteousness, no matter the circumstances.
- **Stanza 7:** The final stanza affirms that compassion is the key to healing the world. By embracing love and kindness, we create a world where all beings can live in peace and harmony.

PHILOSOPHICAL INSIGHTS

This topic explores compassion as a universal force that binds all beings together. In Indian Spirituality, compassion (*karuṇā*) is one of the highest virtues, reflecting divine love and empathy. The Bhagavad Gita teaches that true strength lies in acting with compassion, and the Upanishads highlight the interconnectedness of all beings. The poem illustrates that compassion is not limited by divisions but is the healing force that connects and unites us all, creating a world of peace and harmony.

PRACTICAL GUIDANCE

How often do you practice compassion in your daily life? Are you open to feeling the pain of others and responding with love?

Start by reflecting on how you can cultivate compassion in your life. Practice *ahimsa* (non-violence) by choosing kindness and empathy in all your interactions. Use meditation to connect with the suffering of others and respond with love and kindness. Use affirmations like “I am a compassionate being,” “I connect with the world through love,” and “My compassion heals myself and others.” By embracing compassion, you will create a ripple effect of kindness and contribute to healing the world.

59

The Timeless Bonds of Ancestry

The bonds of ancestry are deep and wide,
They flow through time, they do not hide.
In the blood, in the soul, they reside,
A legacy that we cannot deny.

Through the ancestors, we find our roots,
Their wisdom flows, their spirit shoots.
They guide us in moments of need,
Their stories are the seeds we heed.

The bonds of ancestry give us strength,
They teach us lessons at great length.
In their memory, we find our guide,
A legacy that will never slide.

Through our ancestors, we know our place,
In the cycle of time, in the human race.
They live within us, their wisdom true,
The bonds of ancestry help us through.

In the hearts of our forebears, we find peace,
Their strength and wisdom never cease.
Through their guidance, we find our way,
A light that shines in the darkest day.

The bonds of ancestry are the key,
To understanding who we're meant to be.
They give us purpose, they give us grace,
And help us find our sacred space.

Through the bonds of ancestry, we rise,
Connected to the past, to the skies.
We honour those who came before,
And carry their wisdom forevermore.

INTERPRETATION

The bonds of ancestry connect us to the wisdom and strength of those who came before us

In Indian philosophy, ancestry (*pitr-rishi*) is highly revered, as the knowledge and wisdom passed down through generations are considered sacred. The Bhagavad Gita teaches that we are deeply connected to our ancestors, who guide us in fulfilling our duties and *dharma*. *Krishna* reminds us of the importance of honouring our ancestors and following the path they have set for us.

The Upanishads highlight the connection between the individual self (*atman*) and the collective consciousness, which includes the wisdom of those who came before us. *Yoga* teaches us that by honouring our ancestry, we align ourselves with the universal flow of energy and wisdom, creating a deeper connection with the divine. The bonds of ancestry are not only a source of strength but also a reminder of the continuity of life and wisdom.

STANZA-WISE INTERPRETATION

- **Stanza 1:** The poem introduces the bonds of ancestry as a deep and eternal connection that flows through time. It highlights the significance of the wisdom passed down through generations.
- **Stanza 2:** Ancestry is presented as a source of guidance and strength. The teachings of our ancestors continue to shape us, providing wisdom for every challenge we face.

- **Stanza 3:** The bonds of ancestry are shown as a foundation that strengthens us. The memory and teachings of our forebears provide clarity and direction in life.
- **Stanza 4:** Ancestry is described as the connection that helps us understand our place in the world. It shows us that we are part of a greater cycle of life and wisdom.
- **Stanza 5:** The poem highlights that the wisdom of ancestors continues to guide us. It is a source of peace and strength, helping us navigate life's challenges.
- **Stanza 6:** The bonds of ancestry provide us with purpose and grace. They remind us of our sacred role in the ongoing journey of life and wisdom.
- **Stanza 7:** The final stanza emphasises that by honouring our ancestors, we rise and carry their wisdom forward. We are connected to the past and the future, creating a continuous legacy of strength and understanding.

PHILOSOPHICAL INSIGHTS

This topic explores the timeless bonds of ancestry that connect us to the wisdom and strength of our forebears. In Indian spirituality, the wisdom of ancestors is deeply honoured, as it is seen as a source of guidance and support. The Bhagavad Gita teaches that we are connected to our ancestors through our *dharma* (duty), and the Upanishads speak of the continuity of wisdom across generations. The poem illustrates that by honouring these bonds, we align ourselves with a greater source of wisdom, strength, and purpose.

PRACTICAL GUIDANCE

How often do you reflect on your ancestral roots? Are you aware of the wisdom passed down through generations?

Start by reflecting on your ancestry and the wisdom that has been passed down through your family. Take time to connect with the teachings of your forebears, whether through family stories, cultural traditions, or personal reflection. Practice meditation to honour the guidance and strength of your ancestors. Use affirmations like "I honour my ancestors and their wisdom," "I am connected to the legacy of my family," and "I carry forward the wisdom of the past." By embracing your ancestral bonds, you will find strength, purpose, and guidance in your life.

60

The Oneness of All

We are one in the cosmic sea,
Connected in love, bound to be.
No separation, no distance apart,
In the oneness, we find our heart.

The universe pulses with a single beat,
Every soul, every heart, every street.
In oneness, we find the divine light,
That guides us through the darkest night.

The oneness of all is the truth we seek,
In every soul, we are unique.
Yet, in our hearts, we share one flame,
A light that cannot be put to shame.

In the oneness, we feel no fear,
For all that exists is near.
The divine is in everything, seen and unseen,
In the eternal dance, we are serene.

To see the oneness is to see with love,
A vision that soars, like a dove.
It's the wisdom to know we are all the same,
In the oneness, we rise, we claim.

In the oneness, there is no you or I,
Only the divine, the endless sky.
All are one, and one is all,
The unity that answers life's call.

The oneness of all is the truth we embrace,
It's the path to peace, the sacred grace.
In unity, we rise, we stand,
Bound by the oneness, hand in hand.

INTERPRETATION

The oneness of all is the fundamental truth of existence, highlighting the interconnectedness of all beings

In Indian philosophy, the concept of oneness (*Advitaya*) is central to understanding the nature of reality. The Bhagavad Gita teaches that the individual soul (*atman*) is ultimately united with the universal consciousness (*Brahman*), and through this unity, we transcend the ego and realize our true nature. *Krishna* reminds *Arjuna* that the divine is present in all beings, and true spiritual growth comes from recognizing the oneness of all.

The Upanishads emphasise that everything in the universe, from the smallest particle to the grand cosmos, is part of a single, unified whole. *Yoga* encourages practitioners to meditate on the unity of all life, recognizing that the self and the universe are one. When we realize the oneness of all, we move beyond separation and connect with the divine presence within and around us, leading to peace and spiritual awakening.

STANZA-WISE INTERPRETATION

- **Stanza 1:** The poem introduces the idea of oneness as the underlying truth of the universe. We are all connected, and through this connection, we find the essence of our being.
- **Stanza 2:** The oneness is described as a universal pulse that flows through everything. Every being and every heart is part of this greater unity.

- **Stanza 3:** The poem emphasises that in oneness, we recognise the divine light that unites us all. There is no division; we share the same essence and truth.
- **Stanza 4:** Oneness eliminates fear, as it reveals that everything is interconnected. The divine is present in all things, both seen and unseen.
- **Stanza 5:** The poem shows that to see oneness is to see the world through love. When we embrace oneness, we recognise the unity that binds us all, regardless of outward differences.
- **Stanza 6:** Oneness is presented as the realisation that there is no separation between us. We are all part of the same divine essence, and this unity is the foundation of existence.
- **Stanza 7:** The final stanza affirms that oneness is the path to peace and spiritual growth. By embracing unity, we rise together and live in harmony with the divine.

PHILOSOPHICAL INSIGHTS

This topic explores the oneness of all as the fundamental truth that connects all beings in the universe. In Indian philosophy, *Advitaya* (non-duality) teaches that there is no separation between the individual and the divine; all things are interconnected. The Bhagavad Gita and the Upanishads emphasise the unity of all life, urging us to recognise the divine presence within ourselves and others. The poem illustrates that when we embrace oneness, we transcend the ego and experience the peace, love, and spiritual growth that come from recognizing the unity of all beings.

PRACTICAL GUIDANCE

How often do you recognise the oneness of all? Are you able to see the divine in everything around you?

Start by practising mindfulness to observe the unity in all things. Reflect on how your actions and thoughts are connected to the greater whole. Practice meditation to quiet the mind and connect with the universal consciousness. Use affirmations like "I am one with the universe," "I see the divine in all," and "Oneness brings me peace." Through recognizing the oneness of all, you will experience greater unity, love, and spiritual awakening.

61

The Sacred Circle of Life

Life is a circle, ever spinning,
From birth to death, it keeps winning.
In every turn, we find our place,
A journey of joy, a path of grace.

Through life's circle, we see the truth,
The dance of time, the call of youth.
From the beginning, we are connected,
Through every cycle, we are directed.

In the circle, there is no end,
Only a beginning that we transcend.
The wheel of life turns ever true,
In every moment, something new.

The sacred circle holds us near,
It guides us through every fear.
In its flow, we find our way,
Through the night and into the day.

The circle is endless, ever vast,
It carries us forward, to the past.
Every cycle is a chance to grow,
To learn, to evolve, to let go.

In the circle, there is a plan,
A divine order, a cosmic span.
Through every turn, we understand,
That life is a journey, and we are the land.

The sacred circle is the key,
To understanding life's mystery.
It is the force that moves us along,
To the rhythm of the universe, where we belong.

INTERPRETATION

The sacred circle of life represents the eternal flow of existence, where every cycle brings new growth, understanding, and transformation

In Indian philosophy, life is seen as cyclical, with birth, death, and rebirth forming a continuous loop. The Bhagavad Gita teaches that life is not linear but cyclical, with every action having a cause and effect. The cycle of life is a part of the greater cosmic order, where every being has its role to play. *Krishna* reminds *Arjuna* that by embracing life's cycles, we align ourselves with the divine flow.

The Upanishads describe life as an eternal journey, where the self (*atman*) evolves through countless cycles of birth and rebirth, learning and growing along the way. *Yoga* teaches that by accepting the cyclical nature of existence, we can transcend suffering and achieve spiritual liberation. The sacred circle is a symbol of life's infinite potential and the interconnectedness of all things.

STANZA-WISE INTERPRETATION

- **Stanza 1:** The poem introduces the sacred circle of life as a constant flow. It represents the journey from birth to death, filled with grace and purpose.
- **Stanza 2:** Life's circle is presented as a continuous dance of time. It reminds us that we are all connected through the cycles of existence.

- **Stanza 3:** The poem emphasises that in the circle of life, there is no end, only a beginning. Every cycle is an opportunity for renewal and growth.
- **Stanza 4:** The sacred circle is portrayed as a guiding force that helps us navigate life's challenges. It leads us through fear and uncertainty toward clarity and peace.
- **Stanza 5:** The circle of life is endless and vast, carrying us forward while connecting us to the past. Each cycle offers opportunities to grow and learn.
- **Stanza 6:** The poem highlights that the circle of life operates in divine order, with every turn revealing deeper wisdom and understanding.
- **Stanza 7:** The final stanza reinforces that the sacred circle is the key to understanding life's mystery. It guides us in harmony with the rhythm of the universe.

PHILOSOPHICAL INSIGHTS

This topic explores the sacred circle of life, which represents the eternal cycles of existence. In Indian spirituality, life is seen as a continuous journey of growth and transformation. The Bhagavad Gita teaches that every action and event is part of the greater cosmic order. The poem illustrates that the circle of life is a force that guides us through the cycles of time, offering opportunities for growth, healing, and spiritual evolution.

PRACTICAL GUIDANCE

How do you embrace the cyclical nature of life? Are you open to the lessons that come with each cycle?

Start by reflecting on the cycles of your life. What lessons have you learned from each cycle, and how have they shaped you? Practice mindfulness to observe the patterns in your life and how they reflect the greater cosmic flow. Use affirmations like "I embrace the sacred circle of life," "Every cycle brings me closer to understanding," and "I am part of the eternal flow of existence." By embracing the circle of life, you will align yourself with the rhythm of the universe and experience greater peace and growth.

CHAPTER 6

Preparation for Higher Connection

62

Yoga: Union of Body, Mind, and Soul

Yoga is the path to the soul's delight,
Uniting the body with the spirit's light.
In each movement, a prayer is said,
In every breath, the soul is fed.

Yoga binds us in sacred grace,
A union of mind, body, and space.
Through posture and breath, we align,
The body becomes the sacred shrine.

Yoga is the dance of the soul's intent,
A path to peace, a way to transcend.
It connects us to the divine within,
And frees the heart from every sin.

In every asana, we find the flow,
The rhythm of life, the way to grow.
Through *yoga*, we awaken the truth,
The divine wisdom that is eternal and smooth.

Yoga teaches us to be still,
To quiet the mind, to trust the will.
In stillness, the soul can speak,
And in silence, it is pure and unique.

Yoga is the union of the self with all,
It answers the soul's deepest call.
Through body, mind, and spirit combined,
We rise and open our hearts and mind.

In *yoga*, we are one with the divine,
A path that leads us to the sublime.
It's the sacred journey, the path to peace,
Where body, mind, and soul find release.

INTERPRETATION

Yoga *is the union of the body, mind, and soul, the path that leads to spiritual growth and self-realization*

In Indian philosophy, *yoga* (*yuj*) is a spiritual practice that integrates the physical, mental, and spiritual aspects of life. The Bhagavad Gita teaches that *yoga* is not just a physical practice but a way to unite the self with the divine. *Krishna* instructs *Arjuna* to perform his duties with devotion, showing that *yoga* is about aligning one's actions with a higher purpose. *Yoga* is a path of inner union and spiritual awakening, where the body becomes the temple and the mind aligns with the soul.

The Upanishads describe *yoga* as a practice of connecting with the divine through self-discipline, meditation, and *pranayama* (breathing exercises). *Yoga* leads us to the realisation that the individual self (*atman*) is not separate from the universal self (*Brahman*). It teaches us to go beyond the ego, creating unity between our inner and outer worlds. *Yoga* purifies the body and mind, allowing us to experience oneness with the universe.

STANZA-WISE INTERPRETATION

- **Stanza 1:** The poem introduces *yoga* as a path that unites the body with the spirit. Every movement and breath in *yoga* is a form of prayer, connecting us to the divine.
- **Stanza 2:** *Yoga* is described as a sacred union, aligning the body, mind, and space. Through practice, we transform the body into a vessel for the spirit.

- **Stanza 3:** The poem emphasises that *yoga* is a spiritual practice that transcends physical exercise. It connects us to our inner divinity, helping us overcome limitations.
- **Stanza 4:** *Yoga* is shown as a way to grow and awaken the truth within. Through each posture and breath, we align with the divine wisdom that resides in all of us.
- **Stanza 5:** *Yoga* teaches the importance of stillness, which allows the mind to quiet and the soul to express its true nature. In silence, we can hear the voice of the divine.
- **Stanza 6:** The poem emphasises that *yoga* is the union of the self with the divine. It answers the call of the soul and helps us open our hearts and minds.
- **Stanza 7:** The final stanza affirms that *yoga* is the sacred journey to peace. Through union of body, mind, and spirit, we find spiritual release and harmony with the divine.

PHILOSOPHICAL INSIGHTS

This topic highlights *yoga* as the union of body, mind, and soul, a path to spiritual growth and self-realisation. In Indian spirituality, *yoga* is seen as the practice of aligning oneself with the divine. The Bhagavad Gita and Upanishads teach that *yoga* helps us transcend the ego and experience unity with the universe. The poem illustrates that through *yoga*, we awaken our true selves, creating harmony between our inner and outer worlds, and finding peace in the process.

PRACTICAL GUIDANCE

How can you incorporate yoga into your daily life? Are you open to experiencing the unity of body, mind, and soul?

Start by practising *yoga* daily, even if for a few minutes. Focus on your breath and the movements of your body, allowing each *asana* (pose) to connect you with your inner self. Use meditation to still the mind and connect with your divine nature. Use affirmations like "I am one with my body, mind, and soul," "I find peace through *yoga*," and "*Yoga* brings me closer to my true self." Through regular practice, you will experience the transformative power of *yoga*, leading to inner harmony and spiritual growth.

63

Pranayama: The Breath of Life

Breath is life, the essence we hold,
In every inhale, a story is told.
Through the breath, we connect to all,
The breath of life, the sacred call.

Pranayama is the art to breathe,
To balance the energy, to achieve.
It calms the mind and frees the heart,
A practice that plays a vital part.

Through breath, we find the flow,
The energy that helps us grow.
In each breath, we awaken the soul,
The power within, making us whole.

Pranayama is the breath of peace,
It calms the storm, it grants release.
In each exhale, we let go,
Of tension and worry, all that we know.

The breath is the link to the divine,
It carries us through the unseen line.
Through pranayama, we transcend,
And find the stillness that never ends.

In each breath, we find the key,
To unlocking the divine energy.
Through pranayama, we rise above,
And connect to the source of love.

Pranayama is the breath of life,
It brings us peace, it ends the strife.
In each breath, we align with the flow,
The divine energy, helping us grow.

INTERPRETATION

Pranayama *is the control of breath, the key to harmonizing body, mind, and spirit*

In Indian philosophy, *pranayama* is the practice of controlling the breath to influence the flow of *prana* (life force energy) in the body. The Bhagavad Gita teaches that breath control helps us focus the mind and steady our emotions. *Krishna* encourages *Arjuna* to remain calm and centered, using breath as a tool to stay connected to the divine.

The Upanishads describe breath as the vital force that sustains life. By mastering *pranayama*, we align with the cosmic energy that flows through all beings. In *Yoga*, *pranayama* is seen as a practice that cleanses the body and mind, releasing blockages and allowing the free flow of energy. Through proper breath control, we open ourselves to higher states of consciousness, deepening our connection to the divine.

STANZA-WISE INTERPRETATION

- **Stanza 1:** The poem introduces breath as the essence of life, emphasising that each breath connects us to the universe and to the divine.
- **Stanza 2:** *Pranayama* is described as the practice of breathing with purpose. It is through this practice that we balance our energy and calm the mind.
- **Stanza 3:** *Pranayama* is shown as a practice that helps us align with the flow of energy. Each breath awakens the soul and brings us closer to our true self.

- **Stanza 4:** *Pranayama* is depicted as a peaceful practice that releases tension and clears the mind. With each breath, we let go of worries and stress.
- **Stanza 5:** The breath is shown as the connection to the divine. *Pranayama* allows us to transcend the mundane and connect with the higher consciousness.
- **Stanza 6:** The poem emphasises that *pranayama* unlocks divine energy, allowing us to rise above the ego and align with love and peace.
- **Stanza 7:** The final stanza affirms that *pranayama* is the breath of life, aligning us with the divine flow of energy. It is through breath that we experience growth and spiritual awakening.

PHILOSOPHICAL INSIGHTS

This topic highlights *pranayama* as the key to controlling the breath and harmonizing body, mind, and spirit. In Indian spirituality, *pranayama* is a practice that connects us to the vital energy of the universe. The Bhagavad Gita teaches that controlling the breath helps steady the mind and body, allowing us to focus on the divine. The Upanishads describe breath as the essence of life, and through *pranayama*, we open ourselves to higher states of consciousness and spiritual growth. The poem illustrates that *pranayama* is the practice that leads to peace, balance, and connection with the divine.

PRACTICAL GUIDANCE

How often do you focus on your breath to calm your mind? Are you aware of the power of breath in your spiritual practice?

Start by practising *pranayama* daily, focusing on your breath to center yourself and calm the mind. Try different breathing techniques such as deep breathing, alternate nostril breathing, and belly breathing. Use meditation to deepen your breath awareness and connect with your inner self. Use affirmations like "I breathe with purpose and peace," "My breath connects me to the divine," and "Through pranayama, I align with my higher self." By practising *pranayama*, you will experience greater peace, balance, and spiritual growth.

64

The Art of Meditation

Meditation is the silence we seek,
A place where the mind is calm and meek.
In stillness, the soul finds its way,
A peaceful refuge where thoughts decay.

Through meditation, we dive within,
To find the truth that lies therein.
It is the doorway to the soul's grace,
A sacred space, a divine place.

In meditation, we shed the veil,
We rise above the worldly trail.
With every breath, we feel the light,
Guiding us through the darkest night.

Meditation is the key to peace,
It brings the mind's restless wars to cease.
In its embrace, we find our way,
To serenity, every day.

Through meditation, we rise above,
We connect with the source of love.
It is the force that guides us true,
The path to all that we pursue.

In meditation, the heart is still,
It listens to the divine will.
Through silence, the soul is freed,
And to the divine, it takes the lead.

The art of meditation is the way,
To find peace in the night and day.
Through quiet mind and open heart,
We find the truth, the divine art.

INTERPRETATION

Meditation is the practice of quieting the mind to connect with the divine

In Indian philosophy, meditation (*dhyana*) is a profound spiritual practice that allows us to quiet the fluctuations of the mind and attune ourselves to the higher self. The Bhagavad Gita speaks of meditation as the path to self-realisation, where the individual mind becomes one with the divine. *Krishna* instructs *Arjuna* to practice steady meditation, free from distraction, in order to achieve inner peace and spiritual growth.

The Upanishads describe meditation as the path to discovering our true self (*atman*) and its oneness with the divine (*Brahman*). Through *yoga* and meditation, we align our body, mind, and spirit with the universal consciousness, transcending the ego and experiencing divine peace. Meditation is a key practice for those on the spiritual path, helping us uncover the stillness within and connect with our true nature.

STANZA-WISE INTERPRETATION

- **Stanza 1:** The poem introduces meditation as a practice that brings us into silence. In this silence, the mind finds peace, and the soul connects to its deeper truth.
- **Stanza 2:** Meditation is described as the practice of diving within, where we discover the divine grace that lies within our hearts. It is the sacred space where we find true peace.

- **Stanza 3:** The poem emphasises that through **meditation**, we transcend the distractions of the material world and rise to a higher state of awareness. It is through stillness that we receive guidance.
- **Stanza 4:** Meditation is shown as the key to inner peace. It quiets the mind's restlessness and allows us to experience serenity, free from external disturbances.
- **Stanza 5:** Meditation helps us connect with the divine source of love. It aligns our thoughts and actions with our higher purpose, helping us achieve spiritual fulfilment.
- **Stanza 6:** The poem emphasises that in meditation, the heart becomes still and listens to the divine will. It is through this silence that we find direction and clarity in our spiritual journey.
- **Stanza 7:** The final stanza reinforces that meditation is the path to peace and self-realisation. Through quieting the mind and opening the heart, we discover the truth of our being and connect with the divine.

PHILOSOPHICAL INSIGHTS

This topic explores meditation as the practice of quieting the mind and connecting with the divine. In Indian spirituality, meditation (*dhyana*) is the key to self-realisation and the union of the individual soul (*atman*) with the universal consciousness (*Brahman*). The Bhagavad Gita and the Upanishads teach that through meditation, we transcend the ego and experience inner peace. The poem illustrates that meditation helps us uncover the stillness within and align with our true nature, leading to spiritual growth and fulfilment.

PRACTICAL GUIDANCE

How often do you practice meditation to quiet your mind and connect with your higher self? Are you open to experiencing the stillness that lies within?

Start by setting aside time each day for meditation. Begin with deep breathing exercises to calm your mind, and then focus on your breath or a mantra to quiet the inner chatter. Use affirmations like "I am at peace within," "I connect with my higher self through meditation," and "Meditation leads me to clarity and divine guidance." Through regular practice, you will experience the transformative power of meditation, leading to inner peace and spiritual growth.

65

The Chakras: Portals to Energy Flow

The chakras are the wheels that spin,
The portals where energy flows within.
Each one a center of life's force,
Guiding us through the spiritual course.

In the base, the earth's grounding might,
In the heart, love shines bright.
In the throat, the voice speaks true,
In the mind, wisdom shines through.

Each chakra opens the path to grace,
Transforming energy in its space.
From root to crown, they guide us on,
With each cycle, a new dawn.

The chakras are the keys we hold,
To unlock the truth, the wisdom bold.
They are the bridges to the divine,
A sacred journey, yours and mine.

Through the chakras, we align,
With the energy of the divine.
Each center opens a door,
To greater peace, to love, to more.

In the flow of energy, we are healed,
The chakras unlock, the wounds are sealed.
Through balanced energy, we rise,
To see the world with clear eyes.

The chakras are the sacred flow,
Guiding us where we need to go.
In their energy, we find our way,
To the divine, every day.

INTERPRETATION

The chakras are energy centers in the body that connect us to the spiritual realm

In Indian philosophy, the chakras (*chakra*) are described as spinning wheels of energy that govern various aspects of our physical, emotional, and spiritual lives. The Upanishads describe the human body as having seven main energy centers that align with the divine. Each chakra corresponds to a different level of consciousness, from the base of the spine to the crown of the head. *Yoga* and meditation practices aim to balance and activate these *chakras* to facilitate the free flow of energy, aligning the individual with the universal consciousness.

The Bhagavad Gita teaches that when energy flows freely through the body and mind, we experience harmony and spiritual awakening. By aligning the *chakras*, we achieve a state of balance and connection with the divine. The *chakras* serve as portals through which we can access higher states of consciousness and realize our true potential.

STANZA-WISE INTERPRETATION

- **Stanza 1:** The *chakras* are introduced as spinning wheels of energy. They are the centers through which life force energy flows, guiding us toward spiritual growth.
- **Stanza 2:** The poem describes each chakra and its corresponding energy. From the root chakra that connects us to the earth to the crown chakra that links

us to the divine, each chakra plays a vital role in our journey.

- **Stanza 3:** The *chakras* are shown as transformative energy centers that guide us through the spiritual path. As energy flows through each center, we experience growth and awakening.
- **Stanza 4:** The *chakras* are presented as keys that unlock the divine wisdom and truth within. They are the bridges to spiritual connection and awakening.
- **Stanza 5:** The *chakras* are depicted as pathways to divine energy. As we balance and align them, we experience deeper peace and connection with the divine.
- **Stanza 6:** The poem emphasises that the *chakras* heal us by allowing energy to flow freely. When balanced, the *chakras* help us see clearly and live harmoniously.
- **Stanza 7:** The final stanza affirms that the *chakras* are the sacred flow of energy that guides us toward the divine. By aligning the *chakras*, we move toward spiritual fulfilment every day.

PHILOSOPHICAL INSIGHTS

This topic explores the *chakras* as energy centers in the body that connect us to the divine. In Indian spirituality, the chakras *chakras* govern different aspects of our consciousness and well-being. The Upanishads and Bhagavad Gita teach that by aligning and balancing the *chakras*, we align ourselves with the cosmic flow of energy, leading to spiritual awakening and peace. The poem illustrates that the *chakras* are pathways to greater love, wisdom, and connection with the divine, guiding us toward spiritual growth.

PRACTICAL GUIDANCE

How aware are you of the energy centers in your body? Do you feel the flow of energy through the chakras?

Start by practising meditation and focusing on each of your *chakras*, starting from the root and moving up to the crown. Use affirmations like "I am grounded and connected to the earth," "My heart is open to love," and "I am in harmony with my energy." You can also practice *yoga* to activate and balance the *chakras*, allowing energy to flow freely through your body. By balancing your *chakras*, you will experience greater peace, clarity, and spiritual alignment.

66

Awakening the Third Eye

The third eye sees beyond the veil,
A vision that will never fail.
It opens the doors of the unseen,
And shows the truth, pure and serene.

Through the third eye, the world transforms,
The mundane becomes sacred, warm.
It reveals the paths we must take,
And helps us awaken, for our sake.

The third eye is the inner light,
It guides us through the darkest night.
In its gaze, the truth is clear,
And the divine presence is near.

Awakening the third eye is the way,
To see the world in a brand-new way.
It brings the wisdom of the soul,
And makes the fragmented self whole.

Through the third eye, we transcend,
The illusions that the mind defends.
We see beyond form and face,
And connect with the divine embrace.

The third eye is the key to see,
The infinite possibilities.
It awakens the power within,
And guides us toward the state of bliss.

Awakening the third eye is the light,
That leads us to the truth, burning bright.
Through this vision, we see the divine,
And realize that all is truly mine.

INTERPRETATION

The awakening of the third eye allows us to see beyond the physical and connect with higher consciousness

In Indian philosophy, the third eye (*ajña chakra*) is the center of intuition and spiritual perception. It is often depicted as the sixth chakra, located in the center of the forehead, between the eyebrows. *Yoga* teaches that awakening the third eye allows us to transcend the limitations of the physical senses and access higher realms of perception. The Bhagavad Gita speaks of *Krishna* guiding *Arjuna* to see the truth beyond the apparent world, and this vision can be accessed through the opening of the third eye.

The Upanishads describe the third eye as the key to inner wisdom. Through meditation and spiritual practice, we learn to awaken this eye and perceive the subtle energy that exists beyond the material world. When the third eye is opened, we connect with higher consciousness and experience a deep understanding of our true self and the universe.

STANZA-WISE INTERPRETATION

- **Stanza 1:** The poem introduces the third eye as a gateway to higher perception. It shows that the third eye enables us to see beyond the physical world and grasp deeper truths.

- **Stanza 2:** Awakening the third eye transforms how we see the world. The mundane becomes sacred, and we begin to recognise the divine presence in everything.
- **Stanza 3:** The third eye is presented as a source of inner guidance. Through its perception, we find clarity and understanding, and we are guided by the divine truth.
- **Stanza 4:** Awakening the third eye is the path to seeing the world in a new light. It helps us reconnect with the wisdom of the soul and become whole again.
- **Stanza 5:** The poem emphasises that the third eye helps us transcend illusion. By seeing through the lens of higher consciousness, we perceive the world as it truly is.
- **Stanza 6:** The third eye is shown as a source of infinite potential. When awakened, it allows us to tap into the vast spiritual power that lies within us.
- **Stanza 7:** The final stanza reinforces that the third eye is the key to spiritual awakening. Through its vision, we connect with the divine and understand our true nature.

PHILOSOPHICAL INSIGHTS

This topic explores the awakening of the third eye as a way to connect with higher consciousness and transcend the physical world. In Indian spirituality, the third eye (*ajña chakra*) is a center of intuition and spiritual vision. The Bhagavad Gita and the Upanishads describe the importance of awakening the third eye to perceive the truth beyond the material realm. The poem illustrates that the third eye opens our inner vision, helping us connect with the divine, experience the truth, and see beyond illusion.

PRACTICAL GUIDANCE

How often do you seek to connect with the higher truths of life? Are you open to seeing the world through the lens of spiritual perception?

Start by practising meditation focused on the third eye. Sit in a comfortable position and gently focus your attention on the space between your eyebrows. Visualize light and energy flowing into this space, awakening your inner vision. Use affirmations like "I open my third eye to perceive divine truths," "I trust my intuition and inner guidance," and "My third eye connects me with the divine wisdom within." As you practice, be patient, and trust that your awareness will expand over time.

67

Kundalini: The Serpent's Awakening

Kundalini lies in dormant sleep,
A serpent coiled, so still, so deep.
Within each of us, it resides,
Waiting for the time to rise.

Through the spine, it begins to climb,
Awakening the soul in time.
It rises through each chakra's gate,
A force of love, a force of fate.

Kundalini is the cosmic fire,
That burns away all fear and desire.
Through its flame, we are reborn,
And our true selves are truly sworn.

It ascends with power and grace,
Lighting the path we must embrace.
Through its awakening, we are freed,
From attachments, fear, and need.

The serpent rises to the crown,
Where it lights the soul's great crown.
In its awakening, we find the light,
The ultimate truth, burning bright.

Kundalini is the divine spark,
That ignites the soul, leaving no mark.
It awakens the power within,
And leads us to the state of bliss again.

Through the serpent's rise, we are whole,
The energy ascends, and we become whole.
Kundalini's awakening is the key,
To unlocking our true destiny.

INTERPRETATION

Kundalini is the dormant spiritual energy within us, waiting to be awakened to reach higher states of consciousness

In Indian philosophy, Kundalini (*kundalini-shakti*) is the latent divine energy that resides at the base of the spine. The Bhagavad Gita teaches that awakening this energy through *yoga* and spiritual practices leads to enlightenment and self-realisation. *Krishna* encourages *Arjuna* to perform his duties with devotion, and through awakening *kundalini*, we align ourselves with divine purpose.

The Upanishads describe *kundalini* as a serpent that lies coiled at the base of the spine, and through spiritual practices such as meditation, *pranayama* (breathing techniques), and *asanas* (postures), we awaken this energy. As *kundalini* rises through the *chakras*, it clears blockages and elevates our consciousness, leading to spiritual awakening and ultimate liberation.

STANZA-WISE INTERPRETATION

- **Stanza 1:** The poem introduces *kundalini* as dormant energy, symbolized as a coiled serpent. It lies waiting within each of us, ready to awaken when the time is right.
- **Stanza 2:** *Kundalini* is depicted as rising through the spine, passing through each chakra, awakening our energy and leading us to spiritual growth.

- **Stanza 3:** *Kundalini* is portrayed as a transformative fire that burns away fear and desire, helping us to reconnect with our true self.
- **Stanza 4:** The poem shows that *kundalini* rises with power and grace, clearing obstacles and freeing us from attachments, allowing us to embrace our true path.
- **Stanza 5:** *Kundalini* is shown as the energy that ascends to the crown chakra, where it illuminates our consciousness, bringing us closer to the divine truth.
- **Stanza 6:** The *kundalini* energy is described as the divine spark within us. When awakened, it ignites our soul and leads us to spiritual bliss.
- **Stanza 7:** The final stanza emphasises that *kundalini* awakening is the key to unlocking our true potential. It leads us to a higher state of consciousness and helps us realize our divine purpose.

PHILOSOPHICAL INSIGHTS

This topic explores *kundalini* as the dormant spiritual energy within us, waiting to be awakened. In Indian spirituality, *kundalini-shakti* is the force that elevates our consciousness and connects us with the divine. The Bhagavad Gita and the Upanishads emphasise that through spiritual practices, we can awaken this energy and experience enlightenment. The poem illustrates that as *kundalini* rises through the *chakras*, it clears blockages, elevates our consciousness, and leads us to spiritual fulfilment and self-realisation.

PRACTICAL GUIDANCE

How aware are you of your kundalini energy? Are you open to awakening this powerful force within?

Start by practising meditation and breathing exercises to activate your *kundalini* energy. Focus on the base of your spine and visualize the energy rising through each of your *chakras*, clearing blockages along the way. Use affirmations like "I awaken the divine energy within me," "My *kundalini* leads me to spiritual growth," and "I am connected to my true self through the awakening of *kundalini*." Through consistent practice, you will begin to feel the awakening of this energy, guiding you toward higher consciousness and spiritual enlightenment.

68

The Silence of Samadhi

Samadhi is the stillness of the mind,
A sacred space where peace we find.
In its depths, the self dissolves,
And the divine truth evolves.

In the silence of Samadhi, we see,
The boundless ocean, calm and free.
It is the union with the divine,
Where the soul and spirit intertwine.

Through Samadhi, we transcend time,
The soul is free, the heart sublime.
In stillness, the ego fades away,
And the light of truth leads the way.

Samadhi is the path to bliss,
A place of peace, an eternal kiss.
It is the merging of all that's known,
Where the seeker finds the divine throne.

In Samadhi, the heart is still,
It listens to the divine will.
The mind is calm, the soul is clear,
And the eternal truth is near.

The silence of Samadhi is the key,
To understanding the divine mystery.
In this stillness, we find our way,
And live with peace, come what may.

Through Samadhi, we are whole,
United with the divine soul.
In silence, we are truly free,
Connected to all that is meant to be.

INTERPRETATION

Samadhi *is the state of perfect stillness and union with the divine*

In Indian philosophy, *samadhi* is the ultimate state of meditation, where the individual consciousness merges with the universal consciousness. The Bhagavad Gita speaks of the importance of meditation and *samadhi* as a means to transcend the ego and realize the oneness of all existence. *Krishna* teaches *Arjuna* that the practice of meditation leads to liberation, where the mind becomes still, and the divine presence is felt within.

The Upanishads describe *samadhi* as the state of perfect union with the divine, where the individual self (*atman*) merges with the supreme self (*Brahman*). It is through the practice of meditation and discipline that the seeker attains this state of stillness. *Samadhi* is not just a physical or mental state but an experience of spiritual awakening, where one transcends the limits of the ego and connects with the infinite.

STANZA-WISE INTERPRETATION

- **Stanza 1:** The poem introduces *samadhi* as a state of stillness where peace is found. In this stillness, the self dissolves, allowing the divine truth to emerge.
- **Stanza 2:** *Samadhi* is depicted as a state where the seeker experiences the unity with the divine. In this state, the soul connects with the infinite, free from limitations.

- **Stanza 3:** The poem emphasises that through *samadhi*, the soul transcends time and space. The ego fades, and the divine light guides the way.
- **Stanza 4:** *Samadhi* is portrayed as a state of bliss and peace. It is the ultimate merging of the individual with the divine, where the soul experiences eternal union.
- **Stanza 5:** In *samadhi*, the heart and mind are still, listening to the divine will. The soul is clear, and the eternal truth becomes apparent.
- **Stanza 6:** The poem affirms that *samadhi* is the key to understanding the divine mystery. In stillness, we align with the divine presence and find our true path.
- **Stanza 7:** The final stanza reinforces that through *samadhi*, the seeker becomes whole and united with the divine soul. In silence, we are free, and our connection to all is restored.

PHILOSOPHICAL INSIGHTS

This topic explores *samadhi* as the ultimate state of stillness and union with the divine. In Indian spirituality, *samadhi* (*samādhi*) is the pinnacle of meditation, where the mind is completely still, and the seeker experiences the oneness with the universal consciousness. The Bhagavad Gita and the Upanishads teach that through the practice of meditation, one can attain *samadhi*, transcending the ego and connecting with the divine. The poem illustrates that *samadhi* is the state where the soul is free, the mind is clear, and the seeker is united with the divine truth.

PRACTICAL GUIDANCE

How often do you experience stillness in your life? Are you open to connecting with the divine through the practice of samadhi?

Start by creating a quiet, peaceful space for meditation. Focus on calming your mind and letting go of distractions. Visualize the stillness within and allow your thoughts to dissolve. Use affirmations like "I am one with the divine," "In stillness, I find peace," and "I connect with the truth within." Through regular practice, you will begin to experience the state of *samadhi*, where you are united with the divine and at peace with yourself.

69

Aligning with Cosmic Cycles

The cosmic cycles, they ebb and flow,
A rhythm that the universe knows.
In every turn, there's a divine plan,
Guiding us, as part of the span.

The cycles of time, they shape our fate,
Each moment unfolds at the perfect rate.
We align with the stars and the moon,
To dance with the cosmos, we must attune.

The seasons turn, the tides arise,
The sun sets, and the moon will rise.
Through these cycles, we find our place,
In the cosmic dance, we find grace.

To align with the cycles is to trust,
That the universe knows what's just.
In every moment, we flow with the tide,
And in that flow, we learn to glide.

The cosmic cycles guide our soul,
They teach us to become whole.
Through their rhythm, we understand,
That we are part of the divine plan.

Aligning with the cycles, we find peace,
A harmony that will never cease.
It's the divine flow, the perfect pace,
Guiding us to our sacred space.

Through alignment with the cosmic flow,
We find the strength to truly grow.
In every cycle, we see the truth,
A reflection of our eternal youth.

INTERPRETATION

Aligning with cosmic cycles is the practice of living in harmony with the natural rhythms of the universe

In Indian philosophy, the universe is seen as a living organism that operates in cycles. The Bhagavad Gita teaches that the wise person understands and aligns with the natural rhythms of life, acting in harmony with the cosmic flow. *Krishna* emphasises that by following the divine plan and aligning with the cosmic order, we can live in peace and fulfilment.

The Upanishads speak of the cycles of time, the seasons, and the movements of celestial bodies as manifestations of the divine. These cycles are seen as a reflection of the eternal truth, and aligning with them brings us closer to understanding our true nature. *Yoga* teaches that by attuning ourselves to these cycles, we align with the divine rhythm, allowing us to flow effortlessly through life.

STANZA-WISE INTERPRETATION

- **Stanza 1:** The poem introduces the concept of cosmic cycles as a divine rhythm that governs the universe. These cycles guide us, and we are part of the greater cosmic plan.
- **Stanza 2:** The poem emphasises that everything unfolds in perfect timing according to cosmic cycles. We must align with these cycles to experience harmony and flow in our lives.

- **Stanza 3:** The natural cycles of the universe, such as the turning of seasons and the rise and fall of tides, are presented as guiding forces that help us find our place in the grand design.
- **Stanza 4:** Aligning with the cosmic cycles is shown as an act of trust, knowing that the universe operates with divine wisdom and understanding. By surrendering to this flow, we find ease and grace.
- **Stanza 5:** The poem emphasises that by aligning with the cosmic rhythms, we find inner peace and harmony. We are guided toward our sacred purpose, in sync with the divine plan.
- **Stanza 6:** Cosmic cycles are depicted as guiding us to spiritual growth. By living in alignment with these cycles, we understand our role in the greater divine plan.
- **Stanza 7:** The final stanza reinforces that alignment with the cosmic flow leads to strength, growth, and the realisation of truth. We see the reflection of our eternal self in the cycles of the universe.

PHILOSOPHICAL INSIGHTS

This topic explores the importance of aligning with cosmic cycles to live in harmony with the universe. In Indian spirituality, the natural cycles of time, seasons, and celestial movements are seen as expressions of divine order. The Bhagavad Gita and the Upanishads teach that aligning with these rhythms helps us flow with life, bringing peace and fulfilment. The poem illustrates that by attuning ourselves to the cosmic flow, we understand our place in the universe and align with the divine plan.

PRACTICAL GUIDANCE

How often do you reflect on the natural rhythms of life? Are you aware of the cosmic cycles that govern your existence?

Start by observing the cycles around you—seasonal changes, lunar cycles, and the ebb and flow of your own life. Practice mindfulness to attune yourself to these natural rhythms and allow yourself to flow with them. Use affirmations like "I am in harmony with the cosmic flow," "I trust the divine timing of my life," and "I align with the rhythm of the universe." By recognizing and aligning with the cosmic cycles, you will experience greater peace, growth, and spiritual awakening.

70

The Role of Breath in Spiritual Awakening

Breath is the life force we all share,
It connects us to the earth, the sky, the air.
In every inhale, the soul expands,
In every exhale, it understands.

Breath is the bridge between mind and soul,
It centers us, it makes us whole.
With each breath, we find our peace,
And through breath, our worries cease.

In the breath, we find our truth,
A wisdom that renews our youth.
It is the pulse of the divine,
In every breath, we realign.

Through breath, we awaken the soul's light,
A flame that burns forever bright.
It guides us through the darkened night,
And leads us to the sacred height.

The breath is the gateway to the divine,
It is the force that makes us shine.
Through conscious breath, we find our way,
To the higher self, every day.

Breathing is the key to peace within,
A path to the state where we begin.
In each breath, we are reborn,
And our true nature is adorned.

Through breath, we rise and soar,
To the highest realms, to the divine shore.
The role of breath in awakening is clear,
It takes us to the truth we hold dear.

INTERPRETATION

Breath is the vital force that connects us to our higher consciousness and awakens the soul

In Indian philosophy, breath (*prāṇa*) is seen as the life force that sustains both body and mind. *Yoga* teaches that by controlling the breath through techniques like *pranayama*, we can activate the energy centers in the body and connect with the divine. The Bhagavad Gita teaches that through disciplined practice, the breath can calm the mind and guide us toward self-realisation. *Krishna* emphasises the importance of inner discipline, and breath is one of the key tools in achieving mental and spiritual clarity.

The Upanishads describe *prāṇa* as the force that sustains all life. Through breath control and awareness, we can elevate our consciousness and align with the divine. *Pranayama* is a practice that not only calms the body and mind but also activates higher states of awareness, helping us access our higher self and divine wisdom. Through the role of breath, we move closer to spiritual awakening.

STANZA-WISE INTERPRETATION

- **Stanza 1:** The poem introduces breath as the life force that connects us to all things. It emphasises that through breath, the soul expands and understands its true nature.
- **Stanza 2:** Breath is depicted as a bridge between the mind and soul, helping us find peace and stillness. It is through conscious breathing that we quiet our worries.

- **Stanza 3:** The poem highlights that the breath holds wisdom, renewing us with each inhale. It aligns us with the divine, helping us return to our true state of being.
- **Stanza 4:** Breath is portrayed as the awakening force of the soul. It is through breath that we find guidance and clarity, leading us toward spiritual enlightenment.
- **Stanza 5:** The poem emphasises that breath connects us to the divine. Through mindful breathing, we align ourselves with our higher purpose and the divine will.
- **Stanza 6:** Breath is shown as the key to inner peace and self-realisation. It is through breath that we are reborn, shedding old attachments and returning to our true nature.
- **Stanza 7:** The final stanza affirms that breath is the path to spiritual awakening. It leads us to the highest realms of consciousness and helps us access the divine truth within.

PHILOSOPHICAL INSIGHTS

This topic explores the role of breath in spiritual awakening, emphasising its importance in connecting the body, mind, and soul. In Indian spirituality, breath (*prāṇa*) is seen as the life force that sustains all beings. Through practices like *pranayama*, we can control and direct our breath to awaken higher consciousness. The Bhagavad Gita and the Upanishads teach that breath is not only essential for life but also a key to self-realisation and spiritual growth. The poem illustrates that by mastering the breath, we connect with the divine and awaken to our higher self.

PRACTICAL GUIDANCE

How aware are you of your breath in your spiritual practice? Are you using the power of your breath to connect with your higher consciousness?

Start by practising *pranayama* daily. Focus on deep, conscious breathing, and allow each breath to calm your mind and center your energy. Visualize *prāṇa* (life force) flowing through your body as you inhale and exhale. Use affirmations like "My breath connects me to my higher self," "With every breath, I align with the divine," and "I awaken to higher consciousness through my breath." By incorporating breath awareness into your daily life, you will experience greater peace, clarity, and spiritual awakening.

71

Awakening to Higher Consciousness

Higher consciousness is the state of being,
Where the soul is free, and we start to sing.
It's the awareness that transcends the mind,
A place where the truth we seek, we find.

To awaken the higher self, we must let go,
Of all the illusions we think we know.
It's the release of the ego's grip,
And the surrender to the soul's deep trip.

Through meditation and focused thought,
We open the doors that were once sought.
The veil of ignorance starts to fade,
And we connect to the divine aid.

Higher consciousness is the light we seek,
It's the wisdom that makes us meek.
In its glow, we find our true face,
And align with the universe's grace.

To awaken to higher consciousness is the goal,
It is the path that makes us whole.
It is the realisation of our true self,
And the reunion with the divine wealth.

The higher consciousness opens the gate,
To the infinite love, to the divine state.
Through its awakening, we are free,
And in this state, we simply be.

Awakening to higher consciousness is the key,
To living in peace, to being truly free.
It's the journey to the divine within,
And the sacred light that guides us in.

INTERPRETATION

Awakening to higher consciousness is the realization of our true nature and connection with the divine

In Indian philosophy, higher consciousness (*parama jñāna*) refers to the elevated state of awareness where the individual self (*atman*) recognises its oneness with the universal consciousness (*Brahman*). The Bhagavad Gita teaches that spiritual awakening comes when we transcend the ego and align ourselves with the divine will. *Krishna* emphasises that the path to higher consciousness is through devotion, selfless action, and the pursuit of knowledge.

The Upanishads describe higher consciousness as the state of liberation (*moksha*), where we free ourselves from ignorance and realize our oneness with the divine. *Yoga* practices, including meditation and *pranayama*, are tools to awaken higher consciousness. By quieting the mind and surrendering the ego, we access a higher state of awareness and understanding, aligning ourselves with the divine truth.

STANZA-WISE INTERPRETATION

- **Stanza 1:** The poem introduces higher consciousness as the state where the soul is free, and truth is revealed. It is the awareness that transcends the mind and connects us to the divine.
- **Stanza 2:** To awaken higher consciousness, the poem emphasises that we must let go of the ego and illusions.

This is the release of attachments and the journey toward spiritual awakening.

- **Stanza 3:** Meditation and focused thought are presented as the tools to awaken higher consciousness. As the veil of ignorance fades, we connect to the divine guidance.
- **Stanza 4:** Higher consciousness is shown as the divine light that illuminates our true self. In this state, we align with the universe's grace and wisdom.
- **Stanza 5:** Higher consciousness is the goal of spiritual practice. It is the realisation of our divine nature and the connection to universal wisdom.
- **Stanza 6:** The poem emphasises that higher consciousness opens the gates to infinite love and freedom. It is the state where we are fully aligned with the divine.
- **Stanza 7:** The final stanza affirms that awakening to higher consciousness is the key to living a peaceful, liberated life. It is the journey to the divine within and the light that guides us on our spiritual path.

PHILOSOPHICAL INSIGHTS

This topic explores awakening to higher consciousness as the realisation of our true self and oneness with the divine. In Indian philosophy, higher consciousness (*parama jñāna*) is the state of spiritual awakening where the individual recognises its connection with the universal consciousness. The Bhagavad Gita and the Upanishads teach that through meditation, selfless action, and devotion, we can transcend the ego and experience higher states of awareness. The poem illustrates that higher consciousness is the path to peace, liberation, and spiritual fulfilment.

PRACTICAL GUIDANCE

How often do you seek to awaken to higher consciousness? Are you ready to transcend the ego and connect with the divine?

Begin by practising meditation daily. Focus on quieting the mind and surrendering the ego, allowing the divine truth to emerge. Use affirmations like "I am one with the divine," "I awaken to higher consciousness," and "I am free from the ego's grip." Through consistent practice, you will begin to experience the awakening of higher consciousness, leading to greater peace, wisdom, and spiritual fulfilment.

CHAPTER 7

Spiritual Wisdom and Practices

72

The Sacred Geometry of Life

Life is the pattern, the cosmic design,
In every shape, the divine aligns.
The circle, the square, the spiral so true,
Are symbols of the divine view.

In every form, the truth we find,
A geometry that transcends the mind.
The sacred shapes speak a hidden song,
Guiding us where we belong.

The flower of life, the seed of creation,
Are the codes of cosmic foundation.
Each angle and curve a lesson taught,
In the geometry of life, wisdom is sought.

The geometry of life is divine and pure,
A structure that makes us endure.
Through its patterns, we see the way,
To enlightenment, day by day.

The sacred geometry reflects the divine,
In every shape, the stars align.
It is the blueprint of the universe,
In its sacred design, we immerse.

Through geometry, we touch the divine,
In every curve, in every line.
The sacred patterns guide us true,
To the knowledge of the universe, ever new.

The geometry of life is the key,
To understanding the divine mystery.
It reveals the truth we cannot see,
And connects us to the cosmic sea.

INTERPRETATION

The sacred geometry of life represents the divine patterns and structures inherent in the universe

In Indian philosophy, sacred geometry is seen as the divine blueprint of creation. The Upanishads describe the universe as a manifestation of the divine, governed by patterns and structures that reflect the cosmic order. Yoga teaches that by aligning ourselves with these divine patterns, we can connect with the universe's flow and achieve spiritual awakening.

Indian spiritual practices often involve understanding the geometry of the body, mind, and spirit, seeing them as reflections of the greater cosmic design. The Bhagavad Gita speaks of the universe as a vast, interconnected whole, where every element is part of a divine design. Sacred geometry is the expression of this design, and through it, we can understand the interconnectedness of all things.

STANZA-WISE INTERPRETATION

- **Stanza 1:** The poem introduces sacred geometry as the divine design behind all of life. Every shape and pattern reflects a higher spiritual truth.
- **Stanza 2:** Sacred geometry is described as a language that speaks beyond the mind. It is a tool for understanding the divine and our place within it.
- **Stanza 3:** The poem highlights some key symbols, such as the flower of life and the seed of creation, that are

central to sacred geometry. These symbols represent the essence of the divine.

- **Stanza 4:** The poem describes the geometry of life as a divine structure that supports all of existence. It provides the foundation for spiritual growth and enlightenment.
- **Stanza 5:** The sacred geometry is depicted as the cosmic blueprint, where every shape and pattern aligns with the divine plan. It reveals the interconnectedness of all things.
- **Stanza 6:** Sacred geometry guides us toward spiritual knowledge and understanding. It is through the contemplation of these divine patterns that we gain insight into the mysteries of the universe.
- **Stanza 7:** The final stanza affirms that sacred geometry reveals the divine truth. By understanding these patterns, we align ourselves with the cosmic flow and gain a deeper connection with the divine.

PHILOSOPHICAL INSIGHTS

This topic explores sacred geometry as the divine patterns and structures that govern the universe. In Indian spirituality, geometry is seen as a reflection of the divine order, with each shape and pattern carrying spiritual significance. The Upanishads and Bhagavad Gita emphasise that the universe is a sacred design, and by aligning with this geometry, we can connect with the divine. The poem illustrates that sacred geometry is the key to understanding the interconnectedness of all life and to accessing the divine wisdom of the cosmos.

PRACTICAL GUIDANCE

How often do you reflect on the divine patterns in the universe? Are you aware of the sacred geometry in your own life?

Start by observing the natural forms around you—flowers, trees, the stars, and the movements of the planets. These are expressions of the sacred geometry of life. Practice meditation to connect with these divine patterns and contemplate their meaning. Use affirmations like "I see the divine geometry in all," "I align with the sacred patterns of the universe," and "I am connected to the divine design." By recognizing and aligning with sacred geometry, you will deepen your understanding of the universe and your place within it.

73

The Wisdom of Stillness

In stillness, the soul finds its voice,
A place where the heart can rejoice.
The mind becomes a tranquil sea,
Where peace flows effortlessly.

In silence, we find the truth we seek,
The stillness that makes us meek.
Through quiet, the divine speaks loud,
In stillness, we are unbowed.

Stillness is the path to clarity,
It brings us to inner harmony.
Through silence, we hear the call,
To be still and surrender all.

In stillness, the ego fades,
The heart opens, the soul invades.
It is the space where wisdom dwells,
In stillness, we break the spells.

The wisdom of stillness teaches us,
To trust in the divine, to be just.
Through silence, we connect with grace,
And find the sacred, holy place.

Stillness is the key to peace,
It brings our worries to cease.
In quiet, we find our way,
To the divine, every day.

The wisdom of stillness is clear,
It leads us to the light, drawing near.
Through silence and peace, we grow,
And in stillness, we know.

INTERPRETATION

Stillness is the key to connecting with the divine and accessing the wisdom within

In Indian spirituality, stillness (*maun*) is seen as a sacred state of being where the mind quiets and the soul can hear the divine voice. The Bhagavad Gita teaches that stillness is essential for spiritual growth. *Krishna* encourages *Arjuna* to practice meditation and find inner peace, as it is only in stillness that we can connect with our higher self.

The Upanishads describe stillness as the state where the individual self (*atman*) connects with the universal consciousness (*Brahman*). *Yoga* emphasises the importance of quieting the mind through meditation, allowing the individual to access deeper states of awareness. In stillness, we transcend the ego and open ourselves to divine wisdom and spiritual insight.

STANZA-WISE INTERPRETATION

- **Stanza 1:** The poem introduces stillness as a state where the soul finds peace. In this state, the heart rejoices, and the mind becomes calm, allowing inner peace to flow freely.
- **Stanza 2:** Stillness is described as the place where truth is revealed. In silence, we hear the divine message, and the distractions of the mind fade away.
- **Stanza 3:** Stillness is presented as the path to clarity. Through silence, we align ourselves with the divine, allowing us to surrender and experience true peace.

- **Stanza 4:** The poem emphasises that in stillness, the ego dissolves, and the soul is free to connect with divine wisdom. It is in this quiet space that we find the sacred truth.
- **Stanza 5:** Stillness is shown as the space where wisdom dwells. Through quiet reflection, we connect with divine grace and find our true purpose.
- **Stanza 6:** The poem underscores that stillness brings peace. It allows us to release worries and find the path to spiritual growth and connection with the divine.
- **Stanza 7:** The final stanza affirms that stillness is the key to spiritual growth. Through silence and peace, we find divine wisdom and understanding.

PHILOSOPHICAL INSIGHTS

This topic emphasises the wisdom of stillness as the gateway to spiritual growth and divine connection. In Indian spirituality, stillness (*maun*) is seen as the space where the individual can transcend the ego and connect with the divine. The Bhagavad Gita and the Upanishads teach that through meditation and silence, we can hear the divine voice and align with our higher self. The poem illustrates that in stillness, we find clarity, wisdom, and peace, allowing us to connect with the sacred truth of the universe.

PRACTICAL GUIDANCE

How often do you practice stillness in your life? Are you open to experiencing the wisdom that comes from silence?

Start by creating a quiet space each day for meditation. Focus on silencing the mind and letting go of distractions. Practice *maun* (silence) for short periods throughout the day to experience the peace that stillness brings. Use affirmations like "In stillness, I find the truth," "I am connected to the divine in silence," and "Stillness brings me wisdom and peace." By embracing the wisdom of stillness, you will experience greater clarity, peace, and spiritual growth.

74

The Art of Sacred Rituals

In sacred rituals, we find our place,
A connection to the divine, a moment of grace.
Through offerings, chants, and prayer,
We honour the divine presence, everywhere.

Rituals are the bridge we create,
To the divine, to the cosmic state.
In each action, a blessing is cast,
Linking the present with the divine past.

The art of rituals is the path to peace,
A moment when time seems to cease.
Through sacred acts, we align with the divine,
A reminder that we are a part of the grand design.

In rituals, we honour the sacred space,
And invoke the divine's loving embrace.
It is the act of surrender and grace,
Finding divinity in every place.

Through rituals, we seek to align,
With the divine will, so pure, divine.
It is a dance of faith and trust,
A sacred bond, both strong and just.

The art of rituals leads us home,
To the truth that we are never alone.
Through sacred acts, we find our way,
To divinity's presence, every day.

Rituals remind us of what is real,
A connection that we deeply feel.
In every act, we are blessed anew,
And in the sacred, we find the true.

INTERPRETATION

Sacred rituals are acts of devotion that help us connect with the divine and align ourselves with higher spiritual forces

In Indian spirituality, rituals (*puja*) are sacred practices that help the devotee connect with the divine through offerings, prayers, and meditations. The Bhagavad Gita teaches that all actions, when done with devotion, become a form of worship and connect us with the divine. *Krishna* advises *Arjuna* to surrender all actions to the divine, and through this surrender, all actions are elevated to the level of sacred rituals.

The Upanishads describe rituals as the sacred acts that align us with the universal consciousness (*Brahman*). Through *puja, mantras,* and other rituals, we establish a connection to the divine and transcend the ego. These practices are considered pathways to experiencing divine presence in our daily lives. Rituals are not merely symbolic; they carry the power of intention and reverence, helping the devotee to align with spiritual truth and divine order.

STANZA-WISE INTERPRETATION

- **Stanza 1:** The poem introduces sacred rituals as a means to connect with the divine. Through prayer and offerings, we honour the divine presence that surrounds us.
- **Stanza 2:** Rituals are described as a bridge that links us to the divine and the cosmos. Every action in a ritual is

considered a blessing, connecting the present moment to spiritual truth.

- **Stanza 3:** The poem emphasises that rituals offer a path to peace. Through sacred acts, we align with the divine will and experience a sense of harmony with the universe.
- **Stanza 4:** Rituals are shown as acts of surrender and grace, where we open ourselves to the divine embrace. Every ritual is an opportunity to experience divinity in the present moment.
- **Stanza 5:** The poem highlights that rituals help us align with the divine will. They are acts of trust and faith, creating a sacred bond between the devotee and the divine.
- **Stanza 6:** Sacred rituals are presented as a means to find our true path and connect with divinity. Through these acts, we experience spiritual growth and transformation.
- **Stanza 7:** The final stanza affirms that rituals help us remember our divine connection. They are acts of reverence that help us experience the sacred in every moment of our lives.

PHILOSOPHICAL INSIGHTS

This topic explores sacred rituals as acts of devotion that help us connect with the divine and align ourselves with the cosmic order. In Indian spirituality, rituals (*puja*) are seen as a means to honour the divine and transcend the ego. The Bhagavad Gita and the Upanishads teach that rituals elevate our actions to sacred acts of worship, helping us experience divine presence and spiritual growth. The poem illustrates that through rituals, we align with the divine and experience peace, grace, and spiritual awakening.

PRACTICAL GUIDANCE

How often do you engage in sacred rituals to connect with the divine? Are you open to the transformative power of ritual in your spiritual practice?

Start by incorporating simple rituals into your daily life. Whether it is lighting a candle, offering a prayer, or simply taking a moment of stillness, allow your rituals to be a conscious act of devotion. Use affirmations like "Through my rituals, I connect with the divine," "Every act is an offering to the divine," and "Rituals bring me peace and grace." By dedicating your actions to the divine, you will begin to experience the profound power of sacred rituals in your life.

75

The Divine Feminine and Masculine Within

Within each of us, the balance lies,
The divine feminine and masculine rise.
One brings strength, the other grace,
Together they create a sacred space.

The masculine energy is bold and strong,
It leads the way, it guides us along.
It is the power to act and create,
The will to manifest, the path to fate.

The feminine energy is gentle and deep,
It nurtures life, it helps us sleep.
It is the wisdom, the heart that feels,
The compassion that heals and heals.

Together, they dance in perfect harmony,
The divine union, the cosmic symphony.
The masculine leads, the feminine nurtures,
A balance that brings us to higher cultures.

The divine feminine and masculine are whole,
Together they make us feel whole.
They balance each other in the soul,
And make us ready for the divine goal.

Through the union of these energies, we find,
A deep connection of body and mind.
The divine feminine and masculine unite,
To bring us closer to the divine light.

The balance of these energies is the key,
To living in harmony, living free.
In each of us, both energies reside,
Guiding us with love and wisdom, side by side.

INTERPRETATION

The divine feminine and masculine energies exist within each of us and are essential for spiritual balance

In Indian spirituality, the concepts of *Shakti* (the feminine energy) and *Shiva* (the masculine energy) represent the dual forces that create and sustain the universe. The Bhagavad Gita and the Upanishads teach that these energies are not separate but interdependent, and their balance is key to spiritual awakening and fulfilment. *Krishna* teaches that both energies are needed for the universe to function harmoniously.

The *Tantras* describe the union of *Shakti* and *Shiva* as the ultimate act of creation. The feminine energy is nurturing, compassionate, and intuitive, while the masculine energy is active, willful, and assertive. Together, they create balance and guide the individual toward spiritual growth. *Yoga* emphasises that balancing these energies within oneself is essential for self-realisation and connection to the divine.

STANZA-WISE INTERPRETATION

- **Stanza 1:** The poem introduces the concept of the divine feminine and masculine energies as balanced forces within each individual. They work together to create harmony and spiritual space.
- **Stanza 2:** Masculine energy is described as bold, strong, and creative. It drives action and manifestation, providing the power to create and direct life's course.

- **Stanza 3:** Feminine energy is shown as nurturing, compassionate, and wise. It is the source of healing and emotional connection, providing the wisdom needed for growth and understanding.
- **Stanza 4:** The poem presents the union of the **masculine** and feminine energies as a cosmic dance. They complement and support each other, bringing harmony and spiritual progress.
- **Stanza 5:** The divine feminine and masculine are described as essential for wholeness. When both energies are balanced within, we become aligned with our higher purpose.
- **Stanza 6:** The poem emphasises that the union of these energies leads to spiritual awakening and connection to the divine. They guide us toward higher consciousness and light.
- **Stanza 7:** The final stanza affirms that the balance of the masculine and feminine energies is the key to spiritual fulfilment. When both are in harmony, we experience love, wisdom, and spiritual growth.

PHILOSOPHICAL INSIGHTS

This topic explores the divine feminine and masculine energies as essential aspects of spiritual balance. In Indian spirituality, these energies are seen as complementary forces that govern the universe. The Bhagavad Gita and Upanishads teach that both energies must be balanced within the individual to achieve spiritual harmony and growth. The poem illustrates that when these energies unite, they lead us to enlightenment, peace, and a deeper connection with the divine.

PRACTICAL GUIDANCE

How balanced are the masculine and feminine energies within you? Are you open to embracing both energies to create spiritual harmony?

Start by reflecting on the masculine and feminine energies within you. Are you more active, assertive, and willful (masculine), or more nurturing, compassionate, and intuitive (feminine)? Strive to balance both energies by embracing qualities of both within yourself. Use affirmations like "I honour the divine feminine and masculine within me," "I am balanced in both my actions and emotions," and "I embrace the power of both energies in my spiritual journey." Through practice, you will achieve greater spiritual balance and alignment with the divine.

76

The Power of Prayer and Reflection

In prayer, we speak to the divine,
With open hearts, our souls align.
Through every word, every silent plea,
We draw closer to the eternal sea.

Reflection is the mirror of the soul,
It helps us find and make us whole.
In silence, we hear the divine call,
And in prayer, we surrender all.

Through prayer, we find our strength,
It guides us through the longest length.
In reflection, we see the truth,
And connect with the divine's youth.

Prayer is the light that guides the way,
It calms the storm, it ends the fray.
In reflection, we gain insight,
And in prayer, we find our might.

Through prayer, the soul is healed,
In reflection, the truth is revealed.
Both are paths to inner peace,
Where all conflicts and struggles cease.

Prayer and reflection are the keys,
To connect with the divine with ease.
They open the heart, they quiet the mind,
And in them, the divine is confined.

The power of prayer and reflection is true,
It brings us closer to the divine view.
In prayer and reflection, we grow,
And to the divine, we always flow.

INTERPRETATION

Prayer and reflection are the spiritual practices that allow us to connect with the divine and gain insight into our true nature

In Indian spirituality, prayer (*prārthanā*) is a sacred practice of communication with the divine. Reflection (*svādhyāya*) is the process of self-study and contemplation. The Bhagavad Gita emphasises the importance of devotion through prayer, and how it helps the devotee connect with the divine. *Krishna* teaches that through prayer, one can seek guidance and strength, surrendering all fears and desires.

The Upanishads describe reflection as a means of self-discovery, where the seeker contemplates the truth within. Yoga teaches that through prayer and reflection, we harmonize the mind, body, and soul. These practices purify the mind, remove ignorance, and awaken spiritual wisdom. Both prayer and reflection are integral to the path of self-realisation, allowing us to align with the divine order and experience peace.

STANZA-WISE INTERPRETATION

- **Stanza 1:** The poem introduces prayer as the act of communicating with the divine, drawing us closer to the eternal truth.
- **Stanza 2:** Reflection is presented as the mirror of the soul, helping us hear the divine call and surrender to its guidance. Prayer and reflection work together to guide us spiritually.

- **Stanza 3:** The poem emphasises that prayer provides strength, while reflection reveals the truth within. Both practices lead to spiritual awakening and self-realisation.
- **Stanza 4:** Prayer is depicted as the light that leads us through challenges, calming the mind. Reflection brings insight and clarity, helping us align with the divine.
- **Stanza 5:** Prayer and reflection are shown as healing practices, purifying the mind and soul. They lead us to peace, where struggles and conflicts dissolve.
- **Stanza 6:** Prayer and reflection are presented as keys to spiritual connection. They open the heart, quiet the mind, and bring us closer to the divine truth.
- **Stanza 7:** The final stanza affirms that through prayer and reflection, we align with the divine and experience growth. These practices bring us closer to the eternal light.

PHILOSOPHICAL INSIGHTS

This topic explores the power of prayer and reflection as essential spiritual practices that connect us with the divine and guide us toward self-realisation. In Indian spirituality, prayer (*prārthanā*) is a means of communicating with the divine, while reflection (*svādhyāya*) is the process of introspection and self-study. The Bhagavad Gita and the Upanishads teach that these practices purify the mind, strengthen the connection with the divine, and lead to spiritual enlightenment. The poem illustrates that through prayer and reflection, we gain insight, find inner peace, and align with the divine.

PRACTICAL GUIDANCE

How often do you engage in prayer or reflection in your daily life? Are you open to using these practices to connect with the divine?

Start by setting aside time each day for prayer and reflection. Begin with a moment of gratitude, offering thanks for the blessings in your life. Follow with a period of reflection, contemplating your inner truth and connecting with your higher self. Use affirmations like "I am one with the divine," "My prayer brings me closer to the divine," and "Through reflection, I gain clarity and peace." By incorporating prayer and reflection into your spiritual practice, you will deepen your connection to the divine and experience greater peace and wisdom.

77

The Flow of Spiritual Energy

Spiritual energy flows through the soul,
It is the power that makes us whole.
Through every breath, through every move,
It is the force that helps us improve.

The energy flows like a river of light,
Guiding us through the dark of night.
It flows through us, in every part,
Filling the soul, healing the heart.

In the flow of energy, we find our truth,
A power that renews our youth.
It clears the mind, opens the heart,
And leads us to a sacred start.

Through the flow, we are healed and whole,
The energy fills every part of the soul.
It is the force that brings us peace,
And from its embrace, we never cease.

The flow of energy is the divine breath,
It gives us life, it conquers death.
It flows in cycles, in rhythms so true,
The source of power that guides us through.

Through the flow, we rise and shine,
The divine energy is yours and mine.
It flows through every heart, every soul,
Making us whole, making us whole.

The flow of spiritual energy is the key,
To awakening the truth that's free.
In its flow, we find our way,
To the divine, every day.

INTERPRETATION

Spiritual energy is the force that flows through us, guiding us toward self-realization and spiritual awakening

In Indian philosophy, spiritual energy (*prāṇa* or *shakti*) is the life force that animates all living beings. The Bhagavad Gita teaches that this energy flows through the body and mind, connecting us to the divine. *Krishna* encourages *Arjuna* to recognise the power of this divine energy, which is present in all things. The energy flows through the chakras and is activated through *yoga*, meditation, and *pranayama*.

The Upanishads describe *prāṇa* as the vital energy that sustains life. Through the flow of this energy, we are connected to the universe and the divine. The practice of *yoga* helps us align with this energy, clearing blockages and allowing it to flow freely, bringing balance, peace, and enlightenment. The flow of spiritual energy is essential for personal growth and spiritual realisation.

STANZA-WISE INTERPRETATION

- **Stanza 1:** The poem introduces spiritual energy as the force that sustains us. It flows through every breath and movement, guiding our spiritual journey.
- **Stanza 2:** Spiritual energy is depicted as a river of light that guides us through darkness. It fills every part of our being, healing and nurturing the soul.

- **Stanza 3:** The flow of energy is presented as a source of truth and renewal. It clears the mind and opens the heart, leading us to spiritual growth.
- **Stanza 4:** The poem emphasises that spiritual energy brings healing and peace. It fills the soul, helping us connect with the divine and live in harmony.
- **Stanza 5:** The flow of energy is described as the divine breath that gives life and overcomes death. It moves in cycles and rhythms, guiding us through life's challenges.
- **Stanza 6:** The poem affirms that through the flow of spiritual energy, we rise and shine. This energy connects us to the divine and empowers us to live fully.
- **Stanza 7:** The final stanza reinforces that the flow of spiritual energy is the key to spiritual awakening. By aligning with this energy, we find our path to the divine and experience peace.

PHILOSOPHICAL INSIGHTS

This topic explores the flow of spiritual energy as the life force that connects us to the divine and guides us toward self-realisation. In Indian spirituality, *prāṇa* is the energy that sustains life and connects us to the universe. The Bhagavad Gita and the Upanishads teach that through *yoga*, *pranayama*, and meditation, we can activate and align with this energy. The poem illustrates that the flow of spiritual energy heals, nurtures, and guides us, leading us toward spiritual awakening and peace.

PRACTICAL GUIDANCE

How often do you focus on the flow of energy within you? Are you aware of the divine energy that sustains and guides you?

Begin by practising *pranayama* and meditation to activate and balance your spiritual energy. Visualize the energy flowing freely through your body, clearing blockages and bringing balance. Use affirmations like "I am one with the divine energy," "The flow of energy guides me," and "I am aligned with the flow of spiritual energy." By connecting with this flow, you will experience greater peace, clarity, and spiritual growth.

78

The Light Beyond Fear

Fear is a shadow that clouds the mind,
A veil that makes the soul blind.
But beyond the dark, the light does shine,
A guiding force that's pure, divine.

Fear fades when the truth is known,
It dissolves when the light is shown.
In every heart, this light resides,
Waiting to illuminate, where fear hides.

Beyond the fear, the soul is free,
The light reveals what we can be.
In its glow, we find our strength,
And walk the path of love, at length.

Fear cannot touch the truth we hold,
It dissolves in the light, so bold.
In every step, the light will guide,
And fear will fade, with every stride.

The light beyond fear is love's embrace,
It leads us to a sacred space.
Where peace and joy begin to bloom,
And fear's shadow is consumed.

In the light beyond fear, we rise,
With open hearts, with clear eyes.
We transcend the limitations of the mind,
And in the light, our truth we find.

The light beyond fear is the key,
To living a life that's truly free.
When we walk in this divine light,
Fear disappears, and all is right.

INTERPRETATION

The light beyond fear represents the divine truth and spiritual strength that frees us from fear

In Indian philosophy, fear (*bhaya*) is seen as one of the greatest obstacles to spiritual growth. The Bhagavad Gita teaches that fear arises from attachment and the ego, but through spiritual practice, we can transcend it. *Krishna* advises *Arjuna* to let go of fear and act with faith in the divine will. When we realize our oneness with the divine, we see that fear has no real power over us.

The Upanishads describe the soul as pure light, free from the shadows of fear. In meditation and spiritual practices, we tap into this inner light, which dissolves fear and reveals the truth of who we are. The practice of *yoga*, *pranayama*, and self-inquiry helps us align with this divine light, guiding us to overcome all fears and limitations.

STANZA-WISE INTERPRETATION

- **Stanza 1:** The poem introduces fear as a shadow that clouds the mind, but beyond fear lies the divine light, which guides us toward truth and freedom.
- **Stanza 2:** The light dispels fear, revealing the truth within. When we embrace this light, fear fades away, and we connect with our true nature.
- **Stanza 3:** Fear is shown as an illusion, and beyond it lies the freedom of the soul. The light reveals our inner strength and guides us toward love and spiritual growth.

- **Stanza 4:** The poem emphasises that fear cannot touch the truth. The divine light leads us on the right path, gradually dissolving our fears with each step.
- **Stanza 5:** The light beyond fear is portrayed as the embrace of love, which brings peace and joy. Fear's hold on us weakens in the presence of divine light.
- **Stanza 6:** The final stanza emphasises that by walking in the divine light, we transcend fear and live in alignment with our highest truth.

PHILOSOPHICAL INSIGHTS

This topic explores the light beyond fear as the divine truth and inner strength that helps us transcend fear. In Indian spirituality, fear is considered a barrier to self-realisation and spiritual growth. The Bhagavad Gita and the Upanishads teach that when we align with the divine light within, fear dissolves, and we can live a life of peace and fulfilment. The poem illustrates that the divine light is the key to overcoming fear, revealing our true strength and guiding us to spiritual freedom.

PRACTICAL GUIDANCE

How often do you allow fear to guide your decisions? Are you ready to embrace the divine light within and overcome fear?

Start by practising meditation and focusing on the light within. Visualize the light dissolving any fears or anxieties you may have. Use affirmations like "I am free from fear," "I walk in the divine light," and "Fear has no power over me." Through regular practice, you will experience greater peace, courage, and spiritual growth as you align with the divine light that resides within you.

79

The Role of Silence in Spirituality

In silence, the soul finds its voice,
A space where we can truly rejoice.
It is the realm where truth is known,
And the mind finds peace, fully grown.

Silence is the language of the divine,
In its stillness, we begin to shine.
In quietude, the soul is free,
It connects with the divine, naturally.

Through silence, we listen to the heart,
It guides us to where we must start.
In silence, the mind is still,
And the soul aligns with the divine will.

Silence is the refuge of the wise,
In its depth, the truth lies.
Through silence, we gain clarity,
And see the world in purity.

In silence, we find our way,
It teaches us to live each day.
Through silence, we connect with grace,
And find divinity in every space.

Silence is the path to peace,
In its stillness, we find release.
It is the way to connect within,
And experience the divine within.

The role of silence is the key,
To living in truth, to being free.
In silence, we find the divine voice,
And the soul's true and eternal choice.

INTERPRETATION

Silence is a vital spiritual practice that allows us to connect with the divine and experience inner peace

In Indian philosophy, silence (*maun*) is considered an essential practice for spiritual growth. The Bhagavad Gita teaches that the mind must be still and quiet for true wisdom and self-realisation to emerge. *Krishna* encourages *Arjuna* to transcend mental distractions and focus on the divine, and this is achieved through silence and stillness.

The Upanishads describe silence as the space where the soul connects with the divine. Through meditation and maun, we create the inner stillness necessary to experience our true self (*atman*) and the universal consciousness (*Brahman*). Silence helps us transcend the ego and hear the divine guidance that leads us to spiritual awakening.

STANZA-WISE INTERPRETATION

- **Stanza 1:** The poem introduces silence as the space where the soul finds peace and truth. In silence, the mind becomes still, and the soul can connect with the divine.
- **Stanza 2:** Silence is presented as the language of the divine, where we begin to shine with inner wisdom and spiritual clarity.
- **Stanza 3:** The poem emphasises that silence helps us listen to the heart. It guides us toward spiritual awakening and alignment with the divine will.

- **Stanza 4:** Silence is shown as the refuge of the wise, where clarity and purity are gained. In this stillness, we experience the deeper truth of existence.
- **Stanza 5:** The poem teaches that silence is a guide to spiritual growth. It helps us connect with divine grace and experience the sacredness of every moment.
- **Stanza 6:** Silence is described as the key to peace and release from the distractions of the mind. In silence, we reconnect with our true self.
- **Stanza 7:** The final stanza affirms that silence leads us to truth and spiritual freedom. It is through silence that we experience the divine voice and find the eternal choice of the soul.

PHILOSOPHICAL INSIGHTS

This topic explores the role of silence in spirituality as a tool for self-realisation and divine connection. In Indian spirituality, silence (*maun*) is the practice of quieting the mind and listening to the divine. The Bhagavad Gita and the Upanishads teach that silence is the key to transcending the ego and aligning with the divine will. The poem illustrates that in silence, we find inner peace, clarity, and spiritual awakening, and connect with the eternal truth of the universe.

PRACTICAL GUIDANCE

How often do you allow yourself to experience silence in your life? Are you ready to use silence as a tool for spiritual growth?

Start by creating moments of silence in your day. Practice maun (silence) during meditation, and also throughout your day to create space for spiritual reflection. Use affirmations like "In silence, I find my truth," "I connect with the divine in stillness," and "Silence brings me peace and clarity." Through regular practice, you will experience the deep power of silence to guide you toward spiritual growth and self-realisation.

80

The Sacredness of the Body

The body is a temple, pure and bright,
A vessel for the soul's true light.
In every breath, in every beat,
The divine dwells, so pure, so sweet.

The body is the sacred place,
Where spirit and flesh embrace.
It is the house of the soul's grace,
A temple where we find our space.

Through the body, we express our truth,
In every movement, in every youth.
It is the tool for divine action,
The sacred ground for spiritual satisfaction.

The body is the temple we honour,
With love, we cherish it forever.
Through care, respect, and gratitude,
We align the body with divine attitude.

The body holds the power of creation,
It is the source of transformation.
In its form, the divine resides,
Guiding us to the truth that abides.

Through the body, we find our way,
To live with grace, each day.
It is the sacred path we walk,
A journey where the divine will talk.

The body is the sacred song,
A melody that plays along.
In every cell, the divine does shine,
And through it, we are all divine.

INTERPRETATION

The body is seen as a sacred vessel that houses the divine and supports the soul's journey

In Indian philosophy, the body is not merely a physical structure, but a sacred temple that holds the divine spirit. The Bhagavad Gita teaches that the body is the instrument through which we fulfil our spiritual duties. *Krishna* explains to *Arjuna* that we must care for the body as it is the medium through which we experience the world and connect with the divine.

The Upanishads describe the body as a sacred instrument that channels divine energy. Through practices like *yoga*, we align the body with higher consciousness, recognizing it as a temple for spiritual expression. The act of honouring the body is also a form of honouring the divine within us. The body allows us to express our soul's truth and perform our sacred actions in the world.

STANZA-WISE INTERPRETATION

- **Stanza 1:** The body is introduced as a temple for the soul, a sacred vessel that holds the divine light, allowing us to express our true nature.
- **Stanza 2:** The body is described as the place where the soul and spirit connect. It is the temple where we find divine grace and experience spiritual life.
- **Stanza 3:** The body is shown as the tool for spiritual action. Every movement and expression is an opportunity to connect with the divine and express our truth.

- **Stanza 4:** The poem emphasises the importance of respecting and cherishing the body. By caring for it, we align ourselves with the divine purpose.
- **Stanza 5:** The body is described as the source of transformation. Through spiritual practices, we can transform ourselves and realize the divine within.
- **Stanza 6:** The poem reinforces that the body is the path to living with grace and purpose. It is the sacred journey that allows us to connect with the divine.
- **Stanza 7:** The body is depicted as a sacred song, with every part of it resonating with divine energy. It is the vessel through which the divine shines and communicates with us.

PHILOSOPHICAL INSIGHTS

This topic explores the sacredness of the body as the temple for the soul, where the divine resides and expresses itself. In Indian spirituality, the body is viewed as an instrument for spiritual growth and divine expression. The Bhagavad Gita and Upanishads teach that by caring for the body and recognizing its sacred nature, we honour the divine within and align with higher consciousness. The poem illustrates that the body is not just a physical vessel but a sacred temple that guides us to live our spiritual truth.

PRACTICAL GUIDANCE

How often do you treat your body as the sacred vessel it is? Are you aware of the divine energy within you?

Start by practising self-care and honouring your body as a temple. Incorporate healthy practices such as *yoga*, meditation, and mindful eating into your daily routine. Use affirmations like "My body is a sacred temple," "I honour the divine within me," and "Through my body, I express my soul's truth." By recognizing the sacredness of your body, you align yourself with the divine and experience greater peace and spiritual connection.

81

The Power of Sacred Sound

Sound is the essence of creation's song,
A vibration that's pure, deep, and strong.
It flows through the universe, wide and vast,
Carrying wisdom from the past.

The sound of the universe is divine,
It resonates through space and time.
Every mantra, every chant,
Echoes the divine, ever constant.

In sacred sound, we find our peace,
It brings us closer to release.
Through sound, the soul awakens,
And the mind's clutter is shaken.

Om is the sound that leads the way,
It takes us to the light of day.
In mantras and chants, we find the key,
To unlock the divine mystery.

Sacred sound has the power to heal,
It purifies, it makes us real.
Through its vibration, we are reborn,
To a new dawn, to a new morn.

Through sacred sound, we transcend,
We connect with the divine, without end.
It leads us to the highest state,
And opens the door to the divine gate.

The power of sacred sound is true,
It guides us to the light that's due.
In sound, we find the divine embrace,
And awaken to the divine grace.

INTERPRETATION

Sacred sound is a powerful force that connects us to the divine and guides us toward spiritual awakening

In Indian spirituality, sound (*nāda*) is considered a key element of creation. Om, the primordial sound, is seen as the vibration that created the universe. The Bhagavad Gita and the Upanishads teach that mantras, chants, and the sound of Om are the means by which we connect with the divine and align with the cosmic rhythm. *Krishna* and other sages emphasise that through sound, we can transcend the ego, purify the mind, and awaken the soul.

The Tantras describe the power of sound as transformative. Mantras are powerful sounds that carry the energy to remove obstacles, heal, and bring peace. Through the practice of chanting and listening to sacred sound, we align with the cosmic vibrations and experience spiritual awakening.

STANZA-WISE INTERPRETATION

- **Stanza 1:** The poem introduces sound as the essence of creation, a divine vibration that permeates the universe. It carries ancient wisdom and is the source of all life.
- **Stanza 2:** Sacred sound is described as the divine resonance that transcends time and space. It echoes the truth of the universe and connects us to the divine presence.

- **Stanza 3:** Sacred sound is shown as the means of attaining peace. It helps clear the mind, awakens the soul, and brings us closer to spiritual liberation.
- **Stanza 4:** Om and mantras are presented as the key to unlocking divine wisdom. Through chanting and sound, we connect to the divine and experience spiritual transformation.
- **Stanza 5:** The poem emphasises the healing power of sacred sound. It purifies and transforms us, leading us to spiritual rebirth and inner peace.
- **Stanza 6:** Sacred sound is shown as the means to transcend limitations and connect with the divine. It opens the gate to the highest spiritual state.
- **Stanza 7:** The final stanza affirms that sacred sound is the key to experiencing the divine embrace. Through sound, we awaken to divine grace and align with the universal truth.

PHILOSOPHICAL INSIGHTS

This topic explores the power of sacred sound as the vibration that connects us to the divine and facilitates spiritual awakening. In Indian spirituality, *Om* and *mantras* are seen as powerful sounds that align us with the divine rhythm of the universe. The Bhagavad Gita and the Upanishads teach that through the practice of chanting and listening to sacred sound, we transcend the ego and connect with the divine. The poem illustrates that sacred sound is a transformative force that guides us to spiritual growth, peace, and connection with the divine.

PRACTICAL GUIDANCE

How often do you engage with sacred sound in your spiritual practice? Are you open to the healing and transformative power of sound?

Start by incorporating *mantras* or *Om* chanting into your daily practice. Focus on the vibrations of the sound as you chant, allowing it to align your energy with the divine. Use affirmations like "I am connected to the divine through sound," "Sacred sound brings me peace and healing," and "Through sound, I awaken to my true self." By connecting with sacred sound, you will experience greater peace, clarity, and spiritual awakening.

CHAPTER 8

Celebration and Transcendence

82

The Art of Celebration

Celebration is the soul's delight,
A joyful dance, a radiant light.
In every moment, joy we find,
A celebration of the heart and mind.

Through gratitude, we honour life,
We celebrate in peace, free from strife.
Each small victory, each moment of grace,
Is a celebration of life's embrace.

In celebration, we see the divine,
The presence of God, in every sign.
It is the expression of our soul's truth,
A reminder of our eternal youth.

To celebrate is to connect with love,
To rise above, like the heavens above.
In every smile, in every cheer,
We find the sacred drawing near.

Celebration brings us peace and light,
It fills the soul with endless might.
Through it, we find our way to grace,
And meet the divine in every space.

Celebrate the beauty, celebrate the joy,
Every moment, like a child's toy.
The art of celebration is the key,
To a life of love, wild and free.

In celebration, the soul is whole,
The divine shines, it makes us whole.
Through joy and laughter, we transcend,
And find that love has no end.

INTERPRETATION

Celebration is an act of honouring life and connecting with the divine presence in all things

In Indian spirituality, celebration (*utsav*) is seen as an expression of gratitude and reverence for life. The Bhagavad Gita teaches that every act, when done with devotion, becomes a celebration of the divine presence. *Krishna* encourages us to celebrate life through every act, with a joyful heart and a peaceful mind.

The Upanishads describe celebration as the natural state of the soul, which is ever joyful and free. Through meditation, prayer, and *mantras*, we align with the divine rhythm of life, finding joy in the present moment. Celebration is not just about external events but is an internal attitude of gratitude and recognition of the divine within all things.

STANZA-WISE INTERPRETATION

- **Stanza 1:** The poem introduces celebration as a joyous act that reflects the light of the soul. It emphasises that every moment of life is an opportunity for celebration.
- **Stanza 2:** Gratitude is presented as a key aspect of celebration. By acknowledging life's gifts, we celebrate both the small and significant moments with peace and grace.
- **Stanza 3:** The poem highlights that celebration allows us to recognise the divine in all things. It is the

expression of our inner truth, where we align with the eternal joy within.

- **Stanza 4:** Celebration is depicted as an act of love that connects us to the divine. Every act of joy and cheer brings us closer to the sacred presence.
- **Stanza 5:** Celebration is shown as a path to inner peace and strength. Through it, we align with divine grace and experience the transformative power of joy.
- **Stanza 6:** The poem emphasises that celebration is not limited to grand events but is about recognizing beauty and joy in everyday life. It leads us to freedom and love.
- **Stanza 7:** The final stanza reinforces that celebration makes the soul whole. Through joy, we transcend limitations and connect with the infinite love of the universe.

PHILOSOPHICAL INSIGHTS

This topic explores celebration as an expression of gratitude and reverence for life. In Indian spirituality, celebration (*utsav*) is the act of recognizing the divine presence in every moment. The Bhagavad Gita and the Upanishads teach that every moment is an opportunity to celebrate the divine, and through joy and gratitude, we align ourselves with the universal flow. The poem illustrates that celebration brings peace, joy, and spiritual growth, allowing us to transcend and connect with the divine presence within

PRACTICAL GUIDANCE

How often do you celebrate life, even in the smallest moments? Are you open to seeing the divine in every aspect of your life?

Start by practising gratitude every day. Acknowledge the blessings in your life, both big and small. Use affirmations like "I celebrate the divine in every moment," "My heart is filled with joy and gratitude," and "I find peace in every celebration." By making celebration a regular practice, you will experience greater joy, peace, and spiritual fulfilment.

83

Forgiveness and the Path to Freedom

Forgiveness is the key to the heart,
It's the freedom that sets us apart.
To forgive is to release the pain,
And let go of the past's chain.

In forgiveness, the soul finds peace,
The burdens of hatred and anger cease.
It is the act of love and grace,
That heals the wounds time cannot erase.

Forgiveness is the act of the soul,
It brings healing and makes us whole.
It frees us from the past's embrace,
And guides us toward divine grace.

When we forgive, we set ourselves free,
We let go of the past, and we can see,
The love that flows from the divine,
In forgiveness, we realign.

Forgiveness is the path to peace,
It brings the soul's burdens to cease.
Through forgiveness, we find our way,
And the light shines brighter every day.

To forgive is to free the heart,
To heal the soul, to restart.
In forgiveness, we transcend the pain,
And release the past's hold, again.

Forgiveness is the path of love,
It connects us to the divine above.
In forgiving others, we find grace,
And the peace that transcends time and space.

INTERPRETATION

Forgiveness is the powerful practice that frees us from the past and aligns us with divine grace

In Indian spirituality, forgiveness (*kshamā*) is a path to liberation and inner peace. The Bhagavad Gita teaches that *Krishna* emphasises the importance of forgiveness for spiritual growth. *Krishna* tells *Arjuna* that when we forgive, we let go of the burdens of hatred and anger, allowing ourselves to align with the divine presence.

The Upanishads describe forgiveness as the ultimate act of compassion and spiritual maturity. *Yoga* teaches that through forgiveness, we release the negative energy that holds us back and make space for divine love and healing. By forgiving ourselves and others, we transcend the ego and connect with the eternal peace of the universe.

STANZA-WISE INTERPRETATION

- **Stanza 1:** The poem introduces Forgiveness as the key to unlocking the heart. By forgiving, we release the emotional burdens that keep us tied to the past.
- **Stanza 2:** Forgiveness is presented as a path to peace, where the soul is freed from anger and resentment. It is the act of love and grace that heals the wounds of the past.
- **Stanza 3:** The poem emphasises that Forgiveness is a healing act of the soul. It allows us to transcend the pain and align with divine grace and spiritual truth.
- **Stanza 4:** Forgiveness is shown as the key to freedom. By forgiving, we let go of the past and open ourselves to the divine love that guides us.

- **Stanza 5:** The poem reinforces that Forgiveness brings peace to the soul. It helps us release the burdens of the past and move forward on our spiritual path.
- **Stanza 6:** Forgiveness is depicted as the path to healing and renewal. By forgiving, we transcend the pain of the past and create space for new growth and divine peace.
- **Stanza 7:** The final stanza emphasises that Forgiveness connects us to the divine. It is through forgiveness that we find grace and peace, transcending time and space.

PHILOSOPHICAL INSIGHTS

This topic explores Forgiveness as the path to spiritual freedom and inner peace. In Indian philosophy, Forgiveness (*kshamā*) is the practice of releasing anger and resentment, aligning ourselves with divine love and grace. The Bhagavad Gita and the Upanishads teach that through forgiveness, we heal ourselves and transcend the limitations of the ego. The poem illustrates that Forgiveness frees the soul, bringing peace, love, and divine grace into our lives.

PRACTICAL GUIDANCE

How often do you hold on to anger or resentment? Are you ready to forgive and free yourself from the past?

Start by practising forgiveness in small ways. Reflect on any grudges or resentments you may be holding and consciously release them. Use affirmations like "I forgive myself and others," "Forgiveness brings me peace," and "Through forgiveness, I align with divine grace." By embracing forgiveness, you will experience greater freedom, peace, and spiritual fulfilment.

84

The Courage to Live Authentically

To live authentically, we must be true,
To the self inside, to the essence we knew.
It's the courage to stand, firm and tall,
In a world that tries to make us fall.

Authenticity is the voice of the soul,
The one that makes us feel whole.
It speaks the truth, with no fear,
And guides us to what we hold dear.

Living authentically is a sacred quest,
It leads us to our highest and best.
It's the courage to be who we are,
And to shine brightly like a star.

To live authentically, we must let go,
Of all the masks we wear below.
It's the truth we speak and the love we show,
A path that only the brave will know.

Authenticity is the freedom we seek,
The strength to be gentle, yet bold and unique.
In its embrace, we find our power,
Living truthfully, every hour.

To live authentically is to be real,
To embrace what we feel and heal.
It's the act of living from the heart,
And knowing that we are an essential part.

In authenticity, we are truly free,
It's where we find the divine in me.
By living true, we unlock the door,
To the life we were meant to explore.

INTERPRETATION

Living authentically is the practice of aligning our actions with our true self, unshackled by societal expectations

In Indian spirituality, living authentically (*satya*) is seen as a path to self-realisation. The Bhagavad Gita teaches that truth is the essence of the self (*atman*), and living in accordance with this truth brings spiritual liberation. *Krishna* encourages *Arjuna* to act with integrity, staying true to the soul's purpose, irrespective of external pressures.

The Upanishads emphasise the importance of living authentically as a means of discovering the divine within. *Yoga* teaches that when we align our actions with our deepest truths, we experience spiritual harmony. *Satya* is not only about honesty with others but about being true to the soul and the divine wisdom it holds.

STANZA-WISE INTERPRETATION

- **Stanza 1:** The poem introduces authenticity as living true to the self, standing firm despite external pressures and remaining true to one's essence.
- **Stanza 2:** Authenticity is depicted as the soul's voice, guiding us to speak the truth and live in alignment with what is dear to us.
- **Stanza 3:** Living authentically is shown as a quest for the highest potential. It is about having the courage to be ourselves, shining without fear.

- **Stanza 4:** The poem emphasises that authenticity requires letting go of the false personas we create to please others. It is about living truthfully and courageously.
- **Stanza 5:** Authenticity is described as the freedom to be unique and true to oneself. It gives us strength and empowers us to live with purpose.
- **Stanza 6:** The poem affirms that living authentically means embracing our feelings and experiences, allowing us to heal and grow.
- **Stanza 7:** The final stanza states that authenticity is the key to spiritual freedom and self-discovery. By living authentically, we unlock the path to a divine, meaningful life.

PHILOSOPHICAL INSIGHTS

This topic explores the courage to live authentically as the path to self-realisation and spiritual freedom. In Indian philosophy, *satya* (truth) is considered one of the highest virtues. The Bhagavad Gita and Upanishads teach that living authentically, true to our soul, brings us in alignment with the divine. The poem illustrates that authenticity is about being true to ourselves, shedding the masks, and embracing the divine truth within.

PRACTICAL GUIDANCE

How often do you suppress your true self to fit in or meet external expectations? Are you ready to embrace the courage to live authentically?

Begin by reflecting on areas of your life where you may be holding back your true self. Practice speaking and acting in alignment with your deepest values. Use affirmations like "I am true to myself," "I live with integrity," and "I embrace the truth within me." Through self-reflection and honest action, you will find greater peace and fulfilment as you live authentically.

85

Living with Purpose

Purpose is the force that guides the soul,
It gives us strength, it makes us whole.
In every action, it leads the way,
And fills our hearts with light each day.

To live with purpose is to live with heart,
It's the fire that ignites every part.
It's the reason we rise and strive,
And the reason we feel truly alive.

Purpose is the compass that guides our path,
It's the answer to questions that life hath.
It directs our mind, our soul, and heart,
And aligns us with the divine art.

To live with purpose is to live with clarity,
It removes confusion and brings prosperity.
It brings us peace, it brings us joy,
It is the divine purpose we employ.

Purpose is the reason for every breath,
It frees us from the fear of death.
Through purpose, we find our truth,
And live in alignment, forever new.

Living with purpose is living with love,
It is the force that pushes us above.
It helps us connect with the divine,
And the truth that forever will shine.

The purpose of life is to live with grace,
To find the divine in every space.
When we live with purpose, we find the way,
To love, to serve, and to stay.

INTERPRETATION

Living with purpose is the practice of aligning our actions with a higher divine goal, which brings clarity, joy, and fulfilment

In Indian spirituality, *dharma* is the concept of living with a higher purpose or divine duty. The Bhagavad Gita teaches that each individual has a unique purpose in life that aligns with their soul's essence and contributes to the collective good. *Krishna* advises *Arjuna* to live according to his dharma, without attachment to the results, and by doing so, he finds true fulfilment.

The Upanishads describe *dharma* as the cosmic law that governs the universe. Living in accordance with this law leads to spiritual liberation. *Yoga* teaches that when we align ourselves with our higher purpose, we transcend the ego and live in harmony with the divine order. Purpose guides us through life, bringing meaning and alignment with the divine will.

STANZA-WISE INTERPRETATION

- **Stanza 1:** Purpose is introduced as the guiding force of the soul. It gives us strength and direction, filling our lives with meaning and light.
- **Stanza 2:** Living with purpose is shown as the path that ignites passion and drive. It is the reason we strive and grow, giving us the energy to live fully.
- **Stanza 3:** Purpose is described as the compass that guides our journey. It provides clarity and direction, helping us align with the divine truth.

- **Stanza 4:** Living with purpose brings clarity and removes confusion. It brings peace, joy, and a sense of alignment with the divine.
- **Stanza 5:** The poem emphasises that purpose gives life meaning and helps us transcend fear and death. Through it, we find our true self and live in alignment with our higher purpose.
- **Stanza 6:** Purpose is shown as the force of love that connects us to the divine. It helps us serve others and align with the divine will.
- **Stanza 7:** The final stanza affirms that living with purpose is the path to grace. Through purpose, we find our way to divine love, service, and fulfilment.

PHILOSOPHICAL INSIGHTS

This topic explores living with purpose as the path to spiritual fulfilment and alignment with the divine will. In Indian philosophy, *dharma* is the concept of living according to one's divine purpose, contributing to the greater good. The Bhagavad Gita and Upanishads teach that living with purpose brings clarity, peace, and spiritual growth. The poem illustrates that when we align with our higher purpose, we find meaning, joy, and divine connection.

PRACTICAL GUIDANCE

How often do you feel disconnected from your true purpose? Are you living in alignment with your higher self?

Reflect on your passions and values. What drives you? Start by aligning your actions with your higher purpose, whether it's through your work, relationships, or spiritual practice. Use affirmations like "I am aligned with my higher purpose," "My life is filled with divine meaning," and "I serve with love and grace." By living with purpose, you will find greater fulfilment, peace, and spiritual growth.

86

Honouring the Present Moment

The present moment is all we have,
It is where life's true treasures lie.
In the now, we find our peace,
Where all worries, all doubts cease.

To honour the present is to be alive,
In every moment, we thrive.
It's the space where time stands still,
And our hearts align with the divine will.

In the present, the world unfolds,
In each breath, a new story told.
It is the only time we can know,
Where all wisdom and love flow.

The present is the gift we receive,
It is where our hearts believe.
Through presence, we find our grace,
And the divine shines in every place.

In the now, we let go of the past,
We release all fears that do not last.
In the present, we are whole,
Connected to the truth of our soul.

honouring the present is to live in peace,
To let go and let our worries cease.
Through presence, we awaken the light,
And everything feels pure and right.

To honour the present moment is the key,
To living in truth, to being free.
In the now, we find our way,
To joy, to love, and to divine play.

INTERPRETATION

The present moment is the key to spiritual awakening, where we find peace, wisdom, and connection to the divine

In Indian spirituality, the present moment is regarded as the only true moment. The Bhagavad Gita teaches that the past is gone, the future is uncertain, and the only reality is the present. *Krishna* encourages *Arjuna* to act in the present with full awareness, without attachment to the outcomes.

The Upanishads emphasise the importance of living in the moment and experiencing life as it is. *Yoga* teaches that by focusing on the present, we transcend the mind's distractions and align ourselves with our higher purpose. By honouring the present, we honour the divine that exists in every moment, every breath.

STANZA-WISE INTERPRETATION

- **Stanza 1:** The poem introduces the present moment as the only true reality, where peace and tranquility exist. In the present, we can release all fears and doubts.
- **Stanza 2:** Honouring the present is shown as the way to thrive in life. It is in the now that we find alignment with the divine will, experiencing a deep sense of peace.
- **Stanza 3:** The poem highlights that the present moment is where the world unfolds. It is the time where wisdom and love flow freely, as we experience life in its full glory.

- **Stanza 4:** The present moment is presented as a gift, where our hearts believe and find grace. Through presence, we experience the divine light in every space.
- **Stanza 5:** Living in the present means letting go of the past and releasing fears. In the now, we reconnect with the truth of our soul and find spiritual wholeness.
- **Stanza 6:** The poem reinforces that honouring the **present** brings peace. It allows us to release worries and experience the purity and clarity of the moment.
- **Stanza 7:** The final stanza affirms that the present moment is the key to spiritual freedom. Through presence, we connect with joy, love, and divine play.

PHILOSOPHICAL INSIGHTS

This topic explores the importance of honouring the present moment as the key to spiritual awakening. In Indian spirituality, the present moment is considered the only true moment, where we can find peace and connect with the divine. The Bhagavad Gita and the Upanishads emphasise that by living in the present, we transcend past regrets and future anxieties, aligning ourselves with the divine order. The poem illustrates that by honouring the present, we experience spiritual growth, peace, and divine connection.

PRACTICAL GUIDANCE

How often do you find yourself lost in thoughts of the past or future? Are you fully present in the moment?

Practice mindfulness throughout your day. Begin by setting aside time to simply be present—whether through meditation, deep breathing, or mindful walking. Focus on your breath and bring your attention to the here and now. Use affirmations like "I am present in every moment," "I honour the divine in the now," and "In the present, I find peace." By practising presence, you will experience greater peace, clarity, and spiritual alignment.

87

Finding Peace in Uncertainty

In uncertainty, we find our grace,
It's the place where we learn to embrace.
The unknown is not to fear,
But a place where the truth is clear.

Uncertainty is the space to grow,
It teaches us what we must know.
It challenges us, yet sets us free,
To trust the divine mystery.

In uncertainty, we find our strength,
We rise above, we go the length.
It is the force that makes us strong,
And carries us where we belong.

When life is unclear, we must trust,
That all things will return to dust.
In uncertainty, we learn to flow,
And let the divine energy grow.

Uncertainty is where faith begins,
It's where the soul rises within.
In its depths, we find our peace,
And through it, all worries cease.

In uncertainty, we surrender control,
We let go and open the soul.
It is the space where we find our way,
And trust the divine light each day.

The peace of uncertainty is pure,
It leads us to the truth, so sure.
Through it, we transcend the mind,
And discover the peace we seek to find.

INTERPRETATION

Uncertainty is a space for growth, where we learn to trust the divine and find peace beyond the ego

In Indian philosophy, uncertainty (*avyaktā*) is seen as an inevitable part of life. The Bhagavad Gita teaches that we must trust in the divine plan, even when things are unclear. *Krishna* advises *Arjuna* to surrender to the unknown and act in alignment with his higher purpose, without attachment to the results.

The Upanishads describe uncertainty as the realm where the soul learns to trust the divine wisdom. In *yoga*, uncertainty is embraced as part of the journey to self-realisation. It is through facing the unknown with faith that we transcend the ego and connect with the divine, finding peace and spiritual clarity.

STANZA-WISE INTERPRETATION

- **Stanza 1:** Uncertainty is introduced as the place where we find grace. It is not to be feared but embraced, as it reveals the truth and the divine order.
- **Stanza 2:** Uncertainty is presented as a teacher that helps us grow. It challenges us, yet frees us to trust in the divine mystery and wisdom.
- **Stanza 3:** Uncertainty is described as the force that builds strength and resilience. It guides us on our spiritual path, helping us grow in faith and wisdom.
- **Stanza 4:** The poem emphasises the need to trust during uncertain times, knowing that everything eventually

returns to the divine order. It is a time to let go and flow with divine energy.

- **Stanza 5:** Uncertainty is shown as the beginning of faith. It is through the unknown that we rise to spiritual understanding and find peace within.
- **Stanza 6:** Uncertainty teaches us to surrender control and trust in the divine. It is the space where we find clarity and divine guidance.
- **Stanza 7:** The final stanza affirms that uncertainty is the path to peace. By embracing it with faith, we transcend the mind's limitations and find the peace we seek.

PHILOSOPHICAL INSIGHTS

This topic explores finding peace in uncertainty as the key to spiritual growth and trust in the divine. In Indian spirituality, uncertainty (*avyaktā*) is seen as an inevitable part of the human experience, where we learn to surrender and trust in the divine plan. The Bhagavad Gita and Upanishads teach that by embracing uncertainty with faith, we align ourselves with the divine flow and find peace beyond the mind. The poem illustrates that uncertainty is a powerful tool for spiritual awakening and peace.

PRACTICAL GUIDANCE

How often do you resist uncertainty, and how does it affect your peace? Are you ready to trust the divine during uncertain times?

Begin by practising letting go during uncertain moments. Instead of trying to control outcomes, trust that the divine has a plan for you. Use affirmations like "I trust the divine plan," "I find peace in uncertainty," and "I surrender to the divine wisdom." Through mindfulness and surrender, you will experience greater peace and trust in the divine flow.

88

The Song of the Universe

The universe sings a silent song,
A melody that's ancient and long.
It echoes in the hearts of all,
In every rise and every fall.

The song is heard in every breeze,
In the rustling leaves, the shifting seas.
It's the music of the stars above,
A harmony that speaks of love.

The song of the universe is in the soul,
It guides us, it makes us whole.
In every breath, in every sigh,
The song sings softly, never shy.

It's the rhythm of the earth's pulse,
In every heart, in every impulse.
The universe sings in every sound,
In every vibration, we are found.

In the song, we find our place,
In its notes, we feel divine grace.
It leads us to the higher truth,
Awakening the soul's youth.

The song of the universe never ends,
It's the sound that always transcends.
It carries us on the winds of time,
In its beauty, we climb and climb.

To hear the song is to be free,
To live in harmony with the sea.
The song of the universe calls us home,
To the truth, to the unknown.

INTERPRETATION

The song of the universe represents the divine melody that connects all beings and guides us toward spiritual awakening

In Indian philosophy, sound (*nāda*) is believed to be the primal force of creation. The Bhagavad Gita teaches that everything in the universe is an expression of divine will, resonating with the cosmic song. *Krishna* tells *Arjuna* that the universe itself is a sacred melody, with every action and vibration part of the divine rhythm.

The Upanishads describe the universe as a vast, interconnected whole, where every being and every event is part of the divine song. *Yoga* and meditation practices emphasise listening to the divine sound, connecting with the natural rhythms of the universe, and finding alignment with the cosmic flow. The practice of listening to the song of the universe awakens our soul, guiding us toward inner peace and higher consciousness.

STANZA-WISE INTERPRETATION

- **Stanza 1:** The poem introduces the song of the universe as an eternal melody that is heard in every rise and fall. It is the underlying force that guides all of existence.
- **Stanza 2:** The song is heard in the natural world—wind, leaves, and seas. It is the music of the cosmos, symbolizing the divine love that permeates everything.

- **Stanza 3:** The song is depicted as something that lives in the soul. It is a guiding force that connects us with the divine and reminds us of our true essence.
- **Stanza 4:** The poem emphasises that the rhythm of the universe is in everything, from the earth's pulse to the smallest impulse in our hearts. The song is the divine force that sustains all life.
- **Stanza 5:** The song of the universe is shown as a path to higher truth. It brings grace and spiritual awakening, guiding us toward enlightenment and inner peace.
- **Stanza 6:** The song is portrayed as eternal, transcending time and space. It carries us on a journey through life, constantly leading us to greater understanding and divine connection.
- **Stanza 7:** The final stanza affirms that listening to the song of the universe brings us freedom. It aligns us with the divine, helping us connect with the greater truth of existence.

PHILOSOPHICAL INSIGHTS

This topic explores the song of the universe as the divine melody that connects all beings and guides us toward spiritual awakening. In Indian spirituality, sound (*nāda*) is the primal force of creation. The Bhagavad Gita and the Upanishads teach that everything in the universe is part of the divine song. The poem illustrates that when we align ourselves with the song of the universe, we awaken to our true self and experience divine peace and wisdom.

PRACTICAL GUIDANCE

How often do you listen to the divine rhythm in your life? Are you open to connecting with the cosmic song that guides you?

Start by practising mindfulness and tuning into the natural sounds around you—wind, water, birds, and even the silence. Allow yourself to feel the vibrations and rhythms of life. Use affirmations like "I am one with the song of the universe," "I align with the divine rhythm," and "I am guided by the cosmic melody." Through this practice, you will connect to the divine flow and experience spiritual awakening.

89

The Serenity of Trust

Trust is the foundation of the soul,
It is the power that makes us whole.
In trust, we find our deepest peace,
A place where all fears cease.

To trust is to surrender control,
To open the heart, to make us whole.
It is the faith that guides the way,
And leads us to the light of day.

Trust is the anchor in the storm,
It keeps us safe and keeps us warm.
In the storm of life, it holds us tight,
And guides us to the divine light.

Through trust, we find our strength,
We move forward at great length.
It is the force that guides our path,
And shields us from the world's wrath.

Trust is the key to living free,
It opens the heart, it lets us be.
In its embrace, we find our power,
And rise above in every hour.

Trust is the force that brings us peace,
It is the place where all fears cease.
Through trust, we find our way,
And in its warmth, we always stay.

The serenity of trust is divine,
It aligns us with the sacred design.
Through trust, we transcend the mind,
And in the divine, peace we find.

INTERPRETATION

Trust is the foundation that allows us to connect with the divine and experience inner peace

In Indian spirituality, trust (*śraddhā*) is seen as a form of surrender to the divine. The Bhagavad Gita teaches that we must trust in the divine plan and act with faith, without attachment to the results. *Krishna* encourages *Arjuna* to surrender his doubts and trust in the guidance of the divine will.

The Upanishads describe trust as the quality that allows us to surrender the ego and align with the higher self. Through *yoga* and meditation, we learn to cultivate trust in the divine order, letting go of fear and doubt. Trust opens the heart, allowing us to experience peace, wisdom, and spiritual growth.

STANZA-WISE INTERPRETATION

- **Stanza 1:** Trust is introduced as the foundation of the soul, providing peace and freedom from fear. It is the force that makes us whole.
- **Stanza 2:** Trust is shown as the act of surrender, allowing us to open our hearts and move forward with faith. It guides us to the light and spiritual awakening.
- **Stanza 3:** Trust is depicted as the anchor during life's challenges. It holds us steady in turbulent times and leads us toward divine peace and guidance.
- **Stanza 4:** The poem emphasises that trust is the source of strength. It shields us from the negative forces in the world, guiding us on our path to spiritual growth.

- **Stanza 5:** Trust is presented as the key to freedom. It opens the heart, allowing us to be our true selves and empowering us to live with peace and purpose.
- **Stanza 6:** Trust is shown as the source of serenity. It brings peace, dissolves fears, and provides the guidance we need to navigate life.
- **Stanza 7:** The final stanza affirms that trust is the divine force that aligns us with the sacred order of the universe. Through trust, we transcend the mind and find divine peace.

PHILOSOPHICAL INSIGHTS

This topic explores trust as the foundation for spiritual growth and inner peace. In Indian spirituality, trust (*śraddhā*) is the practice of surrendering to the divine, acting with faith and confidence in the higher will. The Bhagavad Gita and the Upanishads teach that through trust, we align with the divine order and transcend the limitations of the ego. The poem illustrates that trust leads us to peace, wisdom, and spiritual fulfilment, allowing us to live in harmony with the divine.

PRACTICAL GUIDANCE

How often do you struggle with doubt and fear? Are you ready to trust the divine plan and surrender to the flow of life?

Begin by practising trust in small moments of your life. When you face uncertainty or fear, remind yourself that you are supported by the divine. Use affirmations like "I trust in the divine plan," "I surrender my doubts and fears," and "Trust guides me to peace and freedom." By cultivating trust, you will experience greater peace and spiritual growth.

90

Transcending the Self

The self we know is but a mask,
A fleeting image, an endless task.
To transcend the self is to see,
The truth of who we're meant to be.

Beyond the ego, beyond the name,
Lies the truth that's always the same.
The self we cling to fades away,
As the divine light brightens the day.

To transcend the self is to let go,
Of the attachments we've come to know.
It's the release of pride and fear,
And the embrace of the divine that's here.

In transcending the self, we find peace,
A place where all conflicts cease.
We merge with the divine, so true,
And see the world from a higher view.

Transcendence is the way to grace,
It is the act of leaving the chase.
Through surrender, we are free,
To live in the truth of what we see.

The self is but a passing cloud,
In the vast sky, it is not loud.
Through transcendence, we let go,
And allow the divine truth to flow.

To transcend the self is to find,
The peace that lives in the heart and mind.
In this freedom, we are whole,
And merge with the divine soul.

INTERPRETATION

Transcending the self is the practice of letting go of the ego and aligning with the divine truth

In Indian philosophy, the ego (*ahankara*) is considered the source of illusion and suffering. The Bhagavad Gita teaches that the true self (*atman*) is beyond the ego, and that only by transcending the ego can we realize our oneness with the divine. *Krishna* advises *Arjuna* to act without attachment to the ego, surrendering the false sense of self to the higher truth.

The Upanishads describe the process of transcending the self as the realisation that the individual self (*atman*) is identical with the universal consciousness (*Brahman*). *Yoga* and meditation are paths that help us detach from the ego and experience our true nature. By transcending the self, we align with the divine, experiencing peace, freedom, and spiritual growth.

STANZA-WISE INTERPRETATION

- **Stanza 1:** The poem introduces the ego as a mask that hides the true self. To transcend the self is to move beyond the fleeting identity and recognise our divine essence.
- **Stanza 2:** The poem emphasises that the true self is constant and eternal, unlike the ego, which fades away. By transcending the ego, we connect with the divine light.
- **Stanza 3:** Transcending the self requires letting go of attachments, pride, and fear. It is an act of surrender to the divine truth, leading to inner peace.

- **Stanza 4:** The poem emphasises that transcendence leads to peace. When we transcend the ego, we see the world from a higher perspective and experience divine harmony.
- **Stanza 5:** Transcendence is described as the way to grace, where we release the pursuit of material desires and align with the higher truth of existence.
- **Stanza 6:** The poem portrays the ego as a transient illusion, like a passing cloud. By transcending the self, we allow the divine truth to flow freely.
- **Stanza 7:** The final stanza affirms that transcending the self leads to the realisation of divine oneness. In this state, we merge with the divine soul and experience spiritual wholeness.

PHILOSOPHICAL INSIGHTS

This topic explores the concept of transcending the self as the key to spiritual growth and divine realisation. In Indian spirituality, the ego (*ahankara*) is the false sense of self that binds us to illusion. The Bhagavad Gita and the Upanishads teach that transcending the ego allows us to experience our true self, which is one with the universal consciousness (*Brahman*). The poem illustrates that by surrendering the ego and aligning with the divine truth, we achieve peace, freedom, and spiritual fulfilment.

PRACTICAL GUIDANCE

How often do you find yourself acting from the ego? Are you ready to transcend the self and connect with your higher truth?

Start by practising mindfulness and self-awareness. Reflect on moments when your actions are driven by the ego and make an effort to let go of those attachments. Use affirmations like "I am beyond the ego," "I am one with the divine," and "I release all attachments to my false self." Through consistent practice, you will experience greater peace and spiritual growth as you transcend the ego and align with your true essence.

91

Embracing Divine Joy

Joy is the gift that fills the soul,
It is the feeling that makes us whole.
In joy, we find the truth of life,
A respite from the world's strife.

Divine joy is not of the mind,
It transcends all that we find.
It is the light that shines from within,
The source of peace, the end of sin.

To embrace divine joy is to see,
The beauty of life in harmony.
It is the laughter of the soul,
A joy that makes us truly whole.

Divine joy is the music of the heart,
It fills us, never to depart.
In its embrace, we find our way,
To the divine, every day.

In joy, we release all fears,
We transcend sorrow, wipe away tears.
Divine joy is the force of grace,
It brings us peace in every place.

To embrace divine joy is to be free,
It opens the heart and sets us free.
In joy, we live in the divine flow,
And in its light, we grow and glow.

Divine joy is the light we seek,
It is the truth that makes us meek.
Through joy, we awaken the soul,
And find the divine, making us whole.

INTERPRETATION

Divine joy is the inherent state of bliss and peace that arises from spiritual alignment with the divine

In Indian spirituality, joy (*ānanda*) is considered a natural expression of the soul's connection to the divine. The Bhagavad Gita teaches that true joy comes from surrendering to the divine will and aligning with the higher self. *Krishna* emphasises that joy is not found in external pleasures but within, as an expression of divine love and grace.

The Upanishads describe *ānanda* as the ultimate state of being, where the soul is in perfect harmony with the universe. *Yoga* and meditation help awaken this inner joy, allowing us to transcend sorrow and fear. The practice of embracing divine joy leads to spiritual awakening, peace, and fulfilment.

STANZA-WISE INTERPRETATION

- **Stanza 1:** The poem introduces joy as the divine gift that makes us whole. It is the source of peace, providing respite from the struggles of life.
- **Stanza 2:** Divine joy is presented as a transcendent state that goes beyond the mind and the material world. It is the light that shines from within, bringing inner peace.
- **Stanza 3:** The poem emphasises that embracing divine joy allows us to see the beauty of life in harmony. It is the laughter of the soul that brings completeness.

- **Stanza 4:** Divine joy is depicted as the music of the heart, filling us with peace and guiding us toward the divine every day.
- **Stanza 5:** Joy is shown as the force that releases fear and sorrow. Divine joy transcends the pain of life, bringing grace and peace wherever we go.
- **Stanza 6:** Divine joy is presented as the key to freedom. It opens the heart and sets us free, allowing us to live in the divine flow.
- **Stanza 7:** The final stanza affirms that divine joy is the light that leads us to spiritual awakening. Through joy, we find the divine presence within and experience spiritual wholeness.

PHILOSOPHICAL INSIGHTS

This topic explores divine joy as the expression of bliss and peace that arises from spiritual connection with the divine. In Indian spirituality, joy (*ānanda*) is the ultimate state of being, where the soul is in harmony with the divine. The Bhagavad Gita and Upanishads teach that true joy comes from aligning with the higher self and surrendering to divine will. The poem illustrates that by embracing divine joy, we transcend sorrow, fear, and limitations, experiencing peace, freedom, and spiritual fulfilment.

PRACTICAL GUIDANCE

How often do you feel disconnected from joy? Are you ready to embrace the divine joy within?

Begin by practising gratitude and mindfulness each day. Focus on the present moment and allow yourself to experience the joy that arises from being connected to the divine. Use affirmations like “I embrace divine joy,” “Joy is my natural state,” and “Through joy, I connect with the divine.” By embracing divine joy, you will experience greater peace, freedom, and spiritual growth.

CHAPTER 9

The Essence of Practical Wisdom

92

The Power of Sacred Space

Sacred space is where we meet the divine,
In every corner, the light does shine.
It's a space where the soul feels free,
And the heart aligns with eternity.

In sacred space, we find our truth,
A place where we reconnect with our youth.
It is the realm of pure devotion,
Where the mind is calm, like the still ocean.

Sacred space is the altar of the heart,
Where we honour the divine in every part.
It's the space where we surrender our will,
And open ourselves to the divine still.

In sacred space, we release all fear,
We let go of doubts, and draw near.
It is the place where the soul speaks,
And the heart's longing it gently seeks.

The energy of sacred space is pure,
It brings clarity, it makes us sure.
In this space, we connect with grace,
And feel the divine presence in this place.

Through sacred space, we rise above,
We open ourselves to the flow of love.
It is the sanctuary for the soul,
Where we become complete and whole.

The power of sacred space is clear,
It draws us closer, year by year.
It is where the divine unfolds,
And the truth of life is gently told.

INTERPRETATION

Sacred space is a place where we can connect deeply with the divine and find inner peace and clarity

In Indian spirituality, sacred space (*tīrtha*) is considered a powerful space for spiritual practice. The Bhagavad Gita teaches that we must cultivate inner stillness and connect with the divine, and sacred space provides the environment for such connection. *Krishna* encourages *Arjuna* to create a space of peace where the soul can align with divine wisdom.

The Upanishads describe sacred space as a realm where the soul connects with the ultimate reality (*Brahman*). *Yoga* teaches that sacred space can be both external (such as a temple or natural surroundings) and internal (created through meditation and mindfulness). By entering this space, we surrender the ego and allow the divine presence to fill our hearts, guiding us to spiritual truth.

STANZA-WISE INTERPRETATION

- **Stanza 1:** The poem introduces sacred space as the realm where we meet the divine, where light and peace reside, and the soul finds alignment with eternity.
- **Stanza 2:** Sacred space is described as the place where we reconnect with our higher self. It is a space of devotion and peace, where the mind quiets and the soul feels free.
- **Stanza 3:** The sacred space is shown as a space for surrender. In this space, we open ourselves to divine

will and experience a deep connection with the divine presence.

- **Stanza 4:** Sacred space is depicted as a place where fear is released, and the soul finds comfort. It is a space of seeking divine truth and guidance.
- **Stanza 5:** The energy of sacred space is presented as pure and clarifying, bringing a sense of certainty and connection to the divine.
- **Stanza 6:** Sacred space allows us to transcend limitations and connect with divine love. It is a sanctuary that brings the soul to its fullest expression.
- **Stanza 7:** The final stanza affirms that the power of sacred space is transformative, drawing us closer to divine truth and spiritual wholeness.

PHILOSOPHICAL INSIGHTS

This topic explores the power of sacred space as a tool for spiritual awakening and inner peace. In Indian spirituality, sacred space is where the divine presence can be felt and experienced. The Bhagavad Gita and Upanishads teach that by entering a sacred space, we align with the divine, release the ego, and experience clarity, peace, and spiritual connection. The poem illustrates that sacred space is where we can surrender, find guidance, and connect deeply with our true self.

PRACTICAL GUIDANCE

How often do you create sacred space in your life? Are you open to experiencing the divine presence in stillness and quiet?

Begin by creating a sacred space in your home or daily routine. It can be a physical space like a meditation corner or a mental space where you enter stillness and silence. Use affirmations like "I create sacred space for the divine," "In sacred space, I find clarity," and "The divine speaks to me in silence." By regularly entering your sacred space, you will deepen your connection to the divine and experience peace.

93

The Path of Inner Peace

Inner peace is the soul's desire,
It is the flame that never tires.
It is the stillness within the storm,
A place where the heart feels warm.

To find inner peace is to surrender,
To release the need to defend or render.
It's the acceptance of what is,
And the freedom to simply exist.

In the silence of the mind, peace is found,
It is the space where truth is crowned.
Through acceptance, we find our way,
And in inner peace, we always stay.

Inner peace is the calm of the sea,
It is the stillness where we are free.
Through the storms of life, it remains,
A guiding force that sustains.

To walk the path of inner peace,
Is to let go of all that deceives.
It's the surrender of the mind's demands,
And the trust in the divine's hands.

Inner peace is the light we seek,
It is the strength when we are weak.
In its embrace, we find our way,
And in peace, we choose to stay.

The path to inner peace is clear,
It's the journey we must revere.
Through surrender and trust, we find,
The peace that resides in the heart and mind.

INTERPRETATION

Inner peace is the state of tranquility and acceptance that arises when we align with our true nature and trust the divine order

In Indian spirituality, inner peace (*śānti*) is the state of being at ease with oneself and the world. The Bhagavad Gita teaches that inner peace comes from surrendering to the divine will and living in alignment with the soul's truth. *Krishna* encourages *Arjuna* to release attachment to the fruits of action and find peace through devotion.

The Upanishads describe inner peace as the natural state of the soul. Through meditation, *yoga*, and self-inquiry, we release the distractions of the mind and align with the peaceful essence of the divine. By embracing acceptance, we move beyond fear and desire, finding tranquility in every moment.

STANZA-WISE INTERPRETATION

- **Stanza 1:** The poem introduces inner peace as the soul's true desire, a constant flame that provides warmth and calm amidst life's storms.
- **Stanza 2:** Inner peace is described as the result of surrender and acceptance. It is the freedom to be in the moment without needing to control or defend.
- **Stanza 3:** The poem emphasises that inner peace is found in the silence of the mind. By accepting what is, we align with our true essence and find peace within.

- **Stanza 4:** Inner peace is depicted as the calm of the sea, constant and unwavering, even in life's challenges. It is the guiding force that sustains us.
- **Stanza 5:** To walk the path of inner peace requires surrendering the ego's demands and trusting in the divine plan. It is about letting go and allowing peace to guide us.
- **Stanza 6:** Inner peace is described as the light and strength we seek. It is the state in which we feel centered, balanced, and aligned with the divine.
- **Stanza 7:** The final stanza affirms that the path to inner peace is clear: through surrender and trust in the divine, we align with our true essence and find lasting peace.

PHILOSOPHICAL INSIGHTS

This topic explores inner peace as the state of alignment with the true self and divine will. In Indian spirituality, inner peace (*śānti*) arises from surrender, acceptance, and devotion. The Bhagavad Gita and Upanishads teach that by releasing the ego and trusting in the divine order, we find tranquility and spiritual freedom. The poem illustrates that inner peace is a state of harmony, freedom from fear, and alignment with divine wisdom.

PRACTICAL GUIDANCE

How often do you experience inner peace? Are you open to embracing the path of surrender and acceptance?

Practice meditation and *yoga* to quiet the mind and align with your true self. Begin by accepting the present moment as it is, without judgment or resistance. Use affirmations like "I am at peace with myself," "I surrender to the divine will," and "Peace flows through me in every moment." By practising surrender and acceptance, you will cultivate lasting inner peace and spiritual fulfilment.

94

Aligning with Divine Timing

Divine timing moves with grace,
It guides us through the endless space.
Every moment is part of a plan,
Written by the divine hand.

In divine timing, all things unfold,
The future, the present, the stories untold.
Patience is the key to see,
The divine's timing in you and me.

Trust in the flow of the divine,
It takes us on a path so fine.
When the time is right, we will see,
The perfect place where we are meant to be.

Divine timing is the hand that leads,
It nurtures us, it plants the seeds.
It is the rhythm of the heart,
Guiding us, from the start.

In divine timing, there is no rush,
All happens in the perfect hush.
Every step, every action, each thought,
Is guided by the divine that we sought.

Trust the pace, trust the way,
The divine will lead you, day by day.
In alignment, you will find,
The path that is yours, one of kind.

Divine timing is the key to peace,
It brings us rest, it brings release.
By trusting the divine flow,
We align with what we are meant to know.

INTERPRETATION

Divine timing is the process by which the universe unfolds in alignment with a higher plan, guiding us toward our true purpose

In Indian spirituality, divine timing (*īśvara-prakṛti*) refers to the idea that all events in life occur at the right moment, orchestrated by the divine will. The Bhagavad Gita teaches that life unfolds in accordance with the divine plan, and we must act with patience and trust in the timing of the universe. *Krishna* encourages *Arjuna* to surrender to the divine will and understand that everything happens at its appointed time.

The Upanishads describe the divine as an eternal, unchanging force that governs all life. Through meditation and surrender, we align ourselves with this cosmic rhythm, trusting that everything will unfold when it is meant to. Divine timing is about trusting the universe's flow, surrendering control, and knowing that the divine has the perfect plan for us.

STANZA-WISE INTERPRETATION

- **Stanza 1:** The poem introduces divine timing as a graceful, guiding force that leads us through the various stages of life, according to a divine plan.
- **Stanza 2:** Divine timing unfolds in its own way, and with patience, we come to understand that every moment is part of a greater design.

- **Stanza 3:** Trust in the flow of the divine is emphasised. The poem reassures that when the time is right, everything will align perfectly, and we will be in the place we are meant to be.
- **Stanza 4:** Divine timing is described as a nurturing force that plants seeds of growth and guides us through the rhythm of life from the very beginning.
- **Stanza 5:** The poem reminds us that there is no need to rush, as everything happens in its own time, guided by the divine hand.
- **Stanza 6:** The final stanza affirms that trusting divine **timing** leads to peace. By aligning with the divine flow, we come into harmony with our true path.

PHILOSOPHICAL INSIGHTS

This topic explores divine timing as the force that guides our lives according to a divine plan. In Indian spirituality, divine timing (*īśvara-prakṛti*) teaches that everything happens in its own perfect moment, governed by the divine will. The Bhagavad Gita and the Upanishads stress the importance of trusting in the timing of the universe and surrendering to the divine flow. The poem illustrates that by trusting divine timing, we experience peace, patience, and alignment with our true purpose.

PRACTICAL GUIDANCE

How often do you struggle with impatience or try to control outcomes? Are you ready to trust the divine timing in your life?

Begin by practising patience and mindfulness. Reflect on moments when you feel rushed or impatient, and consciously surrender control to the divine. Use affirmations like "I trust divine timing," "I align with the cosmic flow," and "Everything unfolds at the perfect time." By cultivating trust and patience, you will experience greater peace and alignment with your soul's purpose.

95

The Healing Power of Nature

Nature is the healer of the soul,
Its beauty makes us feel whole.
The earth, the sky, the trees, the seas,
They all bring comfort and inner peace.

In nature's arms, we find our rest,
It's where we can be at our best.
Through nature's touch, we heal and grow,
In its presence, we truly know.

The rivers flow with healing grace,
The mountains stand with steady pace.
The forest whispers ancient truth,
And the sun gives life to the youth.

Nature's rhythm guides the heart,
In its dance, we play our part.
It is the song of the divine,
Echoing in every tree and vine.

In nature, we are reborn,
We leave behind the stress we've worn.
Through its beauty, we find our way,
To inner peace, every day.

The wind carries messages of love,
It reminds us of the stars above.
In nature, we find our strength,
It fills us with peace at great length.

The healing power of nature is real,
It is the truth we can feel.
In nature, we find our place,
And connect with the divine grace.

INTERPRETATION

The healing power of nature is a divine force that restores balance and harmony to the body, mind, and spirit

In Indian spirituality, nature (*prakṛti*) is revered as the embodiment of the divine. The Bhagavad Gita teaches that the universe is a manifestation of *Ishvara's* divine energy, and nature is an extension of that divine presence. *Krishna* encourages *Arjuna* to observe the beauty and balance of nature, as it reflects the divine order.

The Upanishads describe nature as a source of wisdom and healing, where every element—the earth, water, fire, and air—is infused with divine energy. *Yoga* and meditation practices teach us to connect with nature as a means of grounding ourselves and healing. By spending time in nature, we reconnect with the divine flow and restore our inner balance.

STANZA-WISE INTERPRETATION

- **Stanza 1:** The poem introduces nature as the healer of the soul, providing comfort and peace through its beauty and presence.
- **Stanza 2:** Nature is presented as the space where we find rest and healing. In its embrace, we reconnect with our true essence and experience spiritual growth.
- **Stanza 3:** The elements of nature—rivers, mountains, forests, and the sun—are shown as the divine forces

that nourish and heal us, guiding us to inner truth and peace.

- **Stanza 4:** Nature's rhythm is described as the divine song that guides our hearts and connects us to the universal truth. Through nature, we participate in the divine dance of life.
- **Stanza 5:** The poem emphasises that in nature, we are reborn. It allows us to release stress and find clarity, peace, and balance.
- **Stanza 6:** The wind and other elements of nature are shown as carriers of divine messages, offering love, strength, and healing. Nature renews us and helps us align with the divine.
- **Stanza 7:** The final stanza affirms that the healing power of nature is real and tangible. It is in nature that we find our connection to the divine and experience its grace.

PHILOSOPHICAL INSIGHTS

This topic explores the healing power of nature as a divine force that restores balance and peace. In Indian spirituality, nature (*prakṛti*) is the embodiment of the divine, providing nourishment, healing, and spiritual wisdom. The Bhagavad Gita and the Upanishads teach that by connecting with nature, we align with the divine flow and experience inner peace and harmony. The poem illustrates that nature is not just a physical environment but a sacred space where we reconnect with the divine and heal on all levels.

PRACTICAL GUIDANCE

How often do you spend time in nature, allowing it to heal and restore you? Are you open to connecting with nature's divine energy?

Begin by spending time in nature each day. Whether it's a walk in the park or sitting by a tree, allow yourself to be present with the natural world. Use affirmations like "Nature heals me," "I am one with the divine energy of nature," and "Through nature, I find peace and balance." By immersing yourself in nature, you will experience spiritual renewal and inner harmony.

96

The Force of Non-Resistance

To resist is to fight the flow,
To swim against the current's glow.
But in non-resistance, we find our peace,
A place where struggles cease to increase.

Non-resistance is the art of surrender,
Letting go of control, with a heart that's tender.
It's the wisdom to flow with life's pace,
And accept each moment with grace.

In non-resistance, we find our strength,
We move forward, going great lengths.
It is not weakness, but pure might,
To embrace life and let go of the fight.

When we stop resisting, we find our way,
The path opens up, clear as day.
With non-resistance, we are free,
To live in harmony with all we see.

Non-resistance is the key to peace,
It brings us release, and our struggles cease.
Through surrender, we find our truth,
And open ourselves to eternal youth.

In non-resistance, we find the divine,
We align with the cosmic design.
It's in letting go that we find,
A life of grace, so calm, so kind.

To resist is to limit our soul,
To non-resist is to make us whole.
The force of non-resistance is true,
It opens the heart to the divine view.

INTERPRETATION

Non-resistance is the practice of surrendering to life's flow, allowing us to connect with the divine and find peace

In Indian philosophy, non-resistance (*anavaraṇa*) is seen as the path to inner peace and spiritual awakening. The Bhagavad Gita teaches that resistance is a form of attachment, which leads to suffering. *Krishna* encourages *Arjuna* to act without attachment to the outcome, surrendering control to the divine plan.

The Upanishads describe non-resistance as a state of grace, where we align with the cosmic order. Through meditation, *yoga*, and self-inquiry, we learn to release resistance and flow with the divine energy that governs the universe. By letting go of the need to control, we transcend the ego and connect with the eternal truth.

STANZA-WISE INTERPRETATION

- **Stanza 1:** The poem introduces non-resistance as the act of letting go of control and surrendering to the divine flow of life. By doing so, we find peace and freedom from struggle.
- **Stanza 2:** Non-resistance is shown as the art of surrender, where we accept each moment with grace and trust in the divine timing of life.
- **Stanza 3:** The poem highlights that non-resistance brings strength, not weakness. It is an empowering choice that aligns us with life's natural flow.

- **Stanza 4:** When we stop resisting, the poem suggests, we find clarity and peace. Non-resistance opens the path to freedom, allowing us to live in harmony.
- **Stanza 5:** Non-resistance is the key to peace. By surrendering control, we free ourselves from inner conflict and align with the truth of our soul.
- **Stanza 6:** The poem describes how non-resistance aligns us with the divine and the cosmic design. By letting go, we find grace, peace, and divine connection.
- **Stanza 7:** The final stanza emphasises that non-resistance is the path to wholeness. It allows us to open our hearts and experience the divine truth.

PHILOSOPHICAL INSIGHTS

This topic explores non-resistance as the key to inner peace and spiritual freedom. In Indian spirituality, non-resistance (*anavaraṇa*) is about surrendering to life's flow and releasing control. The Bhagavad Gita and the Upanishads teach that by letting go of resistance, we align with the divine and experience inner peace. The poem illustrates that non-resistance allows us to transcend the ego and connect with the divine, leading to spiritual awakening and peace.

PRACTICAL GUIDANCE

How often do you resist life's challenges? Are you ready to embrace non-resistance and flow with the divine will?

Start by practising acceptance in small moments. When you face challenges, instead of resisting, surrender to the moment and trust in the divine plan. Use affirmations like "I flow with life," "I release resistance and embrace peace," and "Non-resistance brings me harmony." By practising non-resistance, you will experience greater peace and alignment with your true purpose.

97

The Truth of Impermanence

All things are fleeting, all things shall pass,
Like sand slipping through the hourglass.
The truth of impermanence is clear,
Nothing in life stays the same, my dear.

In every moment, change is near,
It comes with joy, it comes with fear.
Yet in this truth, we find our peace,
For impermanence brings release.

What was once here, will fade away,
Like the dawn turning to day.
In change, we find our growth,
For life moves forward, to the unknown, we go.

Impermanence teaches us to let go,
To release all that we think we know.
It guides us to live in the now,
And trust in the divine's sacred vow.

In impermanence, we find our grace,
We accept each moment, in every place.
Through change, we find our strength,
And align with the divine at length.

To know impermanence is to be free,
To release the past and just be.
We flow with life, we go with the tide,
In impermanence, we learn to glide.

The truth of impermanence is pure,
It helps us endure, it helps us endure.
In its embrace, we find our way,
And live in peace every day.

INTERPRETATION

Impermanence is the truth that all things in life are transient, and understanding this truth leads to peace and freedom

In Indian philosophy, impermanence (*anitya*) is one of the fundamental teachings. The Bhagavad Gita and the Upanishads emphasise that everything in the material world is subject to change, and nothing is permanent. *Krishna* teaches *Arjuna* that attachment to the transient leads to suffering, and true peace comes from realizing the impermanence of all things.

The Buddha also taught that life is impermanent, and it is through accepting this truth that we can overcome suffering. *Yoga* and meditation help us detach from the transient world and find peace in the present moment. By embracing impermanence, we align ourselves with the divine flow and experience spiritual liberation.

STANZA-WISE INTERPRETATION

- **Stanza 1:** The poem introduces impermanence as the truth that everything is fleeting. Nothing in life remains the same forever, and this truth is universal.
- **Stanza 2:** The poem emphasises that change is inevitable and comes with both joy and fear. However, embracing impermanence allows us to find peace and release attachment.
- **Stanza 3:** Impermanence is presented as the force of growth and transformation. What was once here fades away, making room for new experiences and lessons.

- **Stanza 4:** The poem teaches that impermanence encourages us to let go of attachments and live in the present moment. It helps us trust in the divine order of life.
- **Stanza 5:** Impermanence is described as the source of grace. By accepting change, we find strength and align with the divine flow of life.
- **Stanza 6:** The poem affirms that impermanence is the key to freedom. By letting go of the past and living in the now, we experience peace and spiritual growth.
- **Stanza 7:** The final stanza emphasises that impermanence helps us endure life's challenges. By accepting change, we find our way and live with peace every day.

PHILOSOPHICAL INSIGHTS

This topic explores impermanence as the truth that everything in life is transient. In Indian philosophy, impermanence (*anitya*) is the realisation that nothing in the material world lasts forever, and understanding this truth brings freedom from attachment and suffering. The Bhagavad Gita and the Upanishads teach that accepting impermanence helps us align with the divine flow and live in harmony with the universe. The poem illustrates that by embracing impermanence, we find peace, strength, and spiritual growth.

PRACTICAL GUIDANCE

How often do you struggle with attachment to things or people? Are you ready to embrace the truth of impermanence and live with peace?

Begin by reflecting on areas of your life where you may be holding on to the past or fearing change. Practice releasing attachment and embracing the present moment. Use affirmations like "I accept the impermanence of life," "I let go of attachment and trust the flow," and "I find peace in the present moment." By embracing impermanence, you will experience greater freedom and spiritual growth.

CHAPTER 10

The Infinite Journey

98

The Power of Purpose

Purpose is the light that guides our way,
It illuminates every darkened day.
It gives our life meaning and grace,
And shows us the divine's embrace.

To live with purpose is to be free,
It sets the soul's path for all to see.
It is the force that drives the heart,
Guiding us toward our sacred part.

Purpose is the compass that points us true,
To the place where we are meant to pursue.
It's the reason for every step we take,
The road we walk, the path we make.

In purpose, we find our strength,
It drives us forward at any length.
It brings focus, it brings clarity,
And fills us with divine sincerity.

Purpose is the force that makes us whole,
It brings unity to body and soul.
Through purpose, we find our place,
And align with the divine grace.

To live with purpose is to rise,
Above the mundane, the worldly lies.
It leads us to truth, to light,
And gives us the strength to fight.

Purpose is the reason we exist,
A gift from the divine, an eternal twist.
It is the call of the soul's desire,
To ignite our spirit, set it on fire.

INTERPRETATION

Purpose is the force that gives life meaning and direction, aligning us with our true calling and divine path

In Indian spirituality, purpose (*dharma*) is the inherent duty or path that each individual must follow to fulfil their highest potential. The Bhagavad Gita teaches that each person has a unique *dharma* that aligns with their soul's essence. *Krishna* guides *Arjuna* to follow his *dharma*, emphasising that by acting in accordance with one's purpose, one can achieve spiritual fulfilment and liberation.

The Upanishads describe purpose as the alignment of the individual with the universal truth, where one's actions and intentions are directed towards the highest good. *Yoga* and meditation practices help us discover our purpose by quieting the mind and connecting with the divine essence within. Living with purpose leads to a life of meaning, focus, and spiritual peace.

STANZA-WISE INTERPRETATION

- **Stanza 1:** The poem introduces purpose as the guiding light that illuminates our path, giving meaning and grace to our lives while connecting us with the divine.
- **Stanza 2:** Living with purpose brings freedom, as it provides clarity and direction, allowing us to walk confidently toward our sacred mission.

- **Stanza 3:** Purpose is depicted as the compass that guides us toward our highest calling. It shapes our actions and helps us stay aligned with our divine path.
- **Stanza 4:** Purpose is shown as a source of strength, focus, and clarity. It brings divine sincerity to every step we take, aligning us with our true self.
- **Stanza 5:** The poem reinforces that purpose brings unity to our body, mind, and soul. It is through purpose that we find peace and alignment with the divine.
- **Stanza 6:** Living with purpose allows us to rise above worldly distractions and aligns us with the divine truth. It empowers us to face challenges with strength and clarity.
- **Stanza 7:** The final stanza affirms that purpose is the divine gift that fuels our spirit, guiding us to live authentically and with great passion for our highest calling.

PHILOSOPHICAL INSIGHTS

This topic explores purpose as the driving force that aligns our actions with our true calling and spiritual path. In Indian spirituality, *dharma* is the concept of living in alignment with one's true purpose. The Bhagavad Gita and the Upanishads emphasise that by understanding and following our purpose, we experience fulfilment, clarity, and spiritual growth. The poem illustrates that living with purpose leads to divine connection, strength, and peace.

PRACTICAL GUIDANCE

How often do you feel disconnected from your true purpose? Are you ready to align your life with your highest calling?

Reflect on your deepest passions and values. What drives you? Start by living each day in alignment with your purpose, whether through work, relationships, or spiritual practices. Use affirmations like "I am living with purpose," "My actions align with my soul's calling," and "I am guided by divine wisdom." By aligning with your purpose, you will experience greater peace, focus, and spiritual fulfilment.

99

The Gift of Legacy

Legacy is the gift we leave behind,
It is the mark of a life well-defined.
It's the echo of actions we take,
The difference we make, the lives we wake.

A legacy is not in wealth or fame,
But in the love we give, the hearts we claim.
It's in the kindness we sow, the seeds we plant,
And in the peace that we never recant.

Legacy is the story we write,
In every moment, in every fight.
It's the wisdom we share, the love we spread,
And the light we give to others ahead.

A legacy is the love we show,
In every action, in every glow.
It's in the way we heal and care,
And the lives we touch with love so rare.

To leave a legacy is to give of our soul,
To contribute to the whole, to make others whole.
It is to plant the seeds of truth and peace,
And to allow love and kindness to never cease.

The gift of legacy is the gift of grace,
It's the love we leave in every space.
It is the energy that continues to live,
Long after we have something to give.

Legacy is the echo of our being,
It's the love that we're always seeing.
Through our legacy, we transcend time,
And leave a mark that is purely divine.

INTERPRETATION

Legacy is the impact we leave on the world, a reflection of the love, wisdom, and service we offer to others

In Indian philosophy, the concept of legacy is tied to *dharma* (righteous duty) and *karma* (actions). The Bhagavad Gita teaches that every action we perform contributes to our legacy. *Krishna* encourages *Arjuna* to act in a way that serves the greater good, creating a positive impact that lasts beyond one's lifetime.

The Upanishads describe how our actions influence the world, and our legacy is the sum of our deeds. By living with love, wisdom, and compassion, we leave behind a legacy that serves as a guiding light for others. *Yoga* and meditation practices help us align with our true purpose, ensuring that the legacy we create is one of peace, kindness, and spiritual growth.

STANZA-WISE INTERPRETATION

- **Stanza 1:** The poem introduces legacy as the gift we leave behind, which is marked by our actions and the impact we have on others.
- **Stanza 2:** Legacy is shown as the love we give, the hearts we touch, and the peace we create. It is not about wealth or fame but about the kindness we spread.
- **Stanza 3:** The poem emphasises that legacy is written through our daily actions, wisdom, and love. It is the lasting light we leave behind for others to follow.

- **Stanza 4:** Legacy is presented as the love and care we show to others. It is in the healing we offer and the lives we touch with our kindness.
- **Stanza 5:** To leave a legacy is to contribute to the greater good, to plant seeds of truth, peace, and love that continue to grow and inspire others.
- **Stanza 6:** The gift of legacy is shown as the grace we leave behind in every space. It is the energy that transcends time and continues to serve others.
- **Stanza 7:** The final stanza affirms that legacy is the echo of our soul's being. Through it, we transcend time, leaving behind a divine imprint on the world.

PHILOSOPHICAL INSIGHTS

This topic explores the gift of legacy as the impact we leave behind through our actions, love, and service. In Indian spirituality, legacy is linked to *dharma* and *karma*, as every action we perform shapes our legacy. The Bhagavad Gita and the Upanishads emphasise that by living with purpose and compassion, we create a legacy that inspires and serves others long after we are gone. The poem illustrates that legacy is not about material wealth but about the love and wisdom we impart to the world.

PRACTICAL GUIDANCE

What kind of legacy are you creating? Are your actions aligned with the values you want to leave behind?

Reflect on the impact you want to have on the world. What are the values and qualities you want to pass on to future generations? Start living in a way that reflects your deepest values—through kindness, service, and love. Use affirmations like "I create a legacy of love," "My actions inspire others," and "I leave behind a legacy of peace and wisdom." By living intentionally, you will create a legacy that transcends time and continues to serve others.

100

The Echo of Truth

Truth is the echo of the divine voice,
It calls us to make the righteous choice.
In every heart, it resonates clear,
It is the sound we hold most dear.

Truth is not hidden, it's always near,
In the stillness, it whispers clear.
It is the guide that leads the way,
To the light of a brand new day.

Truth is the essence of the soul,
It is the force that makes us whole.
In truth, we find our strength and grace,
It is the divine's eternal embrace.

The echo of truth is heard in silence,
In every thought, in every guidance.
It calls us to rise, to stand tall,
To live with integrity, above all.

Truth is the force that never fades,
It is the light that never shades.
It shines in the dark, it shines in the light,
Guiding us with its pure sight.

In truth, we find our path so clear,
It leads us forward, away from fear.
To walk in truth is to walk in grace,
It brings us closer to the divine place.

The echo of truth is eternal and pure,
It helps us endure, it helps us secure.
In its embrace, we are made whole,
And the truth shines brightly in our soul.

INTERPRETATION

The echo of truth is the divine call that guides us to live authentically and in alignment with our highest self

In Indian philosophy, truth (*satya*) is considered one of the highest virtues. The Bhagavad Gita teaches that living in accordance with the truth is essential for spiritual growth and liberation. *Krishna* tells *Arjuna* that the truth is eternal and unchanging, and it is the foundation of all life.

The Upanishads emphasise that the essence of truth is the realisation of the self (*atman*), which is identical with the supreme reality (*Brahman*). *Yoga* and meditation help us connect with this truth, allowing us to align our actions with divine will and experience inner peace. The echo of truth is the divine voice that resonates within us, guiding us toward enlightenment and spiritual fulfilment.

STANZA-WISE INTERPRETATION

- **Stanza 1:** The poem introduces truth as the divine echo, guiding us to make righteous choices and align with the highest values.
- **Stanza 2:** Truth is presented as something that is always present and accessible. It whispers in the stillness, offering guidance and clarity.
- **Stanza 3:** The poem highlights that truth is the essence of the soul, the force that brings us strength, grace, and alignment with the divine.

- **Stanza 4:** The echo of truth is shown as the guiding force that calls us to live with integrity and authenticity, transcending ego and illusion.
- **Stanza 5:** Truth is depicted as the eternal light that never fades. It is the force that shines through both dark and light, guiding us toward spiritual realisation.
- **Stanza 6:** The poem emphasises that by walking in truth, we find clarity and freedom from fear. Truth aligns us with grace and spiritual peace.
- **Stanza 7:** The final stanza affirms that the echo of truth is eternal. It sustains us, helping us endure life's challenges and guiding us toward spiritual wholeness.

PHILOSOPHICAL INSIGHTS

This topic explores the echo of truth as the divine call that guides us to live in alignment with our higher self. In Indian spirituality, truth (*satya*) is considered one of the highest virtues, and the Bhagavad Gita teaches that we must live according to this eternal truth. The Upanishads describe the realisation of truth as the key to spiritual liberation. The poem illustrates that by listening to the echo of truth, we connect with the divine, live authentically, and experience peace.

PRACTICAL GUIDANCE

How often do you act in alignment with your truth?
Are you ready to listen to the divine echo within?

Practice mindfulness and self-awareness. Reflect on areas of your life where you may not be living authentically or in alignment with your deepest values. Use affirmations like "I walk in truth," "My actions reflect my higher self," and "I am guided by the divine truth." By living in alignment with your truth, you will experience greater peace, clarity, and spiritual fulfilment.

101

The Call of the Infinite

The infinite calls us from the deep,
It stirs our soul from its peaceful sleep.
It whispers in the winds, it speaks in the sky,
It is the call that never says goodbye.

The infinite is the truth we seek,
It's in the strong, it's in the weak.
It's the force that moves the stars,
It's the light that shines from afar.

To hear the call of the infinite is to see,
The divine in all, the vast sea.
It's the realisation that we are one,
And the journey has only just begun.

The infinite calls us to transcend,
To rise above, to make amends.
It guides us to the truth we know,
And helps us to let go and grow.

In the call of the infinite, we find our place,
A moment of grace, a divine embrace.
It leads us on the path of light,
Through the darkness, to the infinite height.

The infinite is the source of all,
It lifts us up when we fall.
Through the call, we find our way,
To the divine, every day.

The call of the infinite is eternal and pure,
It brings us peace, it makes us sure.
Through its voice, we are reborn,
And the light of the infinite is forever adorned.

INTERPRETATION

The call of the infinite is the divine invitation to transcend our limited perceptions and align with the eternal truth

In Indian philosophy, the infinite (*ananta*) refers to the boundless nature of the universe and the divine. The Bhagavad Gita teaches that we are all part of the infinite, and to realize this truth is to experience liberation. *Krishna* encourages *Arjuna* to recognise the eternal nature of the soul, which transcends the limitations of the physical body.

The Upanishads describe the infinite as the ultimate reality, *Brahman*, which is both transcendent and immanent. Through *yoga*, meditation, and self-inquiry, we are guided to realize our oneness with the infinite, experiencing unity with all of existence. The call of the infinite is the divine invitation to awaken to this truth and live in alignment with the cosmic order.

STANZA-WISE INTERPRETATION

- **Stanza 1:** The poem introduces the call of the infinite as the divine voice that stirs our soul, awakening us to a higher truth and purpose.
- **Stanza 2:** The infinite is presented as the force that moves the universe, from the smallest particle to the largest star. It is the light that guides us toward realisation.
- **Stanza 3:** The call of the infinite is depicted as the realisation that we are one with the universe. It invites us to transcend our ego and connect with the divine.

- **Stanza 4:** The infinite calls us to rise above limitations and ego, guiding us toward spiritual growth and awakening to the truth of our divine nature.
- **Stanza 5:** The poem emphasises that in the call of the **infinite**, we find grace and divine guidance. It leads us on the path of light and spiritual elevation.
- **Stanza 6:** The infinite is described as the source of all existence, lifting us when we fall and guiding us on our spiritual journey.
- **Stanza 7:** The final stanza affirms that the call of the infinite is eternal. It brings peace, and through its voice, we are reborn, finding unity with the divine.

PHILOSOPHICAL INSIGHTS

This topic explores the call of the infinite as the divine invitation to transcend the limitations of the self and align with the eternal truth. In Indian philosophy, the infinite (*ananta*) is the ultimate reality, and by recognizing our oneness with it, we achieve spiritual liberation. The Bhagavad Gita and the Upanishads teach that by answering the call of the infinite, we awaken to the divine and live in harmony with the cosmic order. The poem illustrates that by embracing the infinite, we find peace, wisdom, and spiritual fulfilment.

PRACTICAL GUIDANCE

How often do you listen to the divine call within? Are you ready to transcend your limitations and align with the infinite?

Begin by practising meditation and self-inquiry. Reflect on your connection to the infinite and your place in the grand scheme of the universe. Use affirmations like "I am one with the infinite," "I align with the divine flow," and "Through the call of the infinite, I find peace." By listening to the divine call, you will experience greater spiritual growth and alignment with your true purpose.

102

The Final Note of Creation

Creation sings its final song,
A melody that's pure and long.
It echoes in the hearts of all,
The final note of the divine call.

This note is heard in the stillness, deep,
It stirs the soul from its restful sleep.
In its sound, the universe aligns,
All of existence, the divine defines.

The final note is the essence of grace,
It is the rhythm that fills the space.
It's the sound of the soul's release,
A note that brings eternal peace.

In the final note, we transcend time,
We merge with the rhythm, so sublime.
The past, the future, they all dissolve,
In the final note, we are resolved.

This note is the divine's embrace,
It leads us to a sacred place.
In its sound, we find our way,
To eternal truth, where we stay.

The final note is the completion of all,
It answers the soul's deepest call.
It is the truth we seek to find,
A note that brings the heart to mind.

The final note of creation is pure,
It brings us peace, it makes us sure.
In its embrace, we find our home,
In the divine's eternal dome.

INTERPRETATION

The final note of creation is the sound that transcends all and connects us with the divine essence of the universe

In Indian philosophy, the concept of the final note or the ultimate sound (*nāda*) is considered a representation of the divine. The Bhagavad Gita teaches that creation is a manifestation of divine energy, and every aspect of life is part of the cosmic order. *Krishna* encourages *Arjuna* to understand that all actions, all sounds, and all forms are rooted in the divine essence.

The Upanishads describe the supreme sound as the ultimate reality, *Brahman*, from which all creation emanates. *Yoga* teaches that by attuning ourselves to the divine sound, we can experience oneness with the universe. The final note represents the completion and harmony of all creation, leading us to peace, wisdom, and spiritual liberation.

STANZA-WISE INTERPRETATION

- **Stanza 1:** The poem introduces the final note of creation as a divine melody that resonates in all hearts. It symbolizes the ultimate call from the divine, connecting all beings.
- **Stanza 2:** The final note is depicted as a sound that stirs the soul, awakening it from the illusion of separation and aligning it with the divine order.

- **Stanza 3:** The final note is the essence of grace, bringing peace and release. It represents the divine rhythm that guides the soul toward eternal harmony.
- **Stanza 4:** The poem suggests that the final note transcends time, dissolving the boundaries of past and future. It is the sound of ultimate resolution and spiritual truth.
- **Stanza 5:** The final note is described as the divine embrace, guiding us to a sacred space where we experience oneness with the divine and eternal truth.
- **Stanza 6:** The final note is the completion of all creation. It answers the deepest call of the soul, bringing clarity and understanding of the divine.
- **Stanza 7:** The final stanza affirms that the final note is pure and divine. It is the source of peace and spiritual fulfilment, leading us to the eternal truth and divine presence.

PHILOSOPHICAL INSIGHTS

This topic explores the final note of creation as the divine sound that transcends all forms and connects us to the ultimate truth. In Indian spirituality, the final note (*nāda*) represents the divine essence, the sound from which all creation emanates. The Bhagavad Gita and the Upanishads teach that by aligning with the divine rhythm, we can transcend time, experience oneness with the universe, and reach spiritual liberation. The poem illustrates that the final note is the ultimate expression of the divine, guiding us to peace, wisdom, and fulfilment.

PRACTICAL GUIDANCE

How often do you tune into the divine rhythm in your life? Are you open to the final note of creation?

Begin by practising deep listening through meditation or mindfulness. Allow yourself to be present in each moment and attune to the divine sound that surrounds you. Use affirmations like "I align with the divine rhythm," "I am one with the sound of creation," and "I listen to the final note of truth." By embracing the divine sound, you will experience greater peace, harmony, and spiritual growth.

103

The Path of Resilience

Resilience is the strength within,
The force that helps us rise again.
It is the power to face the storm,
And come out stronger, in new form.

Through resilience, we face the test,
We rise above, we give our best.
It is the courage to stand tall,
And continue on, through it all.

Resilience is the spirit's might,
It is the strength to fight the fight.
It carries us through the darkest times,
And guides us through the steepest climbs.

In resilience, we find our power,
It is the strength that grows by the hour.
Through challenges, we find our way,
And rise again, stronger every day.

Resilience is the heart's deep core,
It is the will to rise and soar.
It lifts us up, it sets us free,
And helps us live with clarity.

Through resilience, we find our truth,
We discover the strength of youth.
It is the force that keeps us whole,
And leads us to the deepest soul.

The path of resilience is divine,
It connects us to the eternal line.
With each step, we rise again,
And find the strength to begin again.

INTERPRETATION

Resilience is the ability to rise above challenges, drawing on inner strength to overcome obstacles and grow stronger

In Indian philosophy, resilience (*duṣkarmanivṛtti*) is considered a vital quality for spiritual and personal growth. The Bhagavad Gita teaches that life's challenges are tests of our willpower and resilience. *Krishna* encourages *Arjuna* to embrace resilience, fight the battle of life with courage, and stay aligned with the divine path.

The Upanishads describe resilience as the strength to overcome fear and doubt, standing firm in the face of adversity. *Yoga* and meditation practices help us cultivate resilience by strengthening the mind, body, and spirit. Through resilience, we align with our higher self and navigate life's challenges with grace and power.

STANZA-WISE INTERPRETATION

- **Stanza 1:** The poem introduces resilience as the inner strength that helps us rise above adversity, facing challenges and emerging stronger.
- **Stanza 2:** Resilience is depicted as the courage to keep going despite difficulties, standing tall and giving our best in the face of life's tests.
- **Stanza 3:** The poem emphasises that resilience is the power of the spirit, carrying us through dark times and helping us overcome challenges.

- **Stanza 4:** Resilience is described as the growing strength that emerges with each challenge. It is the force that propels us forward and helps us rise again.
- **Stanza 5:** Resilience is shown as the heart's core strength, lifting us up and enabling us to live with clarity and purpose.
- **Stanza 6:** The poem affirms that through resilience, we reconnect with our inner strength and find the courage to face any adversity.
- **Stanza 7:** The final stanza states that the path of resilience is divine, aligning us with the eternal flow of life. Through resilience, we rise again and continue our journey.

PHILOSOPHICAL INSIGHTS

This topic explores resilience as the inner strength that allows us to overcome life's challenges and grow stronger. In Indian spirituality, resilience is essential for personal and spiritual development. The Bhagavad Gita and the Upanishads teach that resilience is the ability to face life's trials with courage and perseverance, aligning with the divine will. The poem illustrates that through resilience, we can rise above adversity, discover our true strength, and live in alignment with our higher purpose.

PRACTICAL GUIDANCE

How often do you face challenges with strength and determination? Are you ready to embrace resilience in every area of your life?

Begin by reflecting on past challenges and how you overcame them. Practice cultivating inner strength by remaining calm and centered in the face of adversity. Use affirmations like "I am resilient," "I rise above challenges," and "My strength grows with every challenge." By embracing resilience, you will grow stronger and align with your higher purpose.

104

The Freedom of Letting Go

Letting go is not defeat,
It is the strength that makes us complete.
In releasing, we find our peace,
A place where all worries cease.

Letting go is freedom's key,
It opens the soul to what can be.
In surrender, we find our way,
To live in truth, come what may.

When we let go, we transcend fear,
We release the past, the pain, the tear.
It is the power to choose anew,
And see life from a higher view.

Letting go is the act of grace,
It's the courage to leave a space.
To allow newness to enter in,
And let the divine love begin.

In letting go, we trust the flow,
We let the universe guide where we go.
It's the surrender of the mind's control,
And the opening of the heart and soul.

Letting go is to embrace the now,
To live with peace, without the how.
It is to be free from the past,
And trust that the future will come at last.

The freedom of letting go is pure,
It brings us peace, it makes us sure.
In releasing, we are reborn,
And through it, we are forever adorned.

INTERPRETATION

Letting go is the practice of surrendering control and releasing attachments, allowing us to experience true freedom and spiritual peace

In Indian spirituality, letting go (*tyāga*) is a central concept in the Bhagavad Gita. *Krishna* teaches *Arjuna* that true freedom comes from releasing attachment to the outcomes of our actions. Letting go allows us to align with the divine will, surrendering the ego and trusting in the higher purpose.

The Upanishads describe letting go as a means of transcending the mind's illusions. *Yoga* and meditation practices guide us to release the grip of the ego and experience inner peace. By letting go of attachment and control, we align ourselves with the flow of life, experiencing true freedom, wisdom, and spiritual liberation.

STANZA-WISE INTERPRETATION

- **Stanza 1:** The poem introduces letting go as a strength that leads to peace and freedom. By releasing our grip on life, we find serenity and inner balance.
- **Stanza 2:** Letting go is described as the key to freedom, allowing us to open ourselves to new possibilities and trust the divine flow.
- **Stanza 3:** The poem emphasises that letting go helps us transcend fear, releasing the past and allowing us to embrace the present with a higher perspective.

- **Stanza 4:** Letting go is portrayed as an act of grace. It requires courage and trust to make space for new experiences and divine love.
- **Stanza 5:** The poem reinforces that letting go is about trusting the universe to guide us. It is the surrender of control, allowing the divine flow to lead us to where we are meant to go.
- **Stanza 6:** Letting go is depicted as the embrace of the present moment. It is freedom from past regrets and future anxieties, living fully in the now.
- **Stanza 7:** The final stanza affirms that letting go brings us peace and renewal. By releasing attachment, we experience spiritual rebirth and are aligned with the divine.

PHILOSOPHICAL INSIGHTS

This topic explores letting go as the path to freedom, inner peace, and spiritual growth. In Indian philosophy, letting go (*tyāga*) is the practice of surrendering attachment and control. The Bhagavad Gita and the Upanishads teach that true peace and liberation come when we release our desires and align with the divine will. The poem illustrates that through letting go, we transcend the ego and experience the divine flow of life.

PRACTICAL GUIDANCE

How often do you find yourself clinging to the past or trying to control the future? Are you ready to embrace the freedom of letting go?

Practice surrender by reflecting on areas in your life where you are holding on tightly. Begin by letting go of small attachments and gradually work towards releasing control over larger aspects of your life. Use affirmations like "I release control," "I trust the divine flow," and "I am free from attachment." Through regular practice, you will experience greater peace, freedom, and spiritual alignment.

105

Embracing the Infinite

The infinite is all around,
In every breath, in every sound.
It is the vastness, the cosmic flow,
The divine energy that helps us grow.

The infinite is within our reach,
It speaks to us, it teaches each.
It is the wisdom that lights our way,
And guides us to a brighter day.

In the infinite, we find our place,
It fills us with love, it fills us with grace.
Through the infinite, we are free,
And align with the cosmic sea.

To embrace the infinite is to trust,
In the divine, in love, in the just.
It is to surrender to the unknown,
And know that we are not alone.

The infinite calls us to expand,
To rise above and take a stand.
It shows us that there's more to see,
And helps us reach eternity.

Through the infinite, we transcend time,
We rise above, we are sublime.
It connects us all, it makes us whole,
And leads us to the eternal soul.

To embrace the infinite is to be free,
It opens the heart, it lets us see.
In the infinite, we find our truth,
And in its light, we live our youth.

INTERPRETATION

Embracing the infinite is the practice of recognizing our oneness with the universe and aligning with the boundless energy of creation

In Indian spirituality, the infinite (*ananta*) represents the eternal, unchanging essence of the universe. The Bhagavad Gita teaches that by recognizing our connection to the infinite, we transcend the limitations of the ego and experience divine unity. *Krishna* encourages *Arjuna* to understand the infinite nature of the soul, which is beyond time and space.

The Upanishads describe the infinite as *Brahman*, the supreme reality that encompasses all life. Through meditation, *yoga*, and self-realisation, we learn to embrace the infinite within ourselves and experience unity with the cosmos. Embracing the infinite leads to spiritual liberation, peace, and the realisation of our true essence.

STANZA-WISE INTERPRETATION

- **Stanza 1:** The poem introduces the infinite as the cosmic energy that surrounds us and helps us grow. It is present in every breath and sound, connecting all of creation.
- **Stanza 2:** The infinite is shown as a teacher and guide, offering wisdom that lights our path and helps us grow in consciousness.
- **Stanza 3:** Embracing the infinite is described as finding our true place in the universe. Through this embrace, we experience love, grace, and freedom.

- **Stanza 4:** Embracing the infinite requires trust in the divine. It is about surrendering to the unknown and realizing that we are connected to all that is.
- **Stanza 5:** The infinite calls us to expand our consciousness, to rise above limitations, and to experience the eternal truth of existence.
- **Stanza 6:** The poem describes how embracing the infinite allows us to transcend time and space, connecting with the divine and the eternal soul.
- **Stanza 7:** The final stanza affirms that embracing the infinite opens the heart and reveals the truth of our existence. In the infinite, we find our spiritual youth and divine purpose.

PHILOSOPHICAL INSIGHTS

This topic explores embracing the infinite as the realisation of our oneness with the universe and the divine. In Indian spirituality, the infinite (*ananta*) is the eternal essence of existence. The Bhagavad Gita and the Upanishads teach that by recognizing our connection to the infinite, we transcend the limitations of the ego and experience unity with the cosmos. The poem illustrates that embracing the infinite brings peace, wisdom, and spiritual awakening.

PRACTICAL GUIDANCE

How often do you feel limited by time and space? Are you ready to embrace the infinite within you?

Practice expanding your awareness through meditation and contemplation. Reflect on your connection to the infinite and your place in the universe. Use affirmations like "I am one with the infinite," "I embrace the eternal truth," and "The infinite guides me on my path." By embracing the infinite, you will experience spiritual growth, peace, and divine unity.

106

The Gift of Universal Love

Love is the force that binds us all,
It is the power that answers the call.
It is the light that shines so bright,
Guiding us through day and night.

Universal love is the divine embrace,
It fills every heart, every space.
It transcends boundaries, it transcends time,
It is the rhythm, it is the rhyme.

Love is the source of all creation,
It is the foundation of every nation.
In its warmth, we find our home,
It is the force that helps us roam.

Universal love knows no divide,
It unites us all, side by side.
It is the love that brings us peace,
A love that helps our fears cease.

Love is the answer to every plea,
It is the key to being free.
When we open ourselves to love,
We align with the truth above.

In universal love, we are one,
A journey that has just begun.
It is the force that transcends all,
It is the love that will never fall.

The gift of universal love is here,
It brings us peace, it brings us cheer.
Through love, we are made whole,
And love fills the depths of our soul.

INTERPRETATION

Universal love is the divine force that connects all beings, transcending time, space, and boundaries

In Indian spirituality, love (*prema*) is the ultimate expression of divine energy. The Bhagavad Gita teaches that love is the essence of the soul and the highest path to liberation. *Krishna* encourages *Arjuna* to act with love and compassion, understanding that all beings are connected through the divine.

The Upanishads describe universal love as the fundamental force of creation. *Yoga* and meditation help us cultivate love within ourselves, allowing us to transcend the ego and experience unity with all beings. By embracing universal love, we align ourselves with the divine and experience peace, wisdom, and spiritual fulfilment.

STANZA-WISE INTERPRETATION

- **Stanza 1:** The poem introduces universal love as the divine force that connects all of creation. It is the light that guides us and the energy that unites us.
- **Stanza 2:** Universal love transcends all boundaries and time. It is the divine rhythm that permeates the universe, offering peace and harmony.
- **Stanza 3:** Love is presented as the source of creation, the foundation of all life. In its warmth, we find our true home and purpose.

- **Stanza 4:** The poem emphasises that universal love unites all beings, dissolving divisions and bringing peace to the world.
- **Stanza 5:** Love is shown as the key to freedom. By opening ourselves to love, we align with the divine truth and experience liberation.
- **Stanza 6:** Universal love is depicted as the force that connects all beings. It is a divine journey that transcends all limitations.
- **Stanza 7:** The final stanza affirms that universal love is a gift that fills the soul and brings peace. Through love, we are made whole and connected to the divine.

PHILOSOPHICAL INSIGHTS

This topic explores universal love as the divine force that connects all beings and transcends the limitations of the self. In Indian spirituality, love (*prema*) is the essence of the soul and the highest expression of the divine. The Bhagavad Gita and the Upanishads teach that by embracing love, we align with the divine and experience peace, wisdom, and unity with all of creation. The poem illustrates that universal love is the path to spiritual awakening, freedom, and divine fulfilment.

PRACTICAL GUIDANCE

How often do you open your heart to universal love? Are you ready to embrace love as the guiding force in your life?

Start by cultivating love in your everyday actions. Practice kindness, compassion, and empathy toward others. Reflect on your connections with all beings and how love can transcend any divisions. Use affirmations like "I am love," "I am connected to all beings," and "Universal love flows through me." By embracing universal love, you will experience peace, unity, and spiritual growth.

107

The Eternal Now

The present moment is all we have,
It is the truth that makes us brave.
In the eternal now, we are free,
It is the space where we can simply be.

The past is gone, the future unknown,
Only the present is ours to own.
In this moment, we find our grace,
A space where time has no trace.

The eternal now is where we live,
It is the gift that we must give.
In this moment, we find our truth,
It is the path of eternal youth.

In the now, there is no fear,
There is no pain, there is no tear.
Only peace and clarity,
In the eternal now, we are free.

To live in the now is to surrender,
To let go of the past, to remember.
It is to be fully present here,
And trust that the divine is near.

The eternal now is the source of peace,
It is the place where all fears cease.
In this moment, we are whole,
And align with the divine soul.

The eternal now is where we stand,
In the present, we are in command.
Through this moment, we find our way,
And live in peace every day.

INTERPRETATION

The eternal now is the present moment, the only true time where we find peace, clarity, and spiritual awakening

In Indian spirituality, the present moment (*vartamāna*) is considered the doorway to eternal truth. The Bhagavad Gita teaches that the past and future are illusions created by the mind, and the only true reality is the present moment. *Krishna* encourages *Arjuna* to act in the present, without attachment to the past or future, aligning with the divine flow of life.

The Upanishads describe the eternal now as the realisation of the self (*atman*) in the present moment. *Yoga* and meditation practices teach us to be fully present, to let go of past regrets and future anxieties, and to live in alignment with the divine will. By embracing the eternal now, we experience peace, freedom, and spiritual fulfilment.

STANZA-WISE INTERPRETATION

- **Stanza 1:** The poem introduces the eternal now as the present moment, where we find freedom and peace. It is the space where we simply exist, without the burden of past or future.
- **Stanza 2:** The poem emphasises that the past is gone and the future is uncertain, but the present moment is all we can truly own. In the now, we find grace and truth.

- **Stanza 3:** The eternal now is presented as the space where we live and thrive. It is the gift of the present, where we reconnect with our true self.
- **Stanza 4:** The poem emphasises that in the now, there is no fear or pain. The present moment is a place of peace, clarity, and spiritual freedom.
- **Stanza 5:** To live in the now is to surrender the past and future. It is to be fully present and trust that the divine is guiding us in each moment.
- **Stanza 6:** The eternal now is described as the source of peace, where all fears cease. In the present moment, we align with the divine soul and experience wholeness.
- **Stanza 7:** The final stanza affirms that the eternal now is the place where we find our way. By living fully in the present, we experience peace and spiritual growth.

PHILOSOPHICAL INSIGHTS

This topic explores the eternal now as the present moment, the only true time where we can find peace, clarity, and spiritual alignment. In Indian philosophy, the present moment (*vartamāna*) is the key to spiritual realisation. The Bhagavad Gita and the Upanishads teach that by living fully in the now, we transcend the illusions of the past and future and align with the divine will. The poem illustrates that the eternal now is the space where we find peace, freedom, and spiritual awakening.

PRACTICAL GUIDANCE

How often do you find yourself trapped in the past or worrying about the future? Are you ready to live fully in the present moment?

Practice mindfulness and meditation to ground yourself in the present. When you feel distracted by the past or future, bring your focus back to the present moment. Use affirmations like "I live fully in the now," "The present moment is my path to peace," and "I trust the divine flow in this moment." By embracing the eternal now, you will experience greater peace, clarity, and spiritual fulfilment.

108

The Journey Beyond Life

Life is a journey that we all must take,
A river of time, a path we make.
But beyond the veil, there is more to see,
The journey continues, eternally free.

We are not the body, we are not the mind,
We are the soul, in the divine aligned.
Beyond this life, there's no end to the way,
The spirit ascends, and continues to sway.

The journey beyond life is not a fear,
It is the freedom that draws us near.
It is the realisation that life does not cease,
It is the flow into eternal peace.

Beyond life, the soul is boundless and pure,
It is the love that we can endure.
The spirit transcends, it is never confined,
It merges with the divine, one of a kind.

In the journey beyond life, there is no sorrow,
It is the promise of a bright tomorrow.
It is the peace that comes from within,
Where we reunite, the soul to begin.

Beyond life, the universe is vast,
Time is eternal, and all things pass.
But the soul remains, constant and true,
Guided by the light of the divine hue.

The journey beyond life is the final truth,
It is the wisdom that frees our youth.
We return to the source from where we came,
In the journey beyond life, we transcend the name.

INTERPRETATION

The journey beyond life is the realization that life is eternal and that the soul transcends physical existence to merge with the divine

In Indian spirituality, the soul (*ātman*) is eternal, and life is but a temporary manifestation in the material world. The Bhagavad Gita teaches that the soul is indestructible and that death is not the end, but a transition to another phase of existence. *Krishna* encourages *Arjuna* to understand that the soul is beyond birth and death, and it moves through various forms to fulfil its divine purpose.

The Upanishads describe the soul's journey beyond life as a return to the universal self, *Brahman*. The cycle of birth, death, and rebirth (*samsara*) is a process of spiritual evolution, and through *yoga*, meditation, and spiritual practice, the soul ultimately transcends the cycle and attains *moksha*—the liberation from the material world.

STANZA-WISE INTERPRETATION

- **Stanza 1:** The poem begins by acknowledging that life is a **journey**, but the journey doesn't end with physical death. It continues beyond the physical realm into eternity.
- **Stanza 2:** The poem reminds us that we are not the body or the mind but the soul, and the journey beyond life is a return to the divine essence, which is eternal.
- **Stanza 3:** The journey beyond life is described as a transition into freedom and peace, where the soul continues its journey and unites with the divine truth.

- **Stanza 4:** The poem emphasises that the soul is boundless and pure beyond this life. It is the divine love that transcends any earthly limitations and returns to its source.
- **Stanza 5:** The journey beyond life is shown as free from sorrow, a return to the peace within. It is the reunion of the soul with the divine, where all earthly struggles are left behind.
- **Stanza 6:** The poem acknowledges the eternal nature of the soul, which remains constant throughout the cycles of life and death. The universe is vast, but the soul's essence is unchanging.
- **Stanza 7:** The final stanza affirms that the journey beyond life is the ultimate truth, where we transcend our identities and return to the divine source from which we came.

PHILOSOPHICAL INSIGHTS

This topic explores the journey beyond life as the realisation of the soul's eternal nature and its return to the divine essence. In Indian philosophy, the soul (*ātman*) is considered eternal and beyond the physical body. The Bhagavad Gita and the Upanishads teach that life is a journey of the soul through various stages, and death is merely a transition to a higher form of existence. The poem illustrates that through this eternal journey, the soul ultimately returns to its divine source, transcending time, form, and identity.

PRACTICAL GUIDANCE

How often do you reflect on the eternal nature of the soul? Are you ready to embrace the truth that life is a continuous journey of spiritual evolution?

Begin by contemplating the impermanence of the physical body and the eternity of the soul. Reflect on your connection to the divine and your purpose in this life. Use affirmations like "I am the eternal soul," "My journey is guided by divine truth," and "I am one with the divine." By meditating on the eternal nature of the soul, you will experience peace, liberation, and spiritual fulfilment, understanding that the journey continues beyond this life.

"The journey is not about finding the self, but about realizing that you are the self, beyond the mind and beyond the body. The truth is already within you, waiting to be discovered."

–Jiddu Krishnamurti